AN
AMERICAN
ETHIC

AN
AMERICAN
ETHIC

A Philosophy of Freedom
Applied to
Contemporary Issues

John D. Gerken

THE CASLON COMPANY

First published in 1995 in the United States of America by
THE CASLON COMPANY
Middletown, New Jersey

Library of Congress Cataloging-in-Publication Data

Gerken, John D., 1924–
    An American ethic : a philosophy of freedom applied to
contemporary issues / by John D. Gerken.
        p.   cm.
    Includes bibliographical references and index.
    ISBN 0-391-03936-9
    1. Ethics   2. Liberty.   3. Ethical problems.   4. United States—
Moral conditions.   5. United States—Civilization—Philosophy.
I. Title.
BJ1031.G47   1995
170'.973—dc20   95-10146
                                                                CIP

Printed in the United States of America

For
Michael, Deborah,
Stephen, and Rachel

With gratitude to Dee
who gave them to me

This is the first nation in the world that was ever established on the basis of reason instead of simply warfare.

—Joseph Campbell, *Myth and the Modern World*

[Our] tradition is unambiguous; its meaning is articulated in simple, rational speech that is immediately comprehensible and powerfully persuasive to all normal human beings. America tells one story; the unbroken, ineluctable progress of freedom and equality. . . . There has been no dispute that freedom and equality are the essence of justice for us. . . . Nowhere else is there a tradition or a culture whose message is so distinct and unequivocal—certainly not in France, Italy, Germany, or even England. . . . Frenchness, Englishness, Germanness remain, nonetheless, ineffable. Everybody can, however, articulate what Americanness is.

—Allan Bloom, *The Closing of the American Mind*

CONTENTS

INTRODUCTION

The social institutions of family and church have failed to stem the tidal wave of immoral and unethical conduct, and there is widespread concern that there is something very wrong. Ethics has become a very popular topic and codes of ethics are being designed every day. American pluralism with its consequent emphasis of separation of church and state makes it very difficult to develop a consistent set of moral standards or principles that could hope to receive widespread or universal acceptance. Schools, out of respect for the individual's conscience, avoid presenting or researching and developing for presentation any consistent set of moral/ethical teaching. The closest intellectual challenge they present to the rampant unethical behavior are anthologies of essays on various moral problems. A typical college philosophy course in ethics uses such an anthology.[1] The text is really a collection of ethical positions—often contradictory—about particular moral questions of business, medicine, law, politics, etc.; as if one could discover what it means to be an ethical entrepreneur, doctor, lawyer, or politician without first determining what it means to be an ethical person. The lecturer or professor either ignores or denies the existence of absolutes or assumes the question is irrelevant. And so his[2] purpose is not the communication of knowledge and understanding of absolute principles whereby particular behaviors can be judged as morally good or bad. He is not a facilitator of insight into truths that will guide students for the rest of their lives no matter what their profession or occupation. Therefore the most he can do is get the

---

1. Joram Graf Haber, *Being and Doing, Readings in Moral Philosophy,* Macmillan, N.Y., 1993; Steven Jay Gould, *Moral Controversies, Race, Class, and Gender in Applied Ethics,* Wadsworth Publishing Co., Belmont, CA, 1993. In his Preface (xiii) Gould writes: "A successful moral problems course must largely be discussion. Cases have to be selected that will challenge students to think. The cases in this text were chosen to reflect the tough social problems students read about every day, an approach that enables the students to identify with the problems and get excited." Richard A. Wasserstrom, *Today's Moral Problems,* Macmillan, N.Y., 1985. These texts were found 8/2/93 on the shelves of a Cal State University bookstore.
2. Throughout this essay the male form of the pronoun will be used for antecedents that could be female as well as male. It will also be used of God who is eminently more than either or both. No sexism is intended, nor can it be overcome by the irritating frequent use of "he or she" or "s/he."

students to think and then choose their own ethic. He has no idea what that choice might be, nor does he much care. Everyone has a right to his own opinion. He is successful if his students have labored to form one and he has excited them in the process.

But there are absolutes; and the central absolute is man. Man is the reduplicated constant[3] in the billions of individuals through the centuries. That constant, which is absolutely the same in its essence, but diverse in its accidental modifications, is a naturally complex unit, not a compound of separate and separable units. He is an "I" who belongs to an "us," an individual who is an independent *whole* while yet at the same time a *part* of a larger whole, which we call the human race. He is both supreme and subordinate; supreme in his private responsibility for self-determination, yet subordinate to the common good. That common good is peace in its broadest sense, the necessary condition for his ability to determine himself to the fullest of his relatively unlimited individual potential. What man should do, what man must be, what man's ethic or morality is, is to accept, affirm, and fulfill his independence from and subordination to the human race. He is obliged—if he is to avoid being a bad man, he must—if he is to become a good man—be private and public, an individual and a citizen, actively alone and actively a member, actively independent and actively a participating dependent—because he is in his being both unique and common, individual and social. His morality, his ethic, is to actively and freely choose his complexity, his individuality, and his sociability in some form of harmonious unity so that both essential parts of his complex nature mature into an international civilization of peace—the flower of the just and trusting human race. All this is implied in America's assertion that all men are free and endowed with the inalienable rights of life, liberty, and the pursuit of happiness. The thrust of this essay is to make explicit what is implicit in that assertion.

An American Ethic owes its inspiration not only to the Declaration, Constitution, Bill of Rights, but also to the following authors.

Allan Bloom[4] and Joseph Campbell[5] have emphasized reason, normal human being, simple and rational speech, freedom and equality as characterizing American life. This convinced me that a rational presentation of an American ethic is possible.

---

3. As is evident from his common structure and common ability to use arbitrary signs, language.
4. Allan Bloom, *The Closing of the American Mind*, Simon & Schuster, First Touchstone Edition, New York, 1988, 55.
5. Joseph Campbell, *The Power of Myth*, with Bill Moyers, Betty Sue Flowers editor, Anchor Books Doubleday, New York, 1988, 31.

Lawrence Miller[6] showed me the nobility and social purpose of the corporation in particular and of capitalism in general. His work is important for any discussion of business ethics.

Robert Pirsig's story-essay on quality and morals gave me the insight into the thrust of evolution and the need for one stage of that development (society) to control by law enforcement a lower stage (uncivilized man). My chapter on the need for the brutal in sanction would not have been written were it not for him. I share his concern for both metaphysics and for a morality that is metaphysical but just as real as "rocks and trees."[7] I disagree with him on several points: His rejection of the metaphysical concepts of substance, properties (accidents) inhering in substances, causality, and his creation of a Metaphysics of Quality to support a morality as real as rocks and trees.

The notion of substance, and in my essay "transcendent substance," is not only crucial to American freedom and equality, it is identical with it. The most radical moral act we can perform is the affirmation of this substantial transcendence, which is our nature. A metaphysical analysis of freedom will be the starting point from which we shall develop *An American Ethic.*

Karl Menninger's work *The Crime of Punishment*[8] supports my belief that present forms of incarceration are ineffective sanctions and that there is a need for a more prompt and severe penalty for crime.

Laurence Tribe's work[9] on abortion has to be considered here because the topic is so current. It is first of all a moral question before it becomes a legal one. Further, Tribe's presentation of this "clash of absolutes" is exemplary. When both sides on this issue are moving closer to physical confrontation, Tribe's work is an effective peacemaker. As he so well says, within the limits of democratic behavior all we have is persuasion and the vote.

Laurence Pringle's work[10] on the animal rights controversy is important here for three reasons. First, he is much like Tribe in serving as a model of objectivity in presenting the data on a very emotional topic. He is so fair that one cannot discover his own position on the issue. Secondly, raising this issue in a scholarly manner as he does, compels us to contrast inalienable rights with animal rights. Are they identical? What is a right in the proper, non metaphorical, sense? Thirdly, and perhaps most importantly,

---

6. Lawrence Miller, *The American Spirit,* Visions of a New Corporate Culture, William Morrow and Company, Inc., New York, 1984, 37.
7. Robert M. Pirsig, *Lila, An Inquiry into Morals,* Bantam Books, New York, 1991. "These bads and goods are not just 'customs.' They are as real as rocks and trees." 309.
8.Karl Menninger, M.D., *The Crime of Punishment,* The Viking Press, New York, 1968.
9. Laurence H. Tribe, *Abortion, The Clash of Absolutes,* W. H. Norton & Co., New York, 1990, 240.
10. Laurence Pringle, *The Animal Rights Controversy,* Harcourt Brace Janovich, New York, 1989, 15.

this scholar in the arena of the animal rights controversy moves out of that arena into that of philosophy. In a casual comment he remarks that all men are not equal, that to treat them so is founded in a moral prescription. Thus the morality (justice) that should come from the real equality of human beings, is not as real as "rocks and trees." It is essentially arbitrary, no more than a temporary agreement among men. Such an opinion, casually expressed by an eminently fair and otherwise competent scholar, is dangerous thought. The plausibility of that thought increases its dangerous threat to the very soul of American life. It must be rationally destroyed; the thought of equality must be vindicated.

Karl Rahner[11] has written extensively on transcendence, mystery, experiencing the transcendent, consciousness of transcendence, and symbol. There is much in his writing that is similar to the ideas of Joseph Campbell when the latter writes about mystery, the transcendent, the Being of beings, consciousness, the masks of God and eternity. But Rahner's philosophy conforms more to the American tradition of a personal God and a personal afterlife. Campbell favors an impersonal and absolute energy as the ultimate reality or mystery[12] behind the gods man creates to personify the various forces of this one absolute mystery. Identification with this impersonal absolute apparently results in the loss of personal identity. "Nobody there, no, god, no you."[13]

Karl Rahner, on the other hand, not only sees an ultimate and eternal mystical union of man with God, but sees that experience as the permanent condition of man's being now.[14] Rahner sees man as transcendent trying

---

11. Karl Rahner, "The Experience of Self and the Experience of God, *Theological Investigations,* XIII, Tr. David Bourke, Crossroad, Seabury, New York, 1975, 122-132. "Reflections on the Unity of the Love of Neighbour and the Love of God," T.I., VI, TR. Karl-H and Boniface Kruger, Crossroad, New York, 1982, 231-249. "The Anonymous Christian," T.I., VI 390-398.

12. Campbell, *The Power of Myth,* 260.

13. Ibid., 263. Campbell is not clear as to what actually happens when the mystery of my being is identified with the mystery of the ground of being or how the ultimate mystery of my being is the mystery of the being of the world. "But the ultimate mystical goal is to be united with one's god. With that, duality is transcended and forms disappear. There is nobody there, no god, no you. Your mind, going past all concepts, has dissolved in identification with the ground of your own being, because that to which the metaphorical image of your god refers is the ultimate mystery of your own being, which is the being of the world as well."

14. Rahner, "Exeperience of Self..., T. I., XIII, 123. "The transcendental orientation of man to the incomprehensible and ineffable Mystery which constitutes the enabling condition for knowledge and freedom, and therefore for the subjective life itself as such, in itself implies a real, albeit a non-thematic experience of God."

to achieve himself. The achievement is essentially a moral act and is accomplished by accepting or rejecting his fellow human being.[15]

James Q. Wilson's *The Moral Sense* supports what one might call traditional objective morality. He researches literally hundreds of authors, mostly in the natural and behavioral sciences, in favor of his position that there is a moral sense in all humans. The mechanism for that sense is the desire for attachment[16] which all humans manifest. In my opinion, this is identical with the transcendent substance of man which expresses itself in the unrestricted desire to know and to communicate.

Peter Singer's second edition of *Practical Ethics*[17] is comparable to Wilson's work in its research. His ideas are widely known, his thought is quite plausible. His concern for sentient animals, his courageous thought on suicide, assisted suicide, and euthanasia deserve attention. However, I believe there are several points that deserve criticism, and especially the foundation upon which his theory of ethics rests.

Pirsig, Wilson, and Singer have presented serious thoughts on morality. Those thoughts should not be ignored but rather discussed, critiqued, and used as an occasion for developing a more accurate expression of ethical principles. To that end I have given extended consideration to their thought in my final chapters. Those men deserve to be read; they deserve serious consideration and comment. I trust that I have done that respectfully.

The *American Ethic* is only a beginning. It attempts to establish the fundamentals of ethics and applies those fundamentals to a few contemporary issues: crime, animal rights, business, sexual morality, homosexuality, and abortion. None of these applications constitute the last word on those topics. But they are beginnings. May others revise what is wrong, improve the inadequate, and build upon what is good.

Finally custom suggests that an author express his gratitude to those who have supported him in his work. I am grateful to my teachers, especially to those who introduced me to Aristotle, Aquinas, and Karl Rahner, and then helped me to philosophize. More recently, I am indebted to my friends for their encouragement. John Schwarz, Frank Oppenheim, Bob Sassack, and Jack Caldwell were most supportive. I thank them.

---

15. Ibid., 127. "The original objectivity of the experience of self necessarily takes place in the subjectivity of its encounters with the other persons in dialogue, in trustful and loving encounter. Man experiences himself by experiencing the other *person* and not the other *thing.*
16. James Q. Wilson, *The Moral Sense*, The Free Press, Macmillan, New York, 1993, 127. Almost every page of Wilson's book has two to five references to his thirty-two page bibliography.
17. Peter Singer, *Practical Ethics*, Second Edition, Cambridge University Press, New York, 1993.

1

An American Ethic
and Philosophy

By an American ethic I mean the principles of obligating behavior derived from an analysis of the fundamental values of American life: freedom, equality, inalienable rights, justice for all, government to secure those rights (justice), government by the consent of the governed.

By philosophy I mean the explanation and clarification of the realities contained in those abstract terms.

Metaphysics is the most basic philosophical discipline, for it is the philosophy of being, that which all reality has in common. Ethics is the philosophy of metaphysics applied to the being of man. It takes the concepts of nature, substance, essence, existence, accident, quantity, quality, cause, effect, etc. that apply to all being and applies them to man. For example, man is by nature a rational animal, he can act as a cause and can be acted upon and so experience effects. He has permanent characteristics such as intelligence and weight. He has some characteristics that are transitory such as running, or sleeping. Some actions make him better or worse physically, and others make him better or worse morally. He can be corrupt or a person of integrity. These conditions are modifications and so accidental to his person. Throughout life he is the same person in terms of who he is, but not in terms of what he is or becomes; that condition depends upon his free choice. It is those choices that are the object of study in the discipline called ethics.

At the present time we have no such philosophy, and the basic values of freedom, equality, inalienable rights not only are not clearly defined, but are being undermined by the plausible and erroneous thought of the articulate. The self evident truths of the Declaration are not self-evident at all, but rather the convictions of the founding fathers. Implicitly other contrary convictions are just as valid. All men are not created equal because they clearly differ in capability and capacity. Equality is not a fact of life but a moral prescription. Implicitly therefore the superior can control and command the inferior. How this differs from slavery is not clear. And as for a moral prescription to treat inferiors as equals, by whose authority am I to do so, especially since they are not my equals? And finally, since many of our fellow Americans are atheists, what do we do about the endowment of inalienable rights from the Creator? If no Creator, then whence inalienable rights and why are they inalienable?

Thus a second reason for developing an American ethic is to provide a rational defense of the values found in our most precious legal documents: The Declaration, the Constitution, and the Bill of Rights. Granted those values are supported by religion, the family, and graphically and persuasively presented by television and film when they show the triumph of good over evil. But support is not explanation. One can and should understand how and why one is free, has rights, is morally good or evil, etc. Presenting that understanding is the function of philosophy.

The validity and practicality of such a philosophy and logic can be seen in just a few sentences. I give it at the outset of this book to convince the reader that the hard work of philosophizing about freedom, equality, inalienable rights is really worth the effort.

Let's apply philosophy to the casual remark of Laurence Pringle in his book *The Animal Rights Controversy*.[1] This author and competent scholar philosophizes about the nature of man. The prestige of his competence is associated with his philosophy. Once this is added to the plausibility of his statement, his readers are inclined to accept his position and to doubt the most basic value of American life. Just a few philosophical distinctions can expose the fallacy of his statement and vindicate that value: the equality of all human beings.

There are three distinct realities existing in the one complex human phenomenon we refer to as man. They are the *human nature* (or human essence or human substance), its different *characteristics* (or accidental modifications), and the *person*. All humans are identical and therefore equal in their humanity. Each of us is essentially the same in the reality of our humanness. No one is substantially different from another; each of us is fully human. However many of our characteristics or accidental modifications of our natures are different, e.g., sex, race, size, intelligence, and other capabilities. But we are all equally human. In addition to this identity of nature and diversity of characteristics, we are absolutely different in the matter of our persons. As persons we are not only different, we are unique. There never was nor ever will be another identical to us, no mat-

---

1. Laurence Pringle, *The Animal Rights Controversy*, Harcourt Brace Janovich, New York, 1989. "When people think about it, they recognize that the saying "all men are created equal" is not true. Humans vary considerably in their abilities and capacities. Equality is not a fact of human life; it is a moral idea, a prescription of how we should treat humans." (15)

ter how much one is identical to us in nature and similar to us in characteristics. Identical twins are not identical persons, even though their natures are identical (human) and almost all their characteristics (appearance, behavior) are identical.

Thus philosophy, reason applied to the phenomenon man, shows that the Declaration is correct. All men are equal. And philosophy shows in exactly what respect they are equal (human nature) and in what respects they are not equal, namely, their characteristics and their persons.

One can look at this equality from a negative aspect. Suppose we were not equal in nature or essence, not sharing in the same real human substance. We then would have nothing naturally in common. There would be no general species called man. Thus communication would be impossible because we would have nothing in common.

There is one more reason for developing a philosophy, and hence an ethic, based on American values. American values precede positive law. Freedom, equality, inalienable rights, justice for all, etc. exist prior to the Declaration. America came into being to protect those existing values; America did not establish and institute them. Consequently, those values need to be defined and understood in all their implications if subsequent positive law is to be consistent with them, support them, protect them. Such an understanding can only come from a philosophical analysis of the concrete phenomenon man. In other words, since man is obviously free by nature, and that freedom must be respected by both the state and individuals, there must be a philosophy of that nature, a natural law philosophy. That in turn should provide the guiding principles for all positive law, just as those values were the guiding principles for the Declaration, etc.

THE NATURE OF PHILOSOPHY

The nature of philosophy is that it is a type of knowledge that differs from sense knowledge and is dependent upon sense knowledge. We perceive phenomena and the meaning of phenomena. Our senses give us the phenomena, our intellects give us the meaning of the phenomena. The physical or natural sciences are concerned with the accurate measurement of phenomena and their consistent patterns of behavior. These patterns are referred to as the "laws" of the physical or concrete universe. Knowledge of these laws enables man to live and prosper within this concrete tangible world.

Philosophy, on the other hand, goes beyond the phenomena, abstracts meaning from the phenomena. It discovers identity, similarity, contradiction, cause, effect, substance, accidental modification of substance, etc. And with the aid of logic it expresses those realities abstracted from the real phenomenological world in a consistent manner. An example of this is the philosophical response to Pringle's statement that all men are not as a matter of fact equal. Philosophy and logic show that all humans are equal. Those two disciplines did so by analyzing the phenomenon man and distinguishing within that one complex reality the three different realities of nature, accident (characteristics), and person. None of these three realities is perceived by the senses; they are understood by the intellect with the aid of the senses. The senses give us the concrete human being; the senses give us visual and audial images of language so that we can express in a visible (writing) or audial (speech) way what we understand. But that which we understand is in no sense visible or audible, nor is it imaginable. Cause, effect, nature, being, contradiction, person, etc. are unimaginable realities that we understand and use everyday. The human being is always a philosopher. Our concern here is that he be correct when speaking about the abstracted realities of freedom, equality, inalienable rights, etc.

The Problems Inherent to Philosophy (Metaphysics)

Philosophy, particularly the metaphysics of this essay, is under attack. Stephen Hawking in his *A Brief History of Time,* writes, "Philosophers reduced the scope of their inquiries so much that Wittgenstein, the most famous philosopher of this century, said, 'The sole remaining task for philosophy is the analysis of language.' What a comedown from the great tradition of philosophy from Aristotle to Kant!"[2]

Wittgenstein should have said the task for philosophy has always been the analysis of reality, and ideas and language are the only means we have of grasping it and expressing that analysis. After all, if our ideas do not accurately represent the world outside the mind, we neither know it accurately nor know whether it really is there or not. Each of us is isolated and confined to a perpetual view of the products of his own mind. All our experience rejects such a view of human knowing.

If language is distant from reality; so too is faith. And I suspect that Hawking would find fault with Francis Herbert Bradley who said, "Philosophy demands, and in the end it rests on, what may fairly be termed faith. It has, we may say, to presuppose its conclusion in order to prove it."[3] Faith or belief puts a witness between the knower and the reality known.

Robert M. Pirsig in his *Lila* is little more blunt. "Metaphysics is not reality. Metaphysics is *names* about reality. Metaphysics is a restaurant where

2. Stephen H. Hawking, *A Brief History of Time, From the Big Bang to Black Holes,* Bantam Books, New York, 1988, 175.
3. Francis Herbert Bradley, *Essays on Truth and Reality,* London, 1914, 15.

they give you a thirty-thousand page menu and no food."[4] Extending Pirsig's analogy, one can validate metaphysics by saying the menu is a valid menu. It gives you many valid choices. You order beef, you get real beef. Our immigrant forefathers read the menu from the American restaurant and decided they wanted liberty, equality, inalienable rights, justice for all. They bought their steerage passage, came to the restaurant, and were served the food that exactly matched what was on the menu which they read in their homeland.

When we develop our "menu" (philosophy, metaphysics) from the phenomenon of man, the names of freedom, equality, rights, nature, substance, essence, existence, necessary and contingent accidents, quality, quantity, relation, one, good, true, beautiful—all that food for thought is really there and caught in the focus of the mind working through the senses as it contacts the sensible world—particularly the phenomenon man. And Pirsig says as much with ". . . all legitimate human knowledge arises from the senses or by thinking about what the senses provide."[5] Thinking, philosophizing, as opposed to sensing, is a source of legitimate "human knowledge."

Everyone is fundamentally a philosopher, a metaphysician, a person seeking meaning from the experiential world that he counts, measures and weighs. It is crucial that he and the rest of us do so correctly; it is crucial that we have the right "names" and that we apply them consistently, logically, correctly. There are many difficulties with this process, but the main difficulty is accurate definition of terms and consistent application of terms.

BASIC ASSUMPTION OF PHILOSOPHY

The basic given is that there is a real world outside of my mind and that I can know it. That given is experienced; namely, I distinguish between myself and what I do and the real world in which I act and which I know. I know the difference between being awake and dreaming. I do not experience myself as living in an endless dream. Briefly, evidence is the criterion of truth. It is a given; it is not demonstrable.

Another given is the act of understanding. I do understand, I have some knowledge about a real world, and that knowledge progresses so that I actually grasp and control and master the real world. My knowledge works for me. It is practical. I not only learn to survive in the world, but learn to prosper in it by adapting to its structure, utilizing its powers to realize my own unsuspected potential. All this is obvious to "all normal human

---

4. Robert M. Pirsig, *Lila, An Inquiry into Morals*, Bantam Books, New York, 1991, 63.
5. Ibid., 99.

beings." It is the philosopher who gets us into the trouble of losing the real and getting us imprisoned in a "world" where only ideas, not realities, are known. He does this by trying to demonstrate the "given" validity of thinking, philosophizing. The validity can't be demonstrated because it is evident. One does not demonstrate evidence, one uses it to demonstrate the non-evident. Thus, there are two "givens" or conditions of the act of human knowledge, namely, the testimony of the senses and the testimony of the intellect. Bradley's remark about faith is applicable here. I have "faith" in the testimony of both intellect and sense. One cannot use the act of sensation to demonstrate the validity of sensation, nor can one use the act of understanding to demonstrate the validity of understanding. I understand the principle of contradiction: A thing cannot *be* and *not be* at the same time and under the same circumstances. That is evident; I do not prove it. But I used it to prove other statements. Sensation and intellection are the givens in human life. It is intellectual self-abuse to doubt either one, because by doing so I separate myself from the real world. Reject the evident principle of contradiction and you end up knowing nothing about anything.

THE CHALLENGE FOR PHILOSOPHY (METAPHYSICS)

1. The challenge for philosophy is to understand and then express the unity that exists amidst diversity. Man is experienced as a complex unit. His complexity is immediately observable. He has many different parts. His unity, oneness, is a metaphysical reality not observable but understood. The reality of that unity has to have an explanation, a name, a definition that distinguishes it from the observable complexity. Parts are not wholes juxtaposed along with other wholes and then capriciously given the name "parts." Rather, as parts, they interrelate and cause or effect a whole. The question is what do we call that one thing that causes the unity, that created the unified effect. We must name and define it because we perceive it as different from the diversity of the parts. "Substance" is the most logical term we could use. It describes the non-observable unifying force that stands below and controls the diversity in the one complex phenomenon that is man.

The amazing power of the one human substance to organize the varied physical multiplicity that is the human body is appreciated most perhaps by its absence. As long as the substance is forming, and thereby controlling, this multiplicity of chemicals, fluids, and organs for the purpose of the highest form of life we know, then the result is human, intelligent, trusting behavior. That is a unique effect. That one principle produces the various stages of physical development so that it can actualize and express the fullness that is latent in that substance. It makes its own tools (organs), so to speak, so that the power that it is can be released. What happens when that organizing principle leaves, ceases to form and organize? That organized multiplicity becomes raging diversity. Parts now become wholes. Each new unit runs in its own direction. In death the disintegration and decomposition of what was one whole of many parts, now becomes the juxtaposition of the many. A new product is born—an overwhelming and nauseating stench. Such is the power of the living substance; and such is its absence.

Thus the phenomenon man is not just a mass of juxtaposed chemicals and sub-atomic particles. He is one person, participates permanently throughout life in human nature (human substance or essence). That substance[6] has permanent and transitory modifications (accidents). His nature is permanently intellectual, permanently quantified; but he is not permanently thinking nor permanently the same size. That nature with its permanent and transitory modifications is individualized by the concrete person John Doe.

2. This unity of complexity taxes human expression. The first demand is to remember that these perceived realities are really distinct, but distinctness does not imply separability. The names used to express the distinct are separable. I can put the words "human nature" alongside the word "person." The words are separate. But what they signify cannot be separated one from another. I cannot visually or any other way separate the person John Doe from his human nature. The fact that the person of John Doe is not the same as the nature of John Doe, but still inseparable from that nature, means that the two realities are inadequately distinct one from the other. They are not the same, yet they cannot continue to exist separate one from the other. That is simply the way the complex reality of John

---

6. Substance exists in itself and not in another as accidents exist in another. Accidents always exist in another. They depend upon substance for their manner of being and for their existence. Substance can have different names to express its three different purposes. The one reality described as substance denotes its permanence and ability to remain the same while undergoing accidental changes. The same reality can be called nature. This term calls attention to substance as a source of the proper activity that comes from it. Intelligent and free acts (accidents) are said to be natural to man. Those acts come from his substantial being. Finally, substance can be called an essence. Essence denotes what its nature is, as contrasted with its aspect of being a principle of action. Torturing English we could say that essence refers to the whatness of the substance. Therefore: *Substance*— a permanent principle allowing accidental change while it itself remains the same. *Nature* — substance as a source of action. *Essence* — substance specified as this or that, e.g., man, lion, shark, bee, etc. Substance and accidents are correlative concepts abstracted from the complex living unit that is a permanent individual operating through a permanent nature. Its permanent characteristics (e.g., intelligence, instinct) and transitory activities are determined by and proceed from and therefore exist in that nature (substance, essence).

Doe is. The same is true of any living thing. It is a complex unit of an individual participating in a species. The individual is not identical with its species. There is one species, but many individuals participating in it. Fido is an individual dog, but there are many dogs that are not Fido. I cannot take the dog out of Fido, or Fido out of the dog. But I can understand, know something, about each of them separately. I can distinguish between them, separate them mentally, speak factual truths about both. " Fido is three years old." "A dog is easily housebroken."

3. Our great concern must be with the accurate definition of the metaphysical "names" we use. Science, and metaphysics is the science of being, detests metaphor. Science wants to know what a thing *is*. Science is not satisfied with knowing what a thing is *like*. Science wants to know how a thing is *different and distinct* from other things. Consequently, definition is crucial for all science; it will be crucial for the science of an American Ethic. Our discussion will constantly call attention to proper versus metaphorical language. When I predicate the term "leader" to a dog on a dog sled team, does that mean the same thing as the term "leader" predicated of the head of a business? When I say that the animal has rights and the man has rights, do rights mean the same thing in both cases? When I say the fertilized ovum is a "part" of the mother and the arm is a "part" of the mother, does the word "part" have the same meaning in both instances?

It should be clear, therefore, that there is a difference between *proper* speech and analogical or metaphorical speech. Analogy is a comparison. In analogy the things compared are *simply different*, not identical, but in *some sense the same*. That is why we say they are *similar* and *not identical.*

The problem of metaphorical speech and the importance of accurate definition can be seen in the language of the eminent scholar of mythology, Joseph Campbell in his very influential work, *The Power of Myth.* He uses the term consciousness frequently. Consciousness and energy are the same thing, the vegetable world is conscious, these different consciousnesses relate to themselves, we share plant and animal consciousness, the bile knows, we are manifestations of Buddha consciousness or Christ consciousness, consciousness is the vehicle of the body, and in death consciousness rejoins consciousness.[7]

Clearly our understanding would be aided by a definition of consciousness and a definition of energy. It would also help to know when the term was being used properly and when metaphorically. These comments are not to be mistaken as ridicule. The substantial transcendence (freedom)

---

7. Joseph Campbell, *The Power of Myth*, with Bill Moyers, Betty Sue Flowers, editor, Anchor Books, July, 1991, 18, 69, 88.

of the phenomenon man can imply all that Campbell says about consciousness; but that will be discussed in a later chapter. The point to be made here is that proper speech, the distinction between univocal and analogous predication,[8] the control of language by proper definition, are as crucial to the philosophy of ethics as controlled experimentation is crucial to the physical sciences.

In this essay I shall give a plethora of definitions and their validity will be evident—as sense and intellectual knowledge are evident. If the reader disagrees, then let him show that the definition and phenomena from which it is derived is inaccurate. Then let a substitute definition (not metaphor) be given that is a consistent and comprehensive explanation that supports or rejects freedom, equality, inalienable rights, etc.

4. We must be aware of the difference between imagination and thought, images and understanding. I cannot imagine the reality freedom; I can understand it. I cannot imagine the meaning of the principle of contradiction. I have no proper pictures of "A thing cannot be and not be at the same time and under the same circumstances." But I understand and use that principle all the time in daily life. This distinction between imagining and reasoning is very important for our treatment of freedom. For we will say that freedom is man, a substance that is transcendent. Pirsig, following Locke, will say there is no such thing as substance because it cannot be seen and cannot be reconciled with quantum physics.[9] If Pirsig is correct, then all we have to say about freedom and an American ethic derived from freedom will be invalid.

---

8. In *univocal* predication the predicate noun or adjective fits all subjects in exactly the same manner, e.g., "human" fits Caesar, Teddy Roosevelt, Eddie Murphy, and Sister Teresa in exactly the same way. Each is fully human and no more or less so than the others. In *analogous* predication the predicate noun or adjective fits each subject in a simply different way, but in some sense the same way, e.g., "alive" fits John Doe, his dog, his dog's fleas, his trees, and his flowers. But the type of living in each is simply different, but somewhat the same. They reproduce, grow, metabolize, etc. The philosopher not only wants to know what a thing is, but also exactly how it is like or unlike another. Therefore univocal and analogical predication are very important to his discipline.

9. Pirsig, *Lila*, 104, 105. "No one has ever seen substance and no one ever will. All people see is data. It is assumed that what makes the data hang together in consistent patterns is that they inhere in this "substance." But as John Locke pointed out in the seventeenth century, if we ask what this substance is, devoid of any properties, we find ourselves thinking of nothing whatsoever. The data of quantum physics indicate that what are called "subatomic particles" cannot possibly fill the definition of a substance. The properties exist, then disappear, then exist, and then disappear again in little bundles called "quanta." These bundles are not continuous in time, yet an essential, defined characteristic of "substance" is that it is continuous in time. Since the quantum bundles are not substance and since it is a usual scientific assumption that these subatomic particles compose everything there is, then it follows that there is no substance anywhere in the world nor has there ever been. The whole concept is a grand metaphysical illusion."

Suffice it to say that just because one cannot *imagine* substance existing without any properties (accidents inhering in substance), it does not follow that one cannot *think* (abstract from living phenomena) of a reality that exists in itself (permanently) and not in another. The concept of substance is no more an illusion than any other metaphysical concept, e.g., the metaphysical concept of quality,[10] so dear to Pirsig. That which is conceptualized really exists distinctly, though inseparably, in the phenomenon (man) that is first sensed and then understood.

One can abstract from John Doe 1) the permanent human nature that is there, 2) the permanent person that is there, and 3) the permanent and transitory modifications of that nature and person. These "names" are not synonyms for one and the same reality; they distinguish one reality from the other. Each exists in and with the one complex unit that is John Doe. One can also consider independently the meaning and implications of each of these realities, e.g., the meaning of human nature is that it is both animal and rational; the meaning of rational and free is an ability to understand and the moral necessity to be responsible, etc.

Both Pirsig and Locke fail to admit the obvious data of sense and intellect, namely that the living reality sensed and understood is unified and complex, that some realities are inseparable though distinct from other realities, e.g., the nature of man (which no one has ever seen) his characteristics or properties (some of which are visible and some are not) and his person (which is not visible). Pirsig forgets that a "particle" is precisely that, namely a *part* of the atom, something that *participates* in the unity of the whole atom. The fact that these parts can be distinguished from other parts and from the unifying principle of the atom does not mean that they can be considered substances. That which is distinct does not necessarily exist in and for itself. Particles exist in and for the atom. Whether they appear and disappear is irrelevant to the existence or non existence of substance. What is relevant is the fact that John Doe and Fido exist as individuals, that they share the same nature as others of their species, and yet at the same time have different modifications of that nature (substance). That unit is aptly described as substance, something that exists in and for itself and is the permanent reality in which differences and changes can exist and occur.

Now that we have seen the relevance and importance of philosophy for an American ethic, and now that we have seen some cogent reasons for developing that ethic, we are ready to study the three fundamental principles from which that ethic will evolve, namely, freedom, the need for personal communication, and inalienable rights. What is freedom? Why does

---

10 Ibid., 144, 145, and passim.

freedom demand communication? What is the essence of human communication? What are inalienable rights and why are they inalienable? And how are inalienable rights related to freedom? Once we have answered those questions we shall be able to see that they imply obligations and that by fulfilling those obligations we become moral, ethical, good persons.

2

What Is Freedom?

A new nation, conceived in liberty . . .
                                        Gettysburg Address

Unalienable rights, Life, Liberty, and the pursuit of Happiness . . .
                                        Declaration of Independence

Some time ago I was seated next to a physicist on my return flight from the
Pacific Northwest to Southern California. After the usual pleasantries
whereby we learned about each other, I said, "I have just struggled through
Stephen Hawking's *A Brief History of Time*, and there is a question I'd like
to ask him. Perhaps you wouldn't mind if I were to ask you?" "No, go
ahead," he said. So I asked, "What do you think of freedom? What is it?
We have free acts. Where do they come from? Is their source also free?"
He was puzzled, and I attempted to clarify my question a bit, but the conversation was going nowhere. He really was not interested. So two doctor-
ates sat in awkward silence till the physicist deplaned in San Francisco.
"Too bad," I thought. "Freedom is important to both of us, yet we not only
can't agree on what it is, we can't even talk about it."

Since, as Bloom says, "America tells one story, the unbroken and
ineluctable progress of freedom and equality," and since the thesis of *An
American Ethic* is that morality has it source in freedom, we shall talk about
it. We shall give a brief description and then explain it. We shall show what
man's fundamental obligation is and what his fundamental virtue should be.

Freedom is what man is in his substantial being. Freedom is the transcendent substance of man.

The best way to understand substantial freedom is to start with free *acts*
and then descend to free *being*, start with what we *do* to see what we *are*.
What we shall understand is that freedom is substantial transcendence, i.e.,
we are substances, we exist in and for ourselves. And even though we have
bodies, our minds, our psyches, are transcendent. Transcendent means
not tied down to matter, free from matter. The act of understanding goes
beyond matter; it is a transcendent act. So since we do transcendent
actions, we ourselves are transcendent.

13

Let's start with body language and verbal language, because in this comparison we shall see the first clear instance of free choice and free acts. Body language is universal among humans. The smile, the frown, the quizzical look, the scream of terror or pain, sobbing and weeping on the occasion of death, tears of joy on finding a lost one, all these bodily expressions are immediately intelligible to anyone observing them, no matter what race or country he or she represents. In a word there is a necessary connection between the symbol and what is symbolized. The open-faced spontaneous smile can never be understood as signifying terror. Thus symbol and symbolized are tied together, they are not free of each other.

Just the opposite is true of verbal language. The four-legged animal ridden by soldiers, cowboys, and jockeys has a sign or symbol that people use to communicate with each other about it. The Greeks called it "hippos," the Romans said "equus," the Germans say "Pferd," the French say "cheval," and the English call it "horse." There is no permanent connection between the idea and its symbol. Different nations have freely chosen to use completely different symbols to convey the idea from one to another. The idea is free of an intrinsic connection (unlike the smile) with its verbal (audible or written) expression. If ideas were intrinsically connected to matter, there would be but one language. The arbitrariness of human language is our first evidence of freedom. The act of making, producing, an idea is an act that is intrinsically free of matter.

Though the idea is free of particular matter, it is not totally free of matter. It needs something material for its expression. The reality "horse" cannot be known without some sensory (audible, visual) concomitant. Put another way, there is no such thing as imageless thought. No image = no thought; no image = no idea; no images = no insight or conclusions. As philosophers are wont to say, "There's nothing in the intellect that was not first in the senses in some way or other." If all this is hard to understand, try understanding the sentence "I love my children" without imagining your children, without seeing the sentence, without hearing the sentence. Did anything happen in your intellect?

We can take this a step further. Universal ideas like honor, glory, relation, contradiction do not represent anything material, though they are abstracted meanings from visible and audible phenomena. The act of understanding or insight is real, but it is not sensible or measurable.

Perhaps this whole freedom question involved in language can be expressed humorously by comparing the Gaelic person, the Englishman, Frenchman, German, and Russian with the Irish setter, English bulldog, French poodle, German shepherd, and the Russian wolfhound. The people of those nations do not understand each other's language; the dogs "understand" each other. The only language they have is body language, the bark, the growl, the cry of pain. They cannot use arbitrary signs, which is what language is; they can only use natural signs.

But to understand freedom of the human being we have to go beyond, probe deeper, to see the difference between a free *action* and a free *being*.

SUBSTANCE AND ACCIDENT

These terms are essential for our understanding the human being. A substance is something that exists in itself and not in another, e.g., plants, the insect, snake, fish, bird, animal, the human are substances. Accidental to those substances are color, action, weight, etc. These realities never exist separately, never in themselves, always in another. A substance exists in and for itself; accidents always exist in a substance, never in or for themselves. Whiteness, running, sensation, understanding, 100 pounds of weight do not exist in themselves and they are not essentially and permanently connected to substances. Not all humans are white, the animal does not continuously run, every fish is not six inches long and weighs a quarter of a pound, and the human is sometimes asleep or unconscious and therefore is not always understanding something.

Substances are not directly known, but only through their accidental manifestations. Human nature is known through seeing the individual that is such and such height, weight, with varied colors of hair, eyes, skin, etc. None of these characteristics is permanently identified with the human substance, otherwise all human beings would look the same. The characteristics are accidental modifications of this particular human substance.

The human being is a vital substance that produces ideas and understanding, actions that are independent of matter, immaterial. The idea of blue is not a blue idea, a conclusion, an insight has no material characteristics. Therefore that which produces them is also free of matter. In other words the human being is substantially free because a free transitory act can only come to be from a free permanent substance. I, the human permanent substance, produce the free act naturally because my nature is free. What I am is free. Freedom is not a transitory part of me, it is what I am. It is the most profound aspect of the complex unity that is myself.

The point to be made here about freedom is that it is substantial, permanent; it is not transitory and accidental as is the act of understanding or the act of free choice.

Vital freedom, besides being substantial, is transcendent, is not tied down to particulars, not confined to a particular realm of being, goes beyond any particular. Freedom is, therefore, in some sense infinite. All finite beings can be known by me only because I transcend all of them. If I were not transcendent, I would be stuck on one of them, as animals are confined within the realm of survival, preservation of the species, and natural sign expression. The tiger will never fly, and the eagle will never plumb the depths of the sea or even imagine or express the idea of such actions. But the human can both imagine the possibility and, by understanding the nature of things, determine how to fly and how to probe the depths of the sea. But perhaps the best image of the magnitude of this transcendence is man's comprehension of the universe. He can put the whole thing in his head. He can measure the stars and their distances, and know something of what they are. Any thing that is or is out there, he can grasp and comprehend in some way or other. Though millions of years older, longer lasting, and far larger than he, the totality of the universe is grasped by his mind. This small and transitory reality, man, is larger than the universe; he has to be, if he is to embrace and comprehend it. He is larger than the physical universe by means of his immaterial transcendence, by means of his substantial freedom.

Transcendent life is difficult to understand because, as with all rational thought, it cannot be sensed; and our first knowledge and most common knowledge is sense knowledge. We can see the parent, the child, the insect. But we conclude or abstract from those realities one aspect of them by means of the ideas of *person*, parental *relationship*, and the *being* of each.

An analogy sometimes helps our understanding, especially if the analogy is based on a sensible image. Let's compare the vital and permanent transcendence that is man to a sphere and then add a few negatives.

Imagine a sphere with a point in the center. From that point an infinite number of lines could be extended to touch the interior surface of the sphere. Now for the negatives. Suppose there is no surface, but just lines going out from the center and extending without end. Suppose, too, that this center point and its infinite number of lines is vital, dynamic. It follows that any finite or limited thing outside that center point would be intercepted by one or several of those ever extending vital lines. Thus anything that is, any finite reality, is capable of being intercepted by the dynamism of the center point. In a similar manner the human spirit is infinite and not restricted to any particular but is open to being as being, and therefore can know anything that participates in being. Put another way, since the human spirit is designed for the fullness of being it can grasp anything that is less than the fullness. Since its dynamism is unlimited, it can grasp anything that is limited. This is why a philosopher has said, "Man is the unrestricted desire to know." He meant by that that anything that is can be known by us in some way or other.

There are two points to be made here:

1. This infinite dynamism of my freedom reaches out all the time and is never completely satisfied (happy) when it grasps a particular and limit-

ed or finite object.[1] Put another way, the human person can never be perfectly satisfied with anything that is finite because its dynamic structure is free from limitation in its dynamism or vitality. The only reality that could satisfy it, completely absorb its transcendent activity, persuade it to give up its occupation with particular beings, is the fullness of being itself, infinite being—some people would call that reality God.

2. It seems unreasonable to say that there is no proper object for this appetite for the fullness of being when there are proper objects for all my lesser appetites. There is air for my lungs, food to metabolize, light for my eyes, people to know and love. We are, therefore, naturally inclined to infer there must be some object that can completely satisfy my openness to the fullness of being. In other words this appetite for the infinite suggests that there is an infinite. In fact, if there is no proper object, then life is personally absurd. There is nothing in it for me but a vital abyss of emptiness, since no thing nor particular person can fulfill me.

Our intention has been to illustrate the non-sensible and therefore non-imaginable reality of substantial freedom. The intention was to illustrate the positive and therefore go beyond the purely negative description of freedom. We say "negative" because we kept denying sensible things in the description of the human spirit. We said it was non-material, non-finite, unlimited, not tied down to the sensible, not locked into a particular realm of being. Negatives never tell us what something is, and we want to know what freedom is. Therefore the attempt to illustrate dynamic transcendence by use of the analogy of the dynamic point extending sphere-like in all directions into endless distances.

There are some common experiences that suggest but do not prove our transcendence, as language and immaterial ideas do prove it. What do we do when we go to the beach, ascend a mountain or go to the top of a tall building? At the beach of a great lake or ocean, do we unfold our beach chair and then turn it toward the city from which we came? Or if we have come to the top of a high hill, tall building, or mountain do we constantly look down the path we climbed? Why is it that we enjoy and get great satisfaction from slowly gazing out in all directions to view all the things out there and continue to look beyond them as far as gaze and light permit? And strangely enough at the mountain top or high building there is the urge, frightening urge, to go into that wide openness, as if we had a natural affinity for it, as if that is where we should be. That satisfying and

---

1. I want a Rolls-Royce. I get one. But then I want something else. I get that. I am still not completely satisfied. Amazingly, the only reality that comes close to satisfying me is love and being loved—but more of that later.

attracting experience suggests we are made for openness; it suggests we are made to be free of particulars, yet capable of focusing on any of them. That satisfying experience is an image of the imageless reality that is our transcendence.

Put another way, this transcendent dynamism is the latent power behind the particular expressions of that power, the transitory acts of knowledge and love. Ideas or concepts are limited, finite, transitory. By definition they cannot capture and hold that which transcends them, the infinite, the unlimited, the permanent. Thus substantial and permanent freedom is known not by direct observation and perception, but only indirectly and by inference. Transcendence itself cannot be objectified the way an act of transcendence can be objectified. I can consider the insight I get that leads me to solve a puzzle or some other problem. I say, "Oh, I see the answer, I see how." That is a particular insight produced by my transcendent power. But I cannot experience that power as it is in itself, all by itself when it is at rest and not producing intelligent acts. I cannot make it an object along-side other objects and then compare them for similarities and differences because I use that power itself to understand and compare. One can only conclude from the act that the power must exist as the explanation for the fact of the act of understanding, comparison, free choice, etc.[2]

Transitory freedom found in the passing idea and the arbitrariness (free-dom) of language is caused by the permanent freedom (dynamic tran-scendence) from which it proceeds, as effect from proportionate cause. Since I am the permanent and abiding subject that produces thoughts and choices that are free of matter, then it follows that I, the producer, am per-manently and abidingly free. Hence the term substantial freedom as opposed to transitory or accidental freedom.

Another aspect of this dynamic transcendence that I am is its spirituali-ty. To be substantially independent of matter means to be immaterial. Material is extended, has some length, breadth, width, weight. Here come the negatives again. To be free of matter means to have no extension, no volume, no density, no mass, no weight. As we have seen from the fact of language and universal ideas, we are substantially immaterial. The funda-mental characteristic of what we are is spiritual and naturally incorruptible. If my dynamic transcendence is not extended and has no volume, how can

---

2. An image or analogy of this problem in a physical sense is the human eye. When you are alone and have no person to see and no mirror to see your face, you cannot see your eye or any eye. You can see your hand, your foot, and almost all else around you. But you cannot make your eye the object of your sight. You infer that you have an organ of sight. So it is with your *being* transcendent. You infer your *are* transcendent from your *acts* of transcendence. Just as your eye cannot objectify itself, so your transcendence cannot objectify itself.

it be divided, cut in half, burned, crushed, blown apart, vaporized? It can't. Being naturally spiritual, it is naturally incorruptible and so immortal.

Dynamic transcendence as incorruptible and immortal supposes some sort of purpose for being immortal. Why have it? The suggested answer is that the dynamic transcendence of our person is designed to be united to the Infinite, the fullness of being. Again, that is impossible to imagine because neither finite nor infinite transcendence is an object of our senses. And what is not sensed cannot be imagined. But the real possibility of such a union can be understood from the meaning of the facts, as we shall see.

With this analysis and explanation of what freedom is, we can see what is the radical obligation of the human being. Transcendence is openness. The radical obligation is to become by choice what one is by nature—open. This means that I choose to listen, choose to accept the evident, choose to admit that a problem is still a problem even though I am impatient to accept and employ the solution that is not compelling but only plausible and desirable.

Openness is the opposite of defensiveness, prejudice, bigotry, assumption, and precipitous judgment. But it is not agnosticism. Openness is consistent with moral, scientific, mathematical, and metaphysical certitude. Human beings can be trusted, water will always seek its own level, two plus two will always be four, and every effect will always have its proportionate cause. Certitude depends upon evidence perceived by the normal human being. Openness makes it possible to perceive the evidence. The human being's fundamental moral obligation is to be open to the evidence, accept it, and act in accord with it. This is the obligation freedom (openness) imposes upon each of us. Paradoxically, freedom is determining. We are necessarily free, open—by nature, by what we are. We make that freedom personally ours when we choose to be open to evidence and accept and act in accord with its dictates.

But this freedom is not absolute. It is related to the essential material element of the one human nature that we are. The human spirit does not function in a sensory or intellectual or volitional manner except in conjunction with some material image. The spirit does function in a vegetative manner without images, in a manner that is unconscious to us. The spirit produces all the lower forms of human life—metabolism, growth, circulation, breathing, etc.

This essential relationship between matter and spirit in the one complex human being is a guide to human morality. Though the human being is a rational animal, he is not to live simply as an animal. And though he is rational, spiritual, transcendent, he is not to live as if he were not an animal. He will do injury to himself in both body and spirit if he fails to follow the legitimate demands of both essential parts of his nature. The problem of ethics is, of course, to determine what those legitimate demands are.

It is fairly obvious that man should not live simply as an animal because it is evident that he is more than an animal. It is not so evident that he should not live as a mystic, i.e., as someone living most of his life as remote as possible from corporal and physical activity. It is interesting and attractive to attempt to experience one's own transcendence in some union with the Absolute Transcendent, The Ground of Being, the Divine.

This is not to deny the fact and goodness of mystical experience. It is to deny that such experiences are the natural goal of human existence. Another word for "natural goal" would be the "purpose" or "meaning" or "objective or "good" to which or in accord with which the human person is obligated to strive. Strictly speaking, mysticism is not an escape from the rigors the spirit experiences in trying to express itself through the body in research, study, oral and written work. Mysticism is not something that is achieved by the techniques of silence, prayer, penance, fasting or the straining to effect imageless thought. For all that is to flee and ignore the demands of the body, the world, the society of human beings. Strictly speaking, mysticism is the experience of the divine because the divine chooses to communicate Itself directly—therefore no images—to the relative transcendence that is the human spirit. Genuine mysticism is not a bootstrap lifting of one' s spirit out of the limitations of the body and into an experience of identification with or an absorption into the Absolute, the Ground of Being, God. Granting, for the sake of discussion, that the divine is always in contact with all beings by means of its creative and conserving power, this does not mean that the finite can force the infinite to increase that union to the point of mystical experience, to give more of Itself than it freely chooses to do. For that would be for the absolutely dependent creature to capture and manipulate the absolutely independent Creator— a contradiction and therefore nonsense.

There are two very important consequences for the morality of man that flow necessarily from his essential parts of spirit and matter. Let's first consider the consequence of his being transcendent. As was mentioned earlier, his transcendence cannot objectify itself, cannot look upon itself as distinguished and different from other objects. The fact of transcendence is inferred from the fact of transcendent acts. Since it cannot know itself except by inference, it cannot handle itself, study itself, dispose of itself as it can handle, study and dispose of other things it objectifies and knows, e.g., the body which it animates. What this means is that it has a very hard time knowing and understanding itself. It cannot capture its totality in either an image or concept. Consequently no one act can effect the total giving of oneself to another. Love, and especially marital love, wherein we vow perpetual dedication and loyalty to one another, is not a total gift of self but rather a promise to keep on giving insofar as the giver and the recipient can do this in honesty. It is clearly possible that either or both participants in this love so develop and grow that they are so different from the time they initially made the promise that the giver can on longer honestly give and the recipient can no longer honestly accept the gift of self. The persons have either changed or have discovered themselves to be different from or inconsistent with what they were or thought they were at the time of initial self giving.

The same is true with the love of God. Both the creature and the creator are transcendent, incapable of being completely captured in a concept or image. Therefore the sentences "I love God" or "I surrender myself totally to God" are always somewhat ineffective statements. They do not accomplish (total giving of self) what we want them to accomplish because the word "I" does not adequately represent me nor does the word "God" adequately represent the divine. In a word, I do not know completely what I am talking about. I really don't know me, and my ignorance of the absolute transcendent God is infinitely greater. But if I stay open, if I listen to my fellow man, if I represent myself as I know myself to be, if I accept the facts of life and refuse to delude myself, then I am effective in giving all of myself   to wife, husband, friend, neighbor, God as far as I can. I am accepting the will of God who has put me in his creation and expects me to adapt to it. That adaptation may include my honestly saying the words "I love you," "I love God," "I am totally yours." And those words can and should help me remain open, but the true act of love is the fact of honesty, the fact of trust, the fact of openness,[3] not the words.

This chosen openness cannot be accomplished in one act precisely because we exist in time, exist as animal beings growing physically, intellectually and morally. We grow physically strong for a definite period and

---

3. Arthur Ashe (and Arnold Rampersad) in his beautiful autobiography *Days of Grace: A Memoir*, Ballantine Books, New York, 1993 graphically recommends this openness to his daughter, Camera, thus: "You must learn to feel comfortable in any company as long as those people are good people. Traveling the world as a tennis player, I discovered that deep friendships with an infinite variety of people are not only possible but can definitely enrich one's life beyond measure. Do not hem yourself in, or allow others to do so. I am still dismayed when I go to some college campuses and find out that in the cafeteria, for example, black students, by choice, sit separately at a table with only other black students. Whether from force of habit, thoughtlessness, or timidity, this practice is usually a waste of time—time that should be used by these students to get to know people of other cultures and backgrounds. This mixing is an essential part of education, not something extraneous to it. I hope you will summon the courage to forge friendships with as many different people as you can. Some African Americans may tease you or even scorn you, and other people may rebuff you, but I want you to persevere anyway." 336, 337.

then begin to deteriorate. We grow intellectually all our lives—at least we should—and our characters can grow stronger till our deaths or physical incapacitation. We grow in integrity, courage, temperance, prudence, and justice through this practiced openness and acceptance of reality—in a word we grow through the repeated rewarding experiences of self-controlled openness. Chosen openness becomes ingrained, a learned habit of behaving. Honesty becomes spontaneous and easier even in circumstances that strongly tempt me to lie to myself, to rationalize, to cheat or betray my fellow man and my family. The accomplishment of integrity, the peace-giving union and wholeness of what I am with what I choose to be, is a life long process.

This openness, this transcendence, is so united to the material (animal) element of my nature that that material element is and functions as its natural symbol. And so we come to the second consequence that flows from man's complex essence that is material and spiritual. We speak of body language as manifesting the judgments, attitudes, biases, etc. of the person. We are quite aware that one's verbal language may conflict with one's body language. The words may lie, but the body will always tell us the truth, if we are skilled in reading it. The body is the natural symbol of the spirit that informs and vitalizes it.

Besides being the symbol of the spirit, the human body is the highest animal species on the planet. As animal the human being lives not only in the societies of family, tribe, city, state, nation, inter-nation. He also exists as animal among other animals. He eats vegetation and he himself is biodegradable. He defends himself from them and they do the same. He kills and eats them, they can and do do the same. He is a member of the jungle in which there is no justice, mercy, charity, or generosity. There is no murder, injury, or property damage. There is only survival and propagation of the species. The individual has no rights and exists only for the benefit of the species. The only growth, development and progress is so that the species can survive.

As an animal among animals he has no claims against them. He is not being treated unjustly when the termite ruins his home, when the snake bites and poisons him, when the lion comes down from the mountain or out of the field and kills and devours one of his family. Like all other animals he simply figures out how he can live safely among them; he either kills them or protects himself against them. In one aspect he differs from all of them; he is more than a predator as they are predators. He is a domesticator. He can capture, control and make them serve his needs, wants, and pleasures because he transcends them. He is free of matter therefore can see relationships between and among all things. They cannot because they are not free. He can see how they are related to his needs, his wants, his pleasure, his creative imagination. They are not free so they cannot see to imagine and create. He does not violate their rights because they are not his equals, they are not independent of him as he is independent of them and of his fellow man. They have no rights that are to be respected by him or any of their fellow animate beings, for they and he—insofar as he is animal—are locked into the survival and propagation of the species, and this at the expense of individual members of other species of vegetable and animal life. For they are not free, but he is the only animal that is free.

Animals other than man may be called intelligent, but only analogously. Their intelligence does not transcend survival. Man's intelligence carries him beyond survival to mastery and control of all reality because he understands all of it in ever increasing increments. He sees ever more and more relationships. Each new insight is the basis for insight into a thousand more. Each new technological advance is the basis for a thousand more ways to survive, to utilize, to enjoy. The prospects for a better material, intellectual, and moral life are limitless.

Unfortunately this freedom makes it possible for him to be infinitely immoral. Thus mastery by this intellectual animal makes it possible for him to descend below the purely animal level of survival through violence, to the level of waste, injustice, cruelty, and perversion. He is not only capable of the greatest integrity, but also of the most profound duplicity and corruption. His fellow animals are incapable of any of these. For they are determined substances; he is substantially free.

THE GOD OF PHILOSOPHY

The Declaration speaks of God as the creator of all men. Our bills and coins refer to God in image and word, e.g., *Annuit Coeptis* on the reverse side of the dollar bill is the Latin for "He approved our beginnings." "In God we trust" appears on our bills and coins, and "One nation under God" is in our pledge of allegiance to the flag. As a nation we have a tradition of accepting the fact of God and a reverence for him. Trust in him and being subject to him is implied in all these expressions. Nevertheless, we tolerate, yes, respect the freedom of the atheist to deny His existence and deny being subject to Him. And we are adamant in refusing any organized religion a legal power within the law. At most a religion can function only as any other equal member of the democratic process. It can exercise free speech, attempt to persuade, and its individual members can vote. That is the extent of its legal power. The nation's traditions deal with God as unrelated to any particular religion. In the nation's traditions he is a creator, a benefactor, a superior to whom the nation is subject. We pray to him in song "God bless America" and "God crown thy good with brotherhood." What rationally—not religiously—can be said about this nation's God? Is there any way in which this pluralistic society can be rationally united in agreement about the fact and nature of God? We think "yes."

THE EXISTENCE AND NATURE OF GOD

It is evident that I am not the cause of my own being, nor am I the cause of my continuing to be. There must be some cause that explains my coming to be and staying in being. And since my finite dynamic transcendence was caused, then that which caused it must also be transcendent, and transcendent in a superior sense. Superior in the sense that it itself was not caused and subsists in itself because of itself and not because of another. All this is hard to understand because we have no concrete images of cause as cause, infinite, and uncaused transcendence. As we said earlier, we first know the sensible, and we use the sensible (visual and audible images) as the vehicle of understanding the reality beyond the sensible. But the fact of the matter is that we do understand. We have more than sense knowledge. What we are understanding here is the non-sensible realities of freedom, immortality, the fullness of being as opposed to finite being, participations in being—which is what creatures are.

So when we come to the existence and nature of God and admit we know[4] very little and nothing directly, that does not mean that we know nothing. We do really know something about God, namely he actually exists. And we know something about His nature. That knowledge is not direct, of course. But it is analogous. He is like us but simply different. His existence and nature is like ours, but simply and eminently different. A crude example of one being existing in an eminently different way from another being is that of the life of the worm and the life of a human being. The human life is eminently superior to that of the worm. So analogously and more so God's nature and existence when contrasted with ours. This existence and superiority cannot be seen, but it can in some sense be understood. What is understood, little as it may be, still is a reality that is

---

4. This knowledge of God differs from the knowledge of a believer of revealed religion. The revealed religions present characteristics and messages from the deity. The deity's existence is evident to the believer from his or her religious experience and is accepted as such by the followers of those religious leaders. The knowledge of God of which we speak prescinds from the question whether these religions are true or not. Instead it asks the question: What is the meaning of the fact of contingent being? It answers: The fact of contingent being demands a sufficient explanation. The only reasonable explanation is: The fact of contingency demands the fact of necessity, and the fact of inferiority demands the fact of superiority—otherwise there is no meaning to anything.

understood and must be faced if we are to be honest with ourselves, i.e., if we are to adapt to what we know.

The method of coming to the insight of inference that God exists and is superior to us is commonly called the argument from the existence of *contingent being* to the insight that the principle of causality demands there be a *necessary being* supporting all contingent being. Before presenting this argument, it will be helpful to discuss causality in some detail. We shall do that by way of several definitions that cover most aspects of the nature of causality.

> *Principle:* That from which something proceeds in some manner or other.
>
> *Cause:* A principle that induces some new manner of being into another.
>
> *Effect:* Change, a different manner of being, produced by a cause.
>
> *Cause/Effect:* These are correlatives. One can't come to be without the other coming to be.
>
> *Proportionality of an Effect:* Every effect is proportioned to its cause, i.e., the effect cannot have more being than the cause from which it proceeds.
>
> *Purpose or Final Cause:* Purpose moves the agent to perform or act on an object and change it. If there is no intention to act, there will be no act and no effect.
>
> *Exemplary Cause:* The model or design chosen and used to direct the agent in making the specific effect. The effect imitates the exemplar.
>
> *Efficient Cause:* The agent or producer of the effect is something outside the agent.
>
> *Material Cause:* The physical, extended, stuff which the agent uses to make the effect. One could also say it is that onto which the form is imposed, e.g., the form "house" is imposed upon the building materials by the agent.
>
> *Formal Cause:* The essence, the structure, the specific nature that has been put into or on the matter and causes the new being (new effect) to be this rather than that.
>
> *Instrumental Cause:* Limits the efficient cause to the characteristics of the tool. For example, the writer using chalk is operating under different limitations from those he would experience if he used a ball point pen. The effect, writing, is proportionate both to the instrument and to the author. The writing produced manifests both intelligence and chalk (ink).

Moral Cause: Properly speaking this is not a cause, but only analogously so. It is an occasion for something to result from the activity of
another cause. Essentially it is the act of one free being to get
another free being to act. The moral "cause" presents evidence
to persuade someone to choose a good or avoid an evil. The
moral cause presents the good or apparent good to the perception of the listener. The listener then freely chooses to act. Since
there is a free choice, there is no necessary connection between
cause (the persuader) and effect (decision to act) as there is in all
other causality. The decision to act is made by the one listening
to the moral cause, not by the moral cause himself.

A crass example of all this could be the sculpture or painter. He is an
agent that is intelligent and material. The picture/statue will be proportionate to him, i.e., the statue or painting on the cave wall will manifest
both that he is intelligent and that he had physical movement, a body. That
same effect will show that he had a purpose (final cause). He wanted to
make a picture or statue. He had a model (exemplary cause) or figure in
mind to guide him in producing the statue or painting. The fact that the
picture came to be shows that some intelligent material being went into
action (agent, efficient cause) and at a particular time and place produced
the painting or statue. But he did not create it out of nothing. He used
materials, i.e., stone, brass, the surface of the cave wall, paint (material
cause). The statue or painting is not indeterminate or undefined. Each is
a very specific form (formal cause) imitating the exemplar chosen by the
agent. His tools (brush, fingers, chisel) limit and enhance his activity and
manifest their own specific forms. Brush marks, finger marks, and chisel
marks are evident in the form of the statue or painting. Finally, moral
causality was present at the outset when a patron of the arts persuaded the
artist to create the statue or painting. The good he presented was any of
several things, e.g., a stipend, opportunity to exhibit in a famous gallery,
etc. The patron morally "caused" the painting.

All these many different causes make up the meaning that is found in the
one effect through the testimony of the senses and the mind. Strictly
speaking causality (a metaphysical reality) is not immediately observable,
but it is immediately understood by observing the statue or painting and
"seeing" the meaning implied in it.

That being said, let's be clear about the ideas of contingent and necessary causality. It is impossible to imagine the reality "forever." But one can
understand it. You simply say "No beginning and no end." The words, of
course, don't prove that there is a being that is forever. But suppose for a
moment that there are beings that have a beginning and that do come to

an end. They clearly depend on something to bring them out of the realm of pure possibility into actuality. Here is the application of the principle of causality. Anything that is moved in any way is moved by another; and the effect is always in some sense inferior to the cause. The things that have a beginning are dependent upon or contingent upon that principle which brought them into being. They do not necessarily exist, but rather have a contingent existence.

The most important point here is that they do exist, and their existence has to have an explanation. The only explanation is that they ultimately come from a being that is totally independent of others, e.g., a non-contingent being. The non-contingent is *necessary*.[5]

Necessary means that it exists because its nature is such that it has to be, cannot be otherwise. Why? Because contingent being actually exists independent of my mind, therefore the source of its being has to be "out there," "somewhere." And it is "out there" without beginning and without end. That is hard to imagine. But we are out of the realm of imagination and into the realm of understanding meaning. That is the given structure of our knowing capabilities as they face the real world.

That doesn't tell us an awful lot, but what it does tell us is as valid as the knowledge that the universe exists. Not only that, but the nature of that necessary being is also somewhat revealed. It is characterized by freedom, intelligence, and power. Freedom—because it has brought *free contingent* beings into existence. Intelligence—because it *understands* how to make things come into being and exist according to their individual structures or designs; and Power—because it can *execute* according to chosen design and reduce the pure possibility of a contingent universe to an actually existing contingent universe.

All that insight is the meaning found by the mind when investigating the *fact* of contingent being. All that is metaphysical thought, the testimony of the mind, the evidence of things intelligible, unseen, unimaginable, and undemonstrable—as all evidence is undemonstrable. To reject the *meaning* of contingent being permits the rejection of *all meaning*. It is to refuse to accept the given structure inherent in the acts of human sensation and understanding as they fasten onto the real world. Rejecting sensible evidence and its *meaning* leaves us as dumb spectators with nothing to say about the real world.

---

5. The need for a necessary being can be seen from a slightly different viewpoint of the contingent being. There are two real and distinguishable factors to every being that is not God. Those factors are the being's essence or nature and its existence. These are real but inseparable in every contingent being. In other words every contingent being is a composition or a complex unit. Given composition, there must be a non-contingent and non-composed composer.

It is well to recall here the difference between the natural scientist and the metaphysician. The strict scientist limits himself to the observation and reporting of phenomena. There is chemical movement within the cells. He does not take the next step and settle the abortion controversy by saying "There is the beginning of personal life." Life may be the meaning of the movement, but all he can see is the movement. It is at this point that the scientist disqualifies himself as an expert witness and says "I am no witness to the fact of life." On the other hand, the whole point of all his dogged research is not only to see and record what happens, but to discover relationships and applications that will better human life. He is always radically concerned with meaning. Every scientist is more than a scientist. In the basement of the scientific and human mind sits the metaphysician with his unrestricted desire to know, and he says, "Just as in the past I found out the meaning of some of the phenomena, so tomorrow I'll find out what these new phenomena really mean."

TRANSCENDENCE

The contingent being depends upon the necessary being constantly for both its existence and its nature. Thus the necessary being is constantly present, by its power, to the contingent being. This power is experienced, but not objectifiable. We can't, as it were, look at it. We only know it is there by inference from the facts: 1) Neither I nor my parents caused this *unique* being that I am to come to be (parents cause the common nature, not the person); 2) I am not the one who is keeping myself in being now.

We frequently hear the term "Ground of Being"[6] to describe this situation. The analogy distinguishes the contingent being from the source or cause of its being. It imagines an "earth" or "ground" as some sort of foundation or support upon which the contingent being rests. "Ground of Being" is a metaphor. "Necessary Being" is the proper term to describe God as known by philosophy. Causality, as applied to the necessary being, would be explained thus: 1) Principle—The necessary being is the source from which all contingent reality proceeds and is kept in existence. 2) Cause—The necessary being induces the reality of being into the purely possible contingent being. 3) Cause/Effect—The necessary being is not a cause until it induces reality into contingent being. Contingent being is an effect, the sufficient explanation of which exists outside itself, namely in the necessary being. 4) Purpose or Final Cause—The necessary being has a reason for bringing contingent reality into being. It is a contradiction for an infinitely free and infinitely intelligent necessary being to act ran-

---

6. Campbell, *The Power of Myth*, 46, 48.

domly, without purpose, without knowing what it is doing and why it is creating. That purpose will never be fully known by man (contingent being) either by philosophy, religion, or direct experience with the infinite, unfathomable, and ineffable necessary being. 5) Exemplary Cause—the necessary being "looks" upon itself (for there is nothing else to look at) to see how it can be participated in by contingent being. Thus the law (structure) of the necessary being becomes the guide or model for the intelligence and creative power of the necessary being. That intelligent necessary being then purposefully brings the purely possible contingent being into existence, for example, makes the firecracker for the Big Bang. 6) Efficient Cause—The necessary being is the agent that does two things: a) brings contingent being into existence in imitation of the chosen exemplar, and b) keeps the being in existence. These activities are called creation and conservation. These are the proper finite expressions of the infinite, and might metaphorically be called the unique " language of God." No other being can "speak" or fully understand this " language" because no other being can create and then conserve the created. 7) Formal and Material Causes—These are intrinsic to the contingent being and make up its essence. Crass example: the wood (material cause) is formed by the carpenter into a chair. The necessary cause brings both into being at creation. This does not deny subsequent evolution. Contingent causes (carpenter, etc.) always work with and from preexisting materials. The clearest evidence for the existence of matter and form is metabolism and growth among living substances. The human changes living substances (food) into the one substance that is himself. 8) Instrumental Cause— The all powerful necessary being does not need an instrument (another being) to help it create, whereas contingent causes must use instruments to help them make things, whether it be a symphony, a poem, or an automobile. The body is the most radical instrument of the spirit. 9) Moral Cause—The necessary being can be said to be a moral cause attempting to persuade the free human being to respect its will as manifested both in the structure of the human and in the structure of the universe. Respecting those structures brings peace. Ignoring or rejecting them brings disturbance. Both persuade to proper behavior, yet the person is always free to reject such evidence.

The religious poet, Gerard Manley Hopkins, speaks of that necessary being, the cause of all reality, thus:

> I kiss my hand
> To the stars, lovely-asunder
> Starlight, wafting him out of it; and
> Glow, glory in thunder;
> Kiss my hand to the dappled-with-damson west;

> Since, tho' he is under the world's splendour and wonder,
> His mystery must be instressed, stressed;
> For I greet him the days I meet him, and bless when I understand.[7]

So we come to the answer of our question "What is freedom?" An analysis of the freedom mentioned in the Declaration is: Freedom is the transcendent substance of man. That vital transcendence reaches out to the fullness of being as to its proper object. It is this orientation to the fullness of being that makes possible the knowing, seeking, and loving of particular and lesser beings. This substantial transcendent freedom is contingent, and this fact implies a transcendent necessary being, the God that philosophy, not religion, affirms. That necessary, infinite, personal and all powerful being is the proper object of our finite and personal transcendent nature, the meaning of our lives. Our radical moral obligation is to choose to be open, to become by choice what we are by nature, open or transcendent. This means that we face evidence, admit its meaning, and act upon that. Such choices are the means of acquiring our fundamental virtue— integrity, wholeness, the union of what we *know* as good and true with *doing* what is good and true.

In the following chapter we shall discuss the major choice that effects and deepens our decision to be open.

---

7. "The Wreck of the Deutschland," Stanza 5, *Gerard Manley Hopkins, Poems and Prose*, Selected with an Introduction and notes by W. H. Gardner, Penguin Books, 1985.

3

Communication

What obligation flows from this transcendence? Have we done enough when we attempt to keep an open mind in all things? Is there something more to fulfilling this obligation of openness, this choosing to become in my personal life what I am by my nature, i.e., transcendent, open? Is there a method, that if practiced regularly, will dispose me to be open habitually so that it is almost second nature to me to be open? Is there something that is the proper object of my openness so that if I knew where it is and what it is I could go for it, constantly seek it? And if I thus constantly sought it, would I be doing other moral acts, e.g., temperance, justice, patience, etc. while at the same time fulfilling my radical obligation to be open? Yes, there is such a thing, there is such an object, there is such a method. That object is my fellow human being and that method is communication with him.

Communication is a willingness to be one with him in cooperation, friendship, even marriage. That communication is essentially trust that is at first superficial, then serious, and finally takes on the depth of friendship and/or marital love. Trust is the revealing of who I am and the acceptance of another to the point that I act upon what he tells me and build a part of my life upon that given word—whether it is a serious commitment as in business or marriage, a revelation of a concern, hope, serious problem, or a simple agreement to meet me somewhere. It is in this act of trust and being trusted that I begin to know, possess, and dispose of myself. In this communication I experience my freedom and independence as well as experience the independence of another and respect him. I have the opportunity to see the uniqueness and value and importance of that other person only in the act of communication. All my other volitional and intellectual actions that deal with the non-personal are actions done to objects, and objects only. The person is an object because he has a body, and I do things to his body (senses) when I communicate with him. But I reach more than his bodily senses. I reach his person through those senses. I come to him asking trust and exposing myself as trusting him. This does something to me and him that no other action can do. I am not merely

31

open to evidence, as I am when I meet other objects, but I am at risk not only of being betrayed and deceived by him, but also of being accepted by him and so of coming out of my aloneness and now truly being with another. Instead of being selfish I begin to become selfless through a more or less permanent involvement with another in a part of his or her history and lifelong memory. This is a true going out of oneself and a true reception of another, a true being received by another.

The alternative to communication is selfishness, being absorbed with self and therefore essentially lonely. This loneliness cannot be overcome by dealing with other objects, with other things; nor can it be overcome by treating other persons as things or objects. For to do so is, by definition, to fail to communicate. It is a failure to recognize their freedom and independence from me. It is to dispose of them, manipulate them and to use them to accomplish my needs, wants, and pleasure. It is to be alone—lonely in their presence as if there were no speech between us, even though we do talk to, see, and hear each other. When we use another person or persons, we do not extend trust nor ask for it. There may result a communication of knowledge, insight, and information, but there is no union of persons. This is most evident in organizations. If there is low morale, the members really do not identify with the organization. They feel used. Whereas in an organization with high morale, the people do identify with it and its goals. They feel they belong because in fact they do belong. They are trusted and they trust. The organization deals with them openly and honestly and the members do the same.

Therefore the meaning of transcendence is not merely an openness to all things and objects, and thus obligating me to face the facts, but it is openness to the greatest fact of all, the other transcendent, the person of my neighbor. I can give myself to him and receive him and can be received by him so that there is a union between us. And this I must do under pain of punishment or sanction of loneliness and isolation, but worst of all, under pain of being closed. I close myself if I refuse to accept a fact; I close myself if I shut out the other person or persons, I close myself if I refuse to give myself to others, refuse to accept them. I close myself if I deal only with objects, treat people only as objects and not as persons worthy of my trust and worthy of my respect because of their innate goodness, their freedom and independence from me. This closedness, this exclusive self concern, this refusal to be one with another free and independent being in mutual freedom and independence is radical perversion and the source of all perversion. It is the choice to close that which strives to be open. Incest, rape, enslavement, murder, theft, etc. are essentially selfish acts, acts that do not respect the freedom and independence of the other. This abuse of the other persons, this treating of them as objects, is usually founded in the fact that I have more power than they have. I am physically stronger in the case of murder, rape, incest, etc. I am more clever, experienced, have more information in the case of seduction, fraud, etc. I have more economic and/or political power in the case of economic control and subjection of people's lives. In all those acts there is the failure to respect the freedom and equality of the people I treat as objects precisely because they are weaker than I and because I want something, some object, of theirs for myself. Those acts are the opposite of union through communication of free and independent beings. They are essentially self-destructive and a perversion of my openness to my fellow free and open human being.

There is another aspect of this transcendence that needs to be considered here, namely its boundlessness, its aspect of infiniteness. We said that we cannot grasp, perfectly understand ourselves, cannot capture ourselves (or our neighbor) in a concept or image that gives us understanding of all that he is. In a word we are mysterious, incomprehensible. Consequently when we affirm our openness in the act of trust of our neighbor, we move into that mystery and by that very fact move into, say "Yes" to, the Absolute Mystery, the Absolute Transcendence that is the source of all reality and source of all transcendences (persons). For to be open to the boundless in any form is to be open to the boundless as such. Put another way, the "Yes" to my neighbor's incomprehensibility is a "Yes" to the incomprehensibility of the Absolute, to God.

This can become quite clear when we think of death as the end of our lives. There are just two ways of looking at death. One way is to see that it means that life is absurd. If life is absurd, then the only thing to do in the meantime is to live for myself, to get all that I can out of everything in my experience, and that means that I use people, that all communication with them is to achieve power over them so that they satisfy my needs, wants, and pleasures. It is then foolish to trust, and it is wise to become ever more skilled in deception so that I can continually distract myself from the ever haunting fact that I am alone. The other way is to take the leap of faith and affirm that it is not the end but rather the transition to and beginning of a fuller realization of my transcendent life. This leap of faith takes place in every act of openness and trust toward my neighbor. That act of trust is a refusal to be alone, a refusal to close myself to the mystery that is in every neighbor. It is a refusal to say that life and all that it implies—work, research, affection, love, hugging and sexual union leading to child and family joy and sacrifice—are absurd. This "yes" to life is a "yes" to the Ground of Being that constantly causes and conserves our transcendence, focuses it on the fullness of Itself and thereby makes it possible to focus on things and objects that are less than Itself. In a word every act of openness and love and trust of neighbor is an act of openness and love and trust of the Absolute, the Ground of our being, God. Every act of trust is an acceptance of life and a rejection of the idea that the meaning of death is that life is absurd and that I must live for myself. Every act of trust is a rejection of the idea that I must not communicate in a manner that respects the freedom and equality of others. Trust rejects the idea that I must live for myself, that the meaning of life is to discover how to use things and people to satisfy myself and thereby distract myself from the fact that I am alone. Trust of neighbor is essentially a surrender to and "Yes" to the cause, and therefore the meaningfulness, of the vitality that is my transcendence and openness. Trust means that I am not alone now and will not be alone.

There are two ways in which we actually deal with The Absolute. The first way is by immediate and non objectifiable experience. The Absolute is present to us by His creative and conserving power. The Absolute is the sufficient explanation of the vitality that is our transcendence. We cannot separate ourselves and look upon ourselves as separate from the cause of our being. If we could effect such a separation, we would cease to be. We can only infer, therefore, that as caused we are experiencing the cause. The second way of dealing with the Absolute is to anthropomorphize It. Michelangelo did this when he depicted the creation of Adam. God is a bearded, elderly, muscular man reaching out of the clouds and touching with his finger the finger of Adam. This art is the compression of the Absolute into the form of man. Art thereby makes God an object among other objects, the second or fourteenth etc. in a series of objects that can be counted. This makes it easy for me to focus on God instead of on other things and other persons. I can thereby pray to, adore, praise, and thank the Lord by means of such images and concepts. But they never adequately represent and therefore never adequately put me in contact with Him. For I have unsuccessfully attempted to capture the infinite God with a finite concept. Thus I can say I love Him according to the way I imagine Him to be and at the same time have an abiding rejection of all or one of the following: Serbs, Croats, Muslims, Atheists, Christians, Arabs, Jews, Blacks, Hispanics, Whites, Koreans, Homosexuals, etc. Such a "love" does not keep me open as He has designed me to be open. The rejection of any neighbor is a rejection of Him, because it is a rejection of what he has designed me to be, namely open to trust myself to my neighbor and to be trusted by him.

How to Communicate Effectively

It will be good to look at two examples of ineffective communication, because in seeing what is wrong it will be easier to see what is right.

The first example is that of an undisciplined class of high school students. The teacher attempts to cover the material in the textbook. A few students pay attention. A boy is writing a message in ballpoint on the arm of a smiling girl in the row next to his. Two girls and a boy are sharing snapshots and laughing, many others are talking. A couple of boys have their heads on their desks and hoping they can fall asleep. Several girls are engaged in cosmetics, putting on make-up, brushing and braiding one another's hair. Their is no communication here because all but a few are not listening to the teacher. All but a few are closed to the person of the teacher. The teacher is not respected.

The second example is what frequently occurs in city or town meetings on controversial issues. A council member or citizen speaking from the floor advocates one side of the issue. Other citizens or council members angrily interrupt with questions and objections and groans or boos of disapproval even before the speaker can present the reasons for his position. As with the undisciplined high school students, so with the adult citizens at the council meeting—nobody is listening, nobody is open, nobody respects the speaker. Nobody, for the most part, is willing to hear him out and give the ideas serious consideration. The listeners are closed. They damage themselves by making it impossible for them to benefit from any truth the speaker may have.

Such behavior damages the classroom and democratic process because learning and rational decision making by a group are blocked. The behaviors of the students and the citizens are immoral for they have closed that part of their being, the most radical part, that was meant to be open. They neither give respect to their fellow human being, nor make it possible to be united with him. Their behavior moves in the direction of division, separation, isolation, and loneliness. All of that is unhealthy for the human being as an individual and as participating in a community. He suffers and the whole, of which he is a part, suffers.

Carl Rogers, the famous therapist, has something important to say about communication and the health of the person. His goal was to help the client achieve good communication within himself. "Once this is achieved, he can communicate more freely and effectively with others. We may say then that psychotherapy is good communication, within and between men. We may also turn that statement around and it will still be true. Good communication, free communication, within or between men, is always therapeutic."[1]

How stay open? The first step is to decide personally that I will face facts and adapt to them, i.e. change my position when facts show that I am wrong. The second step is to decide that every person's freedom is worthy of respect. He is not to be subjected to the force of my fist, voice, economic

---

1. Carl Rogers and F. J. Roethlisberger, "Barriers and Gateways to Communication," *Harvard Business Review,* July-August, 1952, 30.

or any other power that I might have over him. In a word he is to be listened to, taken seriously as the evidence he has is serious. Once I internalize such decisions, I am immediately faced with the responsibility of being patient as I listen and temperate in my response, and kind when the evidence I have forces me to disagree with his position. Thus radical and chosen openness imposes upon me the duty of practicing a host of virtues toward my fellow human being. None of these things happens in the undisciplined classroom or in the obstreperous council meeting. It should be clear, therefore, that this communication with the neighbor in openness is the means of developing all sorts of other positive character traits, e.g., courtesy, patience, prudence, justice, temperance, fortitude, kindness, etc. For if I am to stay open, I must be patient as I try to understand him. I must be courageous enough not to let him intimidate me, and so object to what I see as inconclusive presentation of evidence. If I am to respect his freedom and dignity, I must give him what is due, i.e., practice justice to that person whether it is an adult, child, subordinate, peer, superior. Thus the practice of openness forces the practice of virtues, and the practice of the virtues deepens my habitual disposition to be open. This is especially true of the virtue of religion. It is subordinate to the virtue of openness (love) toward God. I go to church, pray, follow the precepts of my religion to help me stay open to the mystery of life, to help me respect and trust my neighbor. Both the soul and the object of all virtue is the decision to be open.

Trust is the accomplishment of peace and union between or among human beings; trust is the first fruit or product of successful communication. It is the win/win situation that occurs in true problem solving.

Consequently, discussion, talking to one another or with a group or committee is a moral function. There is a moral and immoral way of discussing. Put another way, I can harm myself, be immoral, bad, evil in discussion and thereby deprive myself of the good for which I was made, namely union, peace, and a trusting relationship with my fellow discussants. Those "discussants" can be my customers, employers, employees, my children, my clients, my vendors, my students, etc.

Therefore it is necessary at this point in our discussion of moral behavior to consider how speech is to be kept moral and productive of mutual human growth.

SELF-FULFILLING PROPHECY AND TRANSACTIONAL ANALYSIS

The way communication is to be kept moral is for the speaker to be aware of two psychological facts: 1) The expectations of the one initiating the communication can cause the expected to happen, and 2) true union or communication may best be served if the communicators proceed from their adult ego-states.[2]

According to the theory of self-fulfilling prophecy as applied to any communication situation, the positive and negative expectations I have toward those with whom I communicate will positively or negatively influence their behavior. In general they will succeed or fail according to my expectations of them. An example to illustrate this may be found in the McGraw-Hill tape. Dr. Albert Kane conducted an experiment at a vocational training center. Five randomly selected hard-core unemployed were described to the trainer as having a high aptitude for welding. At the end of six months, these "haps" as they were called, had a better attendance record, learned the fundamentals in a little more than half the time, scored ten points higher in their test, and were without exception selected as the ones their peers would most like to work and be with. The only variable in the experiment was in the mind of the instructor. The instructor was shocked by the results; he felt he had treated everyone in the class equally.

This fact that my attitude towards my listener is picked up and "heard" by him as encouraging or indifferent and discouraging puts an obligation on me to *be* and then, from this internalized disposition, *act* out of genuine respect for the listener. A habit of courtesy in communication usually insures this, especially with those whom I first meet. Unfortunately this is not always so with those familiar to me from family or work, or from stereotypical assumptions. And practically all of us have suffered at one time or other from being "typed" by those at home, school, the workplace, or the majority of society. This typing made it difficult for us to listen to the "typers," no matter what they said. This fact is also frightening; for how am I to hide from my spouse, children, friend, peer, superior, etc. the negative and factual judgments I have of them. The only thing I can do is: 1) keep my attention focused as much as possible on the good in them that I genuinely appreciate and, 2) when their faults cause me too much inconvenience, reveal my concern in an attempt to get along more harmoniously

2. The first fact is often referred to as the Self-Fulfilling Prophecy proposed by Robert K. Merton and popularized in *Productivity and the Self-Fulfilling Prophecy: The Pygmalion Effect,* a video tape from CRM Productions, McGraw-Hill, Inc. See also: Robert K. Merton, *Social Theory and Social Structure,* 1968 Enlarged Edition, The Free Press, New York, 1968, especially pages 475-490; Robert Rosenthal and Lenore Jacobson, *Pygmalion in the Classroom, Teacher Expectations and Pupils' Intellectual Development,* Holt Rinhart, and Winston, New York, 1968. The second is part of the theory of transactional analysis of Eric Berne, *Transactional Analysis in Psychotherapy, A Systematic Individual and Social Psychiatry,* Grove Press, New York, 1961 and popularized by Thomas Harris's book *I'm OK, You're OK, A Practical Guide to Transactional Analysis,* Harper and Row, New York, 1969, and the book *Born To Win, Transactional Analysis with Gestalt Experiments,* Addison-Wesley Publishing Co., Reading, Mass., 1971. by Muriel James and Dorothy Jongeward.

with them. An honest request for help is always a sign of respect and trust; and it tends to elicit the same.

Therefore, if I am to be moral in my communications with others, my decision to be open to them really means that I have examined my internal judgments (positive as well as negative prejudices) and attempted to convert myself internally from any and all unfair dispositions and replaced them with a respect for the innate goodness and virtues of that person, that group, that nation, etc. Once that has been done, I am ready for the next step, namely dealing with the listener out of my adult ego state.

Transactional Analysis

A good model to serve as a point of departure for our discussion is that of the parent, adult, and child ego states. According to this model people approach one another or take a stance with one another that is domineering, authoritative, threatening when communicating. They speak as a parent and they are trying to elicit a response from the listener that is childlike, obedient, and submissive. Their goal is to win, to have their opinion prevail. They are not open to change, for really there is nothing new to learn. The listener must be won over to their position.

The discussant who asks questions about the facts surrounding the problem is in the problem solving mode, the rational and inquisitive state. His mind is not made up, he is open to reality whatever it may prove to be. This is referred to as the adult ego state.

The child ego state shows a behavior that is submissive, accepting or sometimes playful, ignoring, distracting. It yields to or ignores the power of the parent. Sometimes it treats the parent in a playful or petulant manner. It tries to change the adult into a parent and make that person assume responsibility, give direction, even take over the task to be done because of its own lack of confidence or irresponsibility.

The point here is that there can be no genuine communication, no union, no development of trust among equals as long as one of the discussants remains in either the parent or child ego state. These two states do not respect the freedom and equality of the other discussant/listener. The intimidating or defensive behavior of the parent will never terminate in honest consensus, honest agreement between parent and child, parent and adult. What this really means is that the discussants are not open and honest. They argue or ignore rather than probe for facts and the significance of the facts. Put another way, they are personally closed. This, of course, is in violation of the openness of their personal structure. They are depriving themselves of that for which they were made, namely the facts of reality and the trust that agreement on those facts will produce. Being deliberately closed and thus deprived of their due good, they are morally evil, personally bad, divided from one another, alone, and this even if one of the two feigns agreement.

This situation can be managed and changed if two things happen. First, one discussant must proceed out of his adult ego state, keep himself open, non-defensive, and really listen to what the parent or child is saying. He must sift through the emotional, the intimidating, the defensive, the petulant, etc. and seek the factual evidence in the position being presented and defended. He should attempt to rephrase the position and ask the parent or child whether he has repeated the position correctly.[3] Phrases like, "Correct me if I am wrong, but this is the situation as you see it . . . etc." This might be called the integrity question, for it proves that the listener is truly open to receive the facts. Openness, of course, is the key to successful communication.

The problem now becomes one of changing the parent and child discussant into the adult mode. The first step in this direction has already been taken, i.e., the adult listener has stayed open, has not allowed the other person to elicit from him either a child like or a parental response. There has been no submission, no retaliatory response, no sarcasm, no mocking. Instead he has listened, sincerely trying to understand the points being made. It is possible that the patience, sincerity, openness, and obvious integrity of the listener will be imitated later on. If so, so much the better.

But the second step is for the listener to ask factual questions, i.e., when and where did it happen, who was present, what did the first person say, how much did it cost, how much time did it take, etc. Factual questions like these focus the discussion on reality and gradually force the parent and child into an adult mode. Data are indifferent to emotion; data force one to confront reality. Facing reality, of course, is being open to reality.

These factual questions must always be sincere. Any hint of sarcasm in tone or phrasing, any mocking or feigned sincerity is really an attempt to demean, put down, humiliate, and punish the parent or child. Such behavior is immoral because one is deceptive; one is pretending by correct grammar to seek the facts but the tone and manner have an entirely different purpose. The purpose is to keep the fight going and to come out a winner. True communication, union with the other(s), consensus, and ultimately solving the problem is impossible with these behaviors. To give the appearance of openness when one is really closed and intent on winning is dishonest. That frustrates the natural tendency, the natural thrust of the

---

3. Carl Rogers suggests the following laboratory technique to achieve this openness in ouselves "Each person can speak up for himself only after he has first restated the ideas and feelings of the previous speaker accurately and to that speaker's satisfaction." Rogers, "Barriers etc.," 30.

human spirit. It prevents union, trust, friendship. That behavior is evil, immoral, a closing of that which was made to be open. Sincere factual questions are the only means of opening the closed person. If factual responses are not given, if the questions are ignored and the same old positions are repeated, communication is impossible. There will be no problem solving. The decisions that result will be made in accord with the opinions of those in power, they will not be made in accord with the facts and their significance.

We have spent much time discussing the importance of trust. We have implied that it is based on the communication of truth to our fellow human being. That truth is not merely that our words match the facts that we know, but more importantly that our words match the facts of what we are. We have looked at a technique that will keep ourselves open to reality, and that will lead our fellow human being out of the closed and manipulative parent and child ego states so that the facts and their significance can be faced and agreed upon. Thus this openness, for which we both are made, is completed both by the facts and the mutual consensus. We now are good, we are better than we were for we now have something that we did not have before the communication. We not only have intellectual completion, but personal completion. We have integrity, we are morally good. None of that could have happened if either of us had been domineering, defensive, petulant, sarcastic, implicitly threatening, using position or seductive power over the other. None of that could have happened while we deprived ourselves of our due openness, while we were evil, morally bad. Integrity, sacred honor, cannot exist in the closed person.

THE AMERICAN ETHIC AND RELIGION

The main purpose of this book is to propose an ethic that can be accepted by all Americans no matter what religious belief they accept. That ethic is based on an understanding of what freedom, equality, and justice mean and imply. The analysis of freedom shows that it is personal transcendence over all particular beings and objects. It reaches out to the transcendent neighbor and thereby affirms and accepts the mystery of life and so reaches out to and accepts God.

Every effort has been made to avoid the debate between the American atheist and the American religious person. The affirmation and proof of a Supreme Being from the principle of sufficient causality is not the affirmation of the God of revelation and religion, whether Christian, Jewish, Muslim, Hindu, or any other. The God known by revelation and the God known by philosophy are one and the same; but none of the precepts of religion are either affirmed or denied by what we have shown in our analysis of freedom and freedom's goal, the Absolute Being. Therefore there is no reason why an American ethic cannot be accepted by the religious person.

Since a great number of Americans are Christian, and since many of these long for some moral teaching in our schools, it is hoped that they could accept what has been presented here. We fear they might object to it as being nothing but secular humanism and therefore inconsistent with their Christian traditions. We shall try to meet that concern with references from Christian scriptures now.

First of all St. Paul and St. John make it quite clear that the universe is a Christian universe. It is not simply a world without any relation to God or Christ. All things were made through Christ, and without him nothing was made that was made (Jn 1:3). And Paul says much the same. All things were created through him and for him. And he is before all things, and in him all things consist (Col. 1: 16, 17). The meaning of these passages is that there is a relationship between reality of this universe and Christ. Even though God could have created a thousand different universes without any relationship to Christ, the one he did create is related to him. The cause of that relationship is real and is in the things related. When God knows and understands the universe, he sees it not just as a thing that he made, but rather as something that characterizes it as Christian, ordered to and related to Christ. Made by him, for him, and consisting in him. What those real characteristics are the scriptures do not spell out for us in scientific terms. What the scriptures do say, though, is that this universe is more than just a universe. It is a universe related to Christ. Consequently, the only humanism possible is a Christian humanism, for the humans of this universe are all related to Christ, whether they know it or not.

Secondly, God wants all men to be saved. The history of the world is essentially a history of salvation from sin and death unto everlasting life in Christ Jesus. Tim. 2:4,5 says, ". . . who desires all men to be saved and to come to the knowledge of the truth. For there is one God and one mediator between God and men, the Man Christ Jesus." Many other passages carry the same message, e.g., 2 Pet. 3:9; 1 Jn. 2:2; Rms 5:12; Mt. 18:11; Rms. 8:32; 2 Cor. 5:14; Ez. 33:11; and Wis. 11:24-12:18. The meaning of such a divine desire is not a simple "It would please me if all men would be saved." The desire is effective, i.e., it produces a result, namely, something is done by God to make it reasonably possible for each and every human being to be saved. Every human being means just that, every one that comes into this world—men, women, children, infants, etc. As with the real relationship to Christ, so this efficacious salvific will is not explained by scripture; it is simply affirmed. To say that God wishes universal salvation without his providing the necessary means for salvation is to say that his will is ineffective. That, of course, is nonsense.

One of the means that is available to all human beings—whether they knew, know, or will know Christ—is love of neighbor. Mt. 25: 31-45 clearly shows that one can love Christ without knowing that he is doing so. "Assuredly, I say to you, inasmuch as you did it to one of these the least of my brothers, you did it to me" (Mt. 25:45). There are many other passages that show the love of neighbor as salvific. 1 Jn. 4:12 is impressive ". . . No one has seen God at any time. If we love one another, God abides in us, and his love has been perfected in us." Further on John asks the question that should frighten the latent hypocrite that might be in any of us: ". . .for he who does not love his brother whom he has seen, how can he love God whom he has not seen" (1 Jn. 4:20). If the love of neighbor is not perfect in us, there still seems to be some hope. Perhaps it can be said of us as Christ said of those who crucified him: "Father, forgive them, for they do not know what they do" (Lk. 23:34). Other passages that support this theme of love of neighbor are: Mt. 22:39, 40; Lk. 10:28; Mk. 12:31; Jn. 2:8; 13:34; 15: 17; Rms. 13: 8 & 10; 1 Cor. 13: 1-13; Gal. 5:14; and Col. 3:14.

There are two objections some Christians may have to the theory that love of neighbor is, strictly speaking, not love of God and not salvific. Perhaps the most common one is that this love of neighbor is nothing but humanism and there is nothing Christian about it. But we have already dealt with that in showing that this is a Christian universe and not simply a natural one that has nothing to do with Christ and God's saving grace. Consequently, any "Yes" to life is not merely a "Yes" to purely human values. For there are no purely human values. The "Yes" to life is a "Yes" to Christian human life, regardless of whether one sees that life as Christian. Further, as St. Augustine said long ago "God is more intimate to us than we are to ourselves (*Deus nobis intimior est quam nos nobismetipsis*)." This intimacy is the first word of God to each individual and prior to any revealed word of scripture. Consequently, anyone following his conscience is adhering to the structure that God in his creative and conserving power is "speaking" to him; in other words he is accepting his Christ orientation to God. Thus even the self-proclaimed atheist who rejects the God of philosophy and the God of revealed religion, yet trusts and loves his neighbor, is still affirming the mystery of life and holding himself open to the mystery of God and God's providence for him. Strictly speaking, the only practical atheist is the loner, the one who lives for himself, for number 1 rather than communicate with others in trust.

The second objection is this: Love of neighbor really is not love of God; rather God just counts it as love of himself. What this really means is that God is a patronizing and paternal pretender who has made the history of salvation a game of "Let's pretend." Let's pretend man is good when he really is bad; let's pretend that man loves me, when the most that can be said for him is that he likes his neighbor very much. It is impossible that the source of all reality pretend that the unreal is real.

THE STATUE OF LIBERTY AND THE NEW COLOSSUS

Openness and communication are the two radical obligations of the human person. These, as we have seen, flow from the transcendent nature of man. That transcendent nature is identical with freedom. Individual Americans dedicated to freedom have developed laws of their nation to overcome institutional slavery, segregation, and discrimination. It is the practice of the basic American principles of openness and respect for the freedom of others that is responsible for any and all ethical goodness that is in American life. This respect for the freedom and dignity of oneself and others is the source of justice, courage, patience, generosity, kindness, industry, persistence and all other virtues because they are the means of realizing in everyday life the freedom and dignity of our fellow man. It is appropriate that we conclude these two chapters explaining freedom/ openness and communication with that famous symbol of freedom and openness: The Statue of Liberty and its sonnet "The New Colossus."

> Not like the brazen giant of Greek fame,
> With conquering limbs astride from land to land;
> Here at our sea-washed, sunset gates shall stand
> A mighty woman with a torch, whose flame
> Is the imprisoned lightning, and her name
> Mother of Exiles. From her beacon-hand
> Glows world-wide welcome; her mild eyes command
> The air-bridged harbor that twin cities frame.
> "Keep ancient lands, your storied pomp!" cries she
> With silent lips. "Give me your tired, your poor,
> Your huddled masses yearning to be free,
> The wretched refuse of your teeming shore.
> Send these, the homeless, tempest-tost to me,
> I lift my lamp beside the golden door!"
> —Emma Lazarus

The flame of "imprisoned lightning" can be interpreted as the great exploits a free person can accomplish once he or she has passed through "the golden door" of the USA. The "world-wide welcome" is the openness that is the Spirit of America, the respect for the freedom and equality of human beings. "Give me your tired, your poor, etc." is our ideal of rejection of class distinction, the ideal of rejection of discrimination, and an implicit affirmation of "liberty and justice for all." That statue is a symbol of the American ideal and the radical American ethic—openness to all our fellow human beings. The goal of that openness is expressed in the prayer in the last few words of the song "America the Beautiful": *America, God shed his grace on thee, and crown thy good with brotherhood from sea to shining sea.* If that grace is granted, we will communicate in trust with each other. Communication is the only way in which brotherhood can be accomplished.

4

Why Are Rights Inalienable?

Endowed . . . with certain unalienable rights . . . Life, Liberty, and the pursuit of Happiness.

It is very clear from the word "endowed" that it is totally American to hold that the basic rights of the American citizen come from what the human person is. It is totally inconsistent with Americanism that rights come from either our Declaration of Independence or our Constitution. It is equally totally American to say that the purpose of the American government is to secure those rights, which already existed prior to the establishment of that government. The words "unalienable rights" also mean in the American conception or philosophy of man that it is beyond the power of government to destroy, negate, remove or deny those rights. That is the consequence of saying rights are "unalienable."

Again, therefore, the very nature of this language forces us to think "natural law." For human nature, according to the Declaration, precedes American government; and American government is instituted to protect the rights found in men who "are created equal."

Let's first determine what a right is and then see what an inalienable[1] right is. Then we will go on to consider the rights to life, liberty, and the pursuit of happiness. This latter right we shall identify with the right to private property. That right will then be developed into an explanation of the purpose of business.

What is a right? We can see who has rights and we can see who must respect rights. We affirm rights and demand they be respected. But we can't see or touch rights. Yet we know they exist because we understand and exercise them, e.g., right of ownership, right of self-defense, right to marry and raise children, etc. But what is a right? A right is two things. First it is a relation and second it is a moral power. Both of these need some explanation.

First, a right is a relation. Three factors constitute a relation: a) a subject related, b) the term to which the subject is related, and c) the cause

---

1. We shall use "inalienable" because "unalienable" is archaic.

or foundation for the relationship that always exists in the subject related to the term. An obvious relation is the mutual relationship between mother and child. In the relationship of motherhood the subject is the mother, the term is the child, and the cause or foundation of that relationship is the acts of conceiving and giving birth to that child. Those actions existed in the mother and caused her to be related to the child. The relation of son or daughter is in the child because he or she was conceived and born of that person now called mother. Those relationships cannot be seen, but the subjects, terms, and causative actions can be seen. The relationships cannot; they can only be understood and what is understood is real. Sonship is real, motherhood is real.

The inalienable rights to life, liberty, and the pursuit of happiness verify the definition of a relation. The subject of those rights is every human being. The term to which the human being is related is the exercise of life, liberty, and the pursuit of happiness. The cause of those relationships are first, the substantial freedom of every human being; second, the fact that each and every one is alive; and finally, each and every one is material. Each one needs material things such as air, food, drink, etc. to stay alive, exercise freedom, and thereby be at peace, experience contentment, etc. The causes of all those relationships to those terms are in every human being. They are not only in human beings, but in them in such a way that those causes cannot be removed without destroying the human being. One cannot take away the substantial freedom of man, nor take away his life, nor separate his material element from his spiritual without at the same time destroying the human nature that is essentially free, alive, and material. That is why the right to life, liberty, and the pursuit of happiness are inalienable—their causes cannot be separated (alienated) from the subject man who is necessarily and permanently related to them. Therefore those rights are not man's by some arbitrary decree of an all powerful God, nor by an arbitrary decree of some government, but rather by the nature of man, by the fact that man is free, alive, and material. An atheist may reject the notion that man was created by God and endowed by him with inalienable rights and still be an American. That same atheist cannot, in the face of the evidence here offered and consistent with American philosophy, hold that some men do not have these inalienable rights.

A right is also a moral power. A moral power is different from physical power. Physical power always implies some local motion, one body is displaced in proportion to the superior force required to overcome resistance or inertia. Superior force is always necessary for the successful exercise of physical power. But moral power is the power of self-determination, the power of free choice, the power to exercise natural and legal rights. The exercise of any right is an instance of free choice. A right, therefore, is the ability or power to exercise and realize the relationships one has to life, liberty, and the pursuit of happiness. It is the ability to act freely and acquire what is good for the person. Such goods are communication, and by communication the acquiring of friends, spouse, and family. It is the power to acquire, own, and dispose of property. In some instances, where free will cannot be exercised, e.g., the infant, child, retarded, insane, the right cannot be exercised. In those cases the rights are protected by relatives, friends, and law.

Obviously, physical power can overcome the exercise of moral power, but it can never destroy that power directly. To destroy the power of a right, physical power must first destroy the free human being.

The same moral power, once it is recognized by another free person, can act as a moral cause and persuade another to respect the freedom he sees in his equal and thereby acquire the good of peace and even friendship with his fellow man. Thus there are two types of moral power: 1) the power of self-determination, and 2) the power of moral causality, whereby one persuades another free being to freely choose what the persuader wants him to do. The moral power of persuasion is subordinate to and dependent upon the power of self-determination.

More needs to be said about the right to the pursuit of happiness because this relation and moral power is caused not merely by the vital freedom of man, but also because he is material. This right implies the right to private property because private property is a necessary condition for happiness. The right also implies the right to entrepreneurship. Therefore the purpose of business will also be discussed.

We have been emphasizing the transcendence, the spirituality, the immateriality of the human being, and have been giving only passing recognition of its materiality. We implied that materiality when we said the human being is complex, has vegetative and sensitive life. We touched on it again when we said that all his thoughts and choices used matter as a vehicle of expression and that there was, therefore, no such thing as imageless thought. It is time, therefore, to consider that material aspect of human nature.

To forestall one's contesting this right at the outset, recall what has happened to communism in the recent past. One of its fundamental tenets was that private property and the means of production belonged to the state. The practical result of that view of the mutual relationship of the state and individual was that free human beings were subordinate to the state. They worked first for the state and indirectly (through the state) for themselves. They were in no sense free to change that condition or even to discuss changing that condition. The permanent communization of property followed from the perversion of individual freedom. The communist state granted rights, gave limited freedom. Americans are free, have unalienable rights, create a state, then give it power to specify the exercise of those rights for the common good.

Why is there an inalienable right to private property? Because man's spiritual-material human nature must necessarily own material things in order to give full expression to the substantial freedom that he is. Just as there can be no intellection or free choice, no imageless thought (images are material), so there can be no survival, growth, development, self-realization without the free disposal of material things. I not only have a right to food because I exist, need food, and food exists; but I have a right to my food, a right to eat when and where I want it and the way I want it. If this were not true, then necessarily someone else would be denying me food, or giving me just so much food, and giving it to me the way he wanted to. I would be his dependent; my innate freedom would be subordinate to that other person; I would not be free.

I not only need food; I also need space, need air, need the opportunity to work with things, try to understand things, try to see the interrelationships among them. To understand them I have to experiment and observe them, for I am the unrestricted desire to know. I can't do that unless I own them. Owning them can be done by the individual person or by the corporate person, e.g., Thomas Edison or the Southern California Edison Company. Both are free, both must be able to dispose of material things if they are to become all that they can be within the moral limitations and then legal limitations of that freedom. We shall say more about moral and legal limitations when we come to the topic of obligation. What we must stress here is that the human species must be able to possess material things if it is to be able to use its material human nature to understand and transcend all that confines the human spirit.

Let's return to the contrived image of transcendence we gave earlier[2], i.e., the vital point extending without end in all possible directions. That is an image of substantial and infinite vitality. It would intercept any finite being out there. Not only that, it would also intercept other beings and whatever relationships existing between or among them.

The mark of greater or less intelligence is the ability to perceive relationships. James Watt watched the moving lid on the steaming tea kettle and understood the power of steam, got the idea of harnessing that power through the piston, saw the relationship of both to metal and the wheel. Something similar happened with the observation of bacteria, mold, disease, and penicillin; with electricity, radio waves, and the wireless; with elec-

---

2. Ch 2, 16.

tricity, binomial numbers, and the computer; with the sun, the chip, and the solar calculator; with fetal tissue and Parkinson's disease. If the human is not free to dispose of any and everything material, his unrestricted desire to know is frustrated. The ever extending lines moving out from the central vital and transcendent point that man is is stopped, and thus its natural tendency is perverted, i.e., frustrated. He must be able to own material things so that he can use them. That ownership must be done by the free person, individual or moral (corporation). Freedom is violated, frustrated, if material things are doled out by the state and their use is directed by the state. That is a type of slavery. For the exercise of the state's power is at the discretion of its leader's. Those leaders become the only truly free persons in the community; the rest are in some true sense slaves, slaves to the few.

What is the connection between the right to private property and the pursuit of happiness? Happiness is a vital activity of the human. It is the result of successful accomplishment of natural appetites, natural human tendencies. That accomplishment is contentment, being at peace. The apex of the human's (individual or corporate) tendencies are knowledge and personal union (friend, lover, child, family, neighbor, etc.). As the human freely, without the restriction of the state or any oppressor, pursues his unrestricted desire to know by the use of private property, as he gives and experiences trust with his fellow workers, friends, family, neighbors, etc., he is at peace, content, vitally happy. Man's pursuit of happiness means to own material things, to exercise his transcendence, to understand and control his world, and thus survive, accomplish, grow, mature, self-actualize, give and experience trust. The right of private property flows from the free and material nature of man. It, too, is inalienable because man's materiality and freedom cannot be separated from him without destroying that nature. Since man's materiality cannot be got rid of, neither can his right to private property. The most that can be done is to pervert that right, i.e., 1) either enslave him and direct his use of material things, or 2) or so control all material things within his purview that neither as an individual nor as a unity of free men (corporation) can he do what he freely wants and is inspired to do with them.

What has the right of private property to do with business, and what has business to do with ethics and morality? The use of private property has evolved from a mere means of survival to a means of fantastic human progress. The transcendent dynamism of the human spirit has discovered how to so use material things that it can conquer terrible disease, distribute goods to multitudes over great distances with amazing speed, conserve knowledge in libraries and computer banks and have both readily available to multitudes, and thus enrich the lives of ever more and more people. This has all happened because the human spirit, free to pursue its unrestricted desire to know, has come to understand more and more over the centuries; it has come to understand the nature of things so that it can create ever new products to change life from an ordeal of survival to the possibility of the pursuit of science and art and peace. The human spirit has done all this through business, i.e., the creation of products to meet human needs, the distribution of those products to satisfy more and more people who could barter or pay for them and thereby improve their standard of living. Trade, business, the corporation is the natural flower of the human spirit as it wrestles with the material world in the hope and desire to make life better, first for oneself and then for others. The human being produces enough for his survival, and then produces more in hope that his neighbor will want some of his product and give him something of value in exchange for his surplus. Through that exchange both now have more than either could produce alone, and their lives are better.

So often it has been said that profit is the purpose of business. There can be no profit without there first being product. There can be no profit if the excess that I produce is not of value to my neighbor, if he has no desire to get it for himself through giving me something of value in exchange. Thus the very nature and

> purpose of the corporation is the creation of wealth, those goods and services that enhance our standard of living. When the corporation increases its productivity, it produces more goods and services at lower cost and thereby increases that which is available for consumption. This is an increase in the aggregate wealth of society. . . . The creation of genuine wealth, goods and services for consumers must be the primary purpose of the corporation. . . . The government can produce money; it does not produce wealth. This is the social purpose, the noble purpose, of our business institutions.[3]

It is extremely important here to note the very nature of business, namely creation of desired products always precedes the creation of profit. There is no way anyone, be it an individual or a corporation, can get profit directly. He must first make a product that someone else wants and will give something of value in exchange for that product. The value exchanged must cover the cost of the materials, it must cover the expense incurred, and it must provide the producer with profit, something of value that now makes his life better than it was before he produced the product. If one wants to survive, he produces for himself; if he wants to do more than survive, he must produce something that is of value to someone else and thereby enhance his fellowman's life.

---

3. Lawrence Miller, The American Spirit, *Visions of a New Corporate Culture*, William Morrow and Company, Inc. New York, 1984, 37.

The so called desire for profit is essentially the pursuit of happiness, the desire to live better, to live up to the creative imaginings of a better life, which creative imaginings are nothing more than the active unrestricted desire to know and to create.

As Miller says on the same page "Achieving financial results is necessary, but secondary in purpose. Financial results will follow as the corporation and its stockholders succeed in their primary aim."[4]

Miller's idea was expressed in another way by a business scholar during a seminar for GM executives. He asked them, "What is the purpose of business?" The great majority of participants agreed: profit. His response went something like this: No. Profit is like air. The human must have it in order to live. But the purpose of life is not breathing. So with business, it must have profit to live; but its purpose is to provide goods and services at a reasonable price.

Profit (the acquisition of money) may be what I want to get from the business so that I can use the money to buy more goods and services for myself; the desire for profit—and so for a better life—may inspire me to work hard to discover and create a product that people will buy. But if I focus more on profit than on product, if I so manage the business that I give ever less value for more costs to the consumer, I expose myself to the successful attacks of competition. Someone will come along and produce the same product for less cost. The consumer will benefit, the new business will make more money through volume sales, and he who had control of the market will lose it. Often price is designed to cover cost of material, expenses, and reasonable or great profit. Price should do much more. It should attract the customer and discourage the competition. Experience in the business should always lead to product improvement and improvement in the means of production. The competition should always be wondering, "How can they give so much value for such a low price." Since the competition does not understand, competition stays out of the market. The only reason for entering the market is the reasonable conviction that I have more to give the consumer and therefore I shall make a good profit. With that money I can then better my life by purchasing wealth (goods and services). My hard work and creativity benefits my fellow man first, and thereby benefits me. Only by working for him (making a product he needs or wants) can I benefit myself; paradoxically, business is naturally and essentially altruistic.

Before concluding, we should quote Miller again:

---

4. Ibid.

Business enterprises do have a noble purpose and we should recognize and proclaim it. The purpose of business is the creation of wealth—not for a few, but for all.

Wealth is not money. It is the goods and services that business provides. It is we who are able to produce wealth who will eliminate poverty, disease and ultimately war, who will free humanity from the chains of mindless toil so that we can pursue and utilize our higher capacities of mind and soul.[5]

What has business to do with rights? It is the natural evolution of the exercise of the inalienable right to private property and the pursuit of happiness. What has business to do with ethics and morality? First, as we see every day, there is so much fraud and corruption in business that there is need for some clarification of moral and ethical principles to guide those who run businesses and those who legislate for them. Second, as Miller suggests, business can and should ennoble those who engage in it.

SUMMARY

A right is a moral power; it is the power to dispose of oneself in a free act that is guided or has as its norm human nature, e.g., tell the truth, marry, divorce, resign a position. Moral power is distinguished from physical power. Physical power is the power to move other bodies, other physical things, e.g., hammer a nail, pull a trigger, etc. Moral power is the power to move myself freely. It is also the power to move other free human beings and yet leave them free. I move them by the presentation of evidence, I persuade them by letting them see the goodness for them in the free choice I want them to make. They are moved by my influence, but they move (choose) freely.

A right is constituted by a relation. A relation consists of a subject, term, cause, and cause of relation existing in the subject. An inalienable right is caused by the nature. As long as the nature exists, it is the cause of that right. That right, therefore, cannot be removed or directly affected. It ceases only when the nature ceases to be. The inalienable right to liberty is caused by the substantial transcendent nature of man. The inalienable right to life is caused by the vital transcendent nature of man. The inalienable right to the pursuit of happiness is caused by the material element of man. This body-person needs to own and dispose of material things in order to exist, survive, and freely mature in accord with his unrestricted

---

5. Ibid. , 44

desire to know and create. Therefore the inalienable right to the pursuit of happiness implies the right to private property.

Business is the creation of products and services, the creation of wealth. Profit is subsequent, in its creation, to the creation of wealth. Business necessarily first considers the needs and wants of people and then creates products to meet those needs. Business must, therefore, consider people before profit. Profit, therefore, can never be directly intended. It can only result from people wanting the product so much that they are willing to pay (barter) more for the product than it cost to produce it.

Functions of price: Cover cost of materials, cover cost of expense, provide reasonable profit, attract consumer, discourage competition. Competition: Constantly considers the needs and wants of the consumer to determine how it can give more or the same value for less cost. Nobility of Business: Creation of wealth for all.

Up to this point we have attempted to clarify the notions of freedom and rights. We have said little about the limitations of freedom. We said it is limited by the need for matter to provide the human being with images as vehicles of thought. But that is the only limitation we mentioned. And we have talked about rights as being inalienable, but we have not dealt with the fact of the limitation of those rights. We have not discussed obligation. We shall do so in the next chapter.

5

Inalienable Obligations or Moral Necessity

Just as inalienable rights flow from the very nature of man's transcendence, so do inalienable obligations. These inalienable obligations are what is commonly referred to as the moral law. Man is morally necessitated to obey these laws. Perhaps the best way to appreciate moral law or moral necessity is to contrast it with physical necessity.

If we consider the physical nature of living things such as plants, insects, fish, and animals, we see they are forced by their natures to act in accord with those natures. The apple tree does not produce oranges, the ant does not produce bees, the dog does not produce cats, etc. All are locked into acting in accord with their natures. The same is true of man, but with a significant difference. His nature is free, transcendent, as we have said and shown many times. He is therefore locked into transcendent acts as well as vegetative and sensory acts. He knows, he sees relationships as he analyzes, he synthesizes; he chooses to engineer, manufacture, communicate, and love. He is a scientist, engineer, artist, friend, and lover. No animal can do these things. This is what his nature can do; but unlike the animal, he is free to violate this complex natural structure. He can deliberately violate his body and do damage to his vegetative and sensory processes. But worse, he can close his openness to his fellow man, choose to use and manipulate him and thereby fail to communicate with and be united to him. He can choose to be alone; and this leads to all sorts of denial of the moral world. He denies the right to private property, and so steals from his neighbor. He ignores the right to life, and so murders his neighbor. He denies his neighbor's right to truth in communication and so lies to him, defrauds him, seduces him. He therefore settles for communication with things rather than with people; he can make himself utterly alone.

Man's nature is to be open or transcendent, but he is not forced to be open. He is not forced by nature to accept evidence, not forced to adapt to it, not forced to reveal himself in trust nor forced to trust the other. He is not forced to communicate, to be a friend, to be a lover, to respect the freedom and dignity of others even though he recognizes those realities. He is not forced by nature to live in peace with his fellow humans. But he is obliged to choose to do all these things, if he is to be in accord with that natural tendency in him to be open. Thus there is no physical necessity in man to choose openness, but only moral necessity, i.e., he is free by nature, yet obliged by nature. The only way he can escape these obligations is for his transcendence to be taken away from him; but that is no escape, only destruction. It is because his transcendence is inalienable that his obligations are inalienable.

We speak of inalienable obligations. There is the obligation to be open, but there also are other obligations. We will mention four which will imply many others. And we want to see how these relate to that obligation to be open. The four major responsibilities are prudence, justice, fortitude, and temperance. They relate to openness as the body is related to the soul.

My commitment to openness makes me prudent, i.e., leads me to carefully consider and weigh the relevant evidence as I am about to act justly, courageously, temperately. And that careful decision making confirms me in my openness towards evidence. But the soul and source and animating life of prudence is openness.

My determination or choice to be open to my fellow man implies that I respect his freedom and rights as well as my own equality and rights and therefore that I give him and myself our due. Justice is to render to each and everyone his due. Consequently, being open implies justice, and the practice of justice confirms me in my openness toward my fellow man. The source or soul of that justice and that which animates justice is the commitment to openness.

The same is true regarding fortitude or courage. Openness to fellow man or openness to life as meaningful is to deny that life with all its trials, illnesses, and ultimately death is absurd. And so one struggles to overcome ignorance and the forces of nature in order to survive, prosper, and experience friendship, love, and peace. "Climb every mountain, ford every stream, etc." supports the validity of the dream that is natural and in-born in each of us. It is the basic commitment to the meaningfulness of life that is the soul of courage, and it is the practice of courage that deepens the commitment to the meaningfulness of life.

So also with temperance. My decision to be open to the evidence of what is good for my physical and personal life, makes me careful in taking pleasurable things into myself. Temperance does not apply merely to things that satisfy my bodily appetites, such as food, drink, and sex, but also to communication, to study, to work, to music, etc. Openness to the good of life is more important than openness to one particular good of life. Temperance helps me avoid extremes in the use of the particular goods of life. The opposite of temperate behavior would be found in the glutton, workaholic, the person, who in his climb up the mountain of maturity, personally stops and atrophies at the level of sexual experience. That commitment to life is the soul and animating principle of temperance. Through temperance I affirm and practice my openness to the good life, and through my openness I am led to practice temperance.

Finally, the virtue of religion should be considered in reference to openness because it is frequently considered to be the most important virtue of all. It is not. It is subordinate to the practice of openness, and governed by prudence and temperance. The virtue of religion or piety is narrowly applied to a particular creed or faith such as Judaism, Catholicism, Islam, Protestantism (in its many forms), Mormonism, etc. These are the human responses to the historical intervention of the divine as alleged by each tradition. That intervention is to be distinguished from the constant creative and conserving power of the divine in every element of the universe. Such religions, as human responses, are capable of corruption; so much so that a particular religion can become over time the source and justification for the culture in which the religion is practiced. The criterion for all valid religious practice is not just the particular sacred writings, creed, dogma, liturgy, and law that this human response has articulated. But rather, like prudence, justice, fortitude, and temperance the validity of religion depends upon how well its practice keeps man open to his fellow man in trust and love. Thus the morality that religion attempts to effect in man is not that he become a better Jew, Catholic, Muslim, Protestant, Mormon, etc., but rather that he become the best possible John/Jane Doe. Religion should assist him in becoming truly open to accept that his particular life has meaning and that meaning is best accepted in his openness to his fellow man. The acts of prayer, adoration, and love of the God of historical intervention specifically deal with a finite object, i.e., the historical intervention and not directly with the God who intervened.

Religion and piety are not the proximate norm of morality, even though they are initiated by the divine contacting particular humans. For the divine is always in contact with the human by its creative and conserving power. The first word of the divine to each person is not the scripture, etc. of his religion, but rather the vital structure of his own being in the daily circumstances of life that have been "spoken" to him by the creator who brought him into being. The individual conscience should control by means of prudence, justice, courage, and temperance the prescriptions of religion. For those dictates are always bound by the culture and history and insights of the religious leaders who received the intervention and interpret it to the members of the religion. History is full of crimes committed in the name of religion. And the unwritten histories of individuals who have submitted themselves to the demands of religion are histories replete with misery—self-inflicted and inflicted on family and friends. At the same time those same religions have been the inspiration of frequent, daily, and often heroic, acts of kindness to fellow human beings. These two facts—the misery and kindness—show that religious practice can spring from prudence and imprudence. Consequently, the truly religious person is first open, then prudent, then religious. Religion should always be subordinate to, controlled by the conscience of the free man whose first obligation is to be open and honest with himself, and only after that to be a good Jew, Catholic, Muslim, Protestant, Mormon, etc.

We Americans are fortunate that our Declaration, Constitution, Bill of Rights, etc. have created a society that supports individual freedom and responsibility but only tolerates religions. America's prudence has put religion in its proper place, subordinate to freedom, openness, transcendence. America thereby has become an exemplar of what every free person should do, control religious demands so that they serve and benefit his free person. Unwittingly, America's tolerance has the same objective as valid religious practice, namely the affirmation of the value and dignity of life for all human beings.

The same mutual relationship between the choice to be open and all the other virtues could be demonstrated, e.g., patience, punctuality, persistence, chastity, industry, generosity, mercy, forgiveness, etc. All of these find their root in the choice to be open and their support in the basic virtues of prudence, justice, fortitude, and temperance. Patience can illustrate this point well. Openness to my fellow man inclines me to listen to him, to try to understand the meaning or reality behind his relatively inarticulate and emotional expressions. The act of successful patience gives me the successful experience of being open and tends to strengthen me in that radical commitment. Practice of patience is also the practice of justice and temperance in my responses and questions to him. Similarly my openness to evidence makes me patient as I study the facts and work to learn their meaning. That patience helps me stay open to more evidence. Prudence takes over when I begin to apply the meaning of evidence to form conclusions that I intend to reveal to others.

On the other hand, the radical decision to be closed is also the implicit decision to be rash, unjust, cowardly (despairing) and intemperate. And so this radical decision becomes the animating principle of all other habitual behaviors (vices). Patience becomes cunning, punctuality a symptom of arrogance, persistence a type of ruthlessness, chastity is cold hostility, industry is the virtue of the workaholic, generosity always looks for recompense, so does mercy, forgiveness is simply delayed vengeance, etc. When this closedness reaches its acme point, it has become boundless pride and arrogance. The person is utterly alone, friendless, corrupt, capable of any vice at any time. It has been said that money is the root of all evil. In support of that cliche a famous and now deceased actor once said, "The only good thing about money is that if you have enough of it, you can tell people to go to hell." The real root of all evil is the lie told to oneself, "Life is absurd, therefore live for yourself and to hell with everyone else." Out of this lie comes the desire for riches and power. When these are obtained, Lord Acton's dictum takes over: "Power corrupts, absolute power corrupts absolutely."

One may be habitually open and still be occasionally impatient, indolent, sarcastic. Or one can be habitually closed and still be occasionally kind, generous, patient. These occasional changes can be the beginning of the conversion of the closed person or the first step toward the ultimate corruption of the open person. The latter is the stuff of tragedy (pity and fear that the person is ruining himself); the former brings joy and the beginnings of hope.

As with inalienable rights so with inalienable obligations. They are metaphysical realities founded in sensible realities. They are real but invisible, objects of the mind and not of the senses. Rights are relations, obligations are relations. The subject of the relation of obligation is the concrete person, who is visible. The term, that to which the person is related, is the action of choosing to be open and to practice prudence, justice, fortitude, and temperance etc. Such actions are sensed and often visible. The cause of that obligation is vital transcendence that is the person and which is the tendency to choose to be open, to affirm that life is meaningful, to trust and be trusted, love and be loved. Those tendencies are also experienced by the concrete person. And of course the cause (transcendence) is in the person, making him obligated.

Finally, the obligation to be open and the consequent obligations of prudence, justice, fortitude, and temperance are natural obligations, and therefore inalienable obligations. Man cannot escape them because they flow from his nature. They are his radical natural law. They are sanctioned by reward or punishment immediately upon violation or fulfillment. The reward is union, peace, trust with one's fellow man; the punishment is isolation, separation, guilt. One could say this another way: the reward is maturity, the punishment is immaturity. All of this, of course, admits of degrees. Just as we legally distinguish misdemeanor, felony, and crime or petty theft, theft, robbery etc., the same is true with the morally good acts, e.g., more and more trust, more and more generosity, more and more industry, etc. Moral maturity depends upon the basic commitment to honesty and integrity. The understanding of what these mean and how to practice them grows with experiencing them. Depending upon that experience one becomes more or less mature. But the obligations to be open, prudent, just, etc. are always present and inalienable. That is because the person is transcendent and needs to communicate with other transcendents. If he fails to communicate, he closes his openness and thereby violates his nature and so becomes a violator of the natural law.

THE OBLIGATION OF CONFORMITY

During the spring semester of 1993 a student at UC Berkeley was dismissed for coming to campus and classes naked. He explained that he was protesting conformism. In his opinion there was just too much conformity being practiced in the university community. There has always been a great concern to protect the individual from the abusive power of authority, and in particular, governmental authority. This concern led to the Declaration and the formulation of the Bill of Rights. But like so many other practices, this concern, too, can be pursued imprudently and thereby lead to pathetic and tragic results.

One obvious example of this is the right of the individual to bear arms. The tragic result of the administration of this right is the proliferation throughout society of weapons designed only to kill human beings quickly. Presently peace officers have less fire power than those who threaten and actually disturb the peace. And that is tragic. What is needed is not less government so that the individual can have more freedom, but rather enforced restrictions of freedom so that citizens can live in peace and enjoy their inalienable rights. The distinction here is freedom vs. freedom under law. There is the freedom of the jungle where there is no law. The freedom in a free society is not that of the jungle, but a freedom that has many restrictions. The restrictions are there for the common good and exist precisely because man is equal to his fellow man and so is common with him. This commonality of being supposes common action. The most radical common action is language. Language is an arbitrary procedure, a set of rules, a "law" to which man must conform if he is to communicate and experience personal peace. Nobody questions the usefulness of the conformity involved in the "rules" of language. And nobody in his right mind questions the usefulness of law, for it is obviously the structure of any civilization. But law, procedures, customs, rules are the means of restricting the individual so that he can enjoy the common good of his society. The rules are effective because they help him acquire the needs, wants, and pleasures that he has in common with his fellow men. Respect for law, respect for conformity, is respect for that element man shares with his fellow man—his nature. Consequently, one is morally obliged to be committed not only to his individual freedom, but also to that which he has in common with all others. He must be committed to a peaceful and just and free life that he shares with his fellow man.

This recognition of and commitment to the commonality of his nature necessarily implies a commitment to common action or behavior, e.g., language, customs, rules, laws, which restrict his individual freedom. Bluntly put, he is obliged to be committed to freedom, and obliged to be committed to the loss of freedom in the form of conformity to the behavior of the group. Every time he leaves private life and enters his automobile, every time he enters the classroom, every time he participates in the town meeting, he affirms his commonality—but only when he respects the procedures, customs, rules, laws of those communities.

There is great concern today for respect for the individual, being one's self, developing a good self-image, and there is the tendency to denigrate conformity. Classroom posters show long lists of children's rights, right to be different, right to be individuals. And that is good and long overdue. At the same time, however, there is the need to stress that the self-image include the self as common with other selves and a member of the group, a member and a part (not a self-sufficient independent whole) whose freedom is rightly limited by the needs, wants, pleasures of other individuals who are also members and parts of something greater than themselves. Yet this same member is unique. Though he must belong to the group, he cannot totally belong nor totally be subject to the group because he is not only common and therefore public, but he is also unique and therefore private.

This commonality is natural to him and inalienable from him. Therefore he is morally obliged to set up and follow common procedures. He must establish language, customs and laws to accomplish the good he can only achieve with others. We call that good the common good. Man has an inalienable obligation to accomplish it.

6

Norms of Morality: Positive Law, Natural Law, Religion, Conscience

Man is morally good or bad insofar as his behavior is in conformity with just laws, natural law, his religion, and his conscience. His radical norm, the proximate norm of all morality, is his conscience. If positive law or the precepts of his religion conflict with his conscience, his duty is to obey conscience. There can be and have been unjust demands made by civil and religious authorities; the just person down through the ages has disobeyed them even at the cost of great physical and psychological pain—the price paid for personal integrity. Natural law, since it is promulgated not by printed word but rather by the structure of nature experienced, understood, and ever more accurately articulated by man is, consequently more difficult to codify and promulgate clearly as is done with positive law. But it is not, therefore, any less a norm—and a sanctioned norm—than is positive law. We shall discuss each of these norms and show how they are to be guides for man's behavior.

But before that is done, we must clarify some basic metaphysical concepts that apply to man's moral nature. Those concepts are: good, imperfect, evil (bad), peace, order. These realities are found in things we perceive with our senses. But they are not directly and separately known. We neither perceive nor know goodness or evil as such. Yet we say the food is good, the music is good, the man is good, etc. It is immediately evident, therefore, that good is an analogous notion. It can be applied to many things. Each application is simply different from the others, but in some sense the same. Thus the concept "good" transcends particular things. It can be called a transcendental concept and is different from a univocal concept which can only be applied to a particular class and fits everything in that class in the same way, e.g., horse, fish, man, etc. Yet I can speak of a good horse, a good fish, good man, etc.

So what is the definition of good? I cannot begin the definition by starting out with

"Good is when . . . etc." For that would be to exemplify, not define. Once the example is given, one still has to explain or define the example. Good is being or reality. Good is being or reality considered as completing or perfecting. When something is perfect it is completed, it has all that it is supposed to have. Light and physical objects complete my power of vision. Water and other liquids complete my thirst. When my body has reached its adult stage of development, it is complete. There is more physical being in the adult than in the child. The adult body has accomplished all the growth it was designed to have. Good therefore is being insofar as it (being) perfects or completes. We can understand "good" a little easier if we contrast it with "imperfect."

Imperfect: This is being on its way to completion. It does not yet have all that it was designed to have. The child is incomplete in its physical development; it is still growing, still on its way to the physical completion called adulthood. Imperfect, therefore is not evil or bad. The child has all it needs to be a child; it does not have all that it will soon have and is meant to have. Physically speaking it is still incomplete. As a human being, it has not yet attained adulthood, and so is a physically imperfect human being.

Evil, Bad: This is the privation of a due good. Thus there is a clear difference between "imperfect" and "deprived." Physical integrity means head, torso, arms, legs. To lose an arm is to lose physical integrity. That body has suffered physical damage or evil. It has been deprived of what should be (due to be) there. Any deprivation of a good that should be present is evil. Evil therefore cannot exist in itself; it always exists in something that still has some element of good or being or perfection. Since all that is is good, i.e., has being that completes or perfects, good therefore is the material cause of evil. Good is the matter in which evil inheres. If there is no good (being), there is no evil. Thus absolute evil[1] is impossible or a contradiction, since privation cannot exist except in something deprived. The body that has lost an arm is still good in all the aspects of what it still is. The head works fine, the right arm is good, so is the torso, and so are the legs. But the body has been deprived of its left arm. We say something bad has happened to that person. The body has evil associated with it.

We could use other examples: fruit that is partially spoiled. It has been deprived of the good that it should have. It differs from unripe fruit. This

---

1. If you admit there is a devil and wish to say he is absolutely evil, realize you are speaking metaphorically, not properly. For Satan is usually considered to be diabolically clever, meaning his intelligence is pretty good. Thus even with Satan, good is the matter in which the privation of good (evil) exists.

latter has all that is due to it at this stage of its development. It is not bad, it has not been deprived of anything that should be there; it is on its way to maturity and ripeness. It is good but imperfect. Evil is a privation that exists in something deprived.

If we apply good, evil, imperfect to man as obliged by the natural law, we would have to say that he is good insofar as he is open, prudent, just, etc. His actions have the being they should have because they equal the norm (nature). He is obliged to be open, etc. and by his actions he is open, prudent, just, etc. He is complete according to the norm. Insofar as he does not fully understand what he should do here and now, he does not understand how the norm applies to him now. The child, the adolescent, the adult acting out of ignorance is, to the extent of his ignorance, morally imperfect, immature we say. He is not morally responsible as he will be after he gets more knowledge/experience. We do not call him irresponsible. In fact, we usually say "That's to be expected, considering his age/experience."

The evil man, on the other hand, is not simply imperfect. He is deprived of conformity to the norm by his free choice. He is deliberately unjust, alone. He deprives himself of that which is due to himself. He should choose the just act, choose to be open to evidence, open to his neighbor in trust, but he deliberately closes himself, deliberately uses and manipulates his neighbor rather than dealing in trust with him. In that act he deprives himself of that for which he was made, of that which is natural for him. Thus he is in violation of the natural law and so is bad or evil. And that evil, that privation is in him. It is in his spirit which is a good spirit, for it has all that it needs to have to function freely. Thus good (his spirit) is that matter or material in which moral evil inheres. The spirit is the material cause of moral evil. There is nothing wrong with the spirit of man, but there is something wrong with the person using its freedom to choose to be closed rather than open.

Notable examples of moral evil existing side by side are the cases of Magic Johnson and President Bush. The immorality of promiscuity, by his own admission[2] existed in Magic Johnson. It is hard to imagine that it exists in him today. This man was and is known and loved by many. And the reason is evident. There is clearly so much good in him—his openness, courage, honesty, love of parents and son. Yet among the high school students interviewed by Connie Chung on the same program, one of them said, "'. . . he kind of let me down. Because sleeping with so many women

---

2. "Morally I was wrong sleeping with a lot of women, yes. I was wrong—it was wrong." CBS, *Face to Face with Connie Chung*, 12/11/91; transcript by Burrelle's Information Services, Livingston, N J, 1, 11.

made me lose respect for him." She, too, agrees with Magic that what he did (promiscuity, not unprotected sex) was wrong. Thus when so much good can exist with evil, that total—yet deprived reality—is still attractive. The immature child can be disappointed in his hero; the mature adult, understanding the cost of integrity, admires the man who has put immorality aside and changed for the better.

More apropos to our discussion than Magic Johnson is President George Bush and personal integrity. Clearly he is a good man; no one gets to that position without many good personal qualities. Proof of that is the obvious love of his wife for him, and of him for her. But evil has to have good in which to inhere. Example: he appeared on national television and showed a package of crack cocaine that had been purchased in front of the White House.[3] The message was obvious: Drugs are everywhere and the nation must be united in its resolve to war against drugs. A few weeks later it was learned that the purchase of crack cocaine was staged. And Bush knew it. When challenged by the news about the obvious deception, he remarked that the bottom line was the drug was sold and the seller detained. And the end (let the nation be united in a war against drugs) justifies the means (it is all right to deceive the nation with a dramatic example). However good George Bush might be, no matter how often he has been a man of integrity, in that moment, the evil of duplicity existed in that man of integrity. And he, better than anyone else, knew it We can be thankful that the free press exposed that act; hopefully he is thankful, too. Hopefully the personal pain of guilt along with the pain of public embarrassment will incline him more to integrity than to duplicity.

There are two other terms that should be defined here because they are closely related to good, imperfect, and evil. They are peace and order.

Peace is the dynamic tranquility of order; order is the organization of parts contributing to form the whole. A corpse, a building, and a piece of furniture are static and immobile. Properly speaking they are not at peace. Peace exists in a nation or among nations when the laws (order) of that society or those societies are being followed. Peace can metaphorically be applied to the person. Man is at peace with himself when his choices are in accord with the natural order of his being, in accord with his openness to his fellow man.

Order supposes a purpose, a unifying principle, a whole. The whole supposes parts, and these are subordinate to the whole. Their meanings are never totally understood in themselves, but only in relation to the whole.

---

3. *Los Angeles Times*, 9/23/89, Part 1, 23. Ramsey Clark, "Drugs, Lies, & TV," *Nation*, 10/16/89, 408, 409.

The peel of the orange is only understood in relation to the segments, pulp, juice, and seeds. Man's spirit cannot be understood except in relation to his body and to his fellow transcendents. His left arm cannot be understood except in relation to his hand, his torso, his head, etc.

How do order, peace, evil, imperfect, good apply to the individual man? His individual choices are parts of his exercising moral life. There is a proper order of his nature leading to a good that that nature is to achieve by free acts. That order is dynamic and therefore he can be at peace if his parts (choices) are in order. That peace can come to him both privately and publicly. It comes to him publicly if, as a member of the city, state, nation, family of nations, he is joined with other members in accomplishing the common good, i.e., acting in accord with just law.

Clearly, as is evident in history and present life there are varying degrees or order, peace, tranquility. America is not totally at peace within herself, nor with the totality of nations. But she is at peace with some nations, and she is at peace in some places within her borders.

PEACE AMONG NATIONS AND ORGANIZATIONS

Just as the individual is made for the peace that comes from trust, so too with societies. Just as that peace can be thwarted by the parent and child ego states of those with whom the individual communicates, and just as those ego states can be changed by the individual remaining open and asking factual questions, so too with societies. If one society is intimidating, domineering, lying, petulant in its dealings with another society or with its own members, then that society is acting out of a parent or child ego state. The punishment for that behavior is immediate. Conflict, verbal or physical, results. The peaceful pursuit of the proper common good is thwarted. The tranquility of order is disturbed. The only true means to peace and growth is to face the facts and agree on them. A clear example of both peace and conflict resulting from the facing or rejecting of facts (reality) is Europe after the fall of communism and the Middle East after Desert Storm. Both locations are both enjoying and suffering. Russia rejected the violations of freedom that was communism; Israel stayed out of the war. But the refusal to work out the age-old ethnic hatreds and distrust (Jew-Arab, Croat-Serb, etc.) results in suffering, death, and sorrow. Things will change for the better when social pain (the privation of the common good) becomes so great that the nations and their leaders can't stand it any more. Hence the almost universal demise of communism. Some way or other, the leaders and their societies (nations or corporations) have to follow the rules for achieving mutual trust, i.e. be open to the facts, have the courage to hear out the others and admit to errors and misunderstanding, accept the facts. But in addition to being open to the facts, the society must ask factual questions and hold its own position until facts necessarily demand otherwise. In other words the parent and child ego states must be pierced and vanquished by a determination to force a facing of the facts. The result of the process will be peace; the failure will be continued social disorder, conflict, delay in achieving the common good. The meaning of that result is that the leaders and members who keep them in power are bad, evil. Those word seem harsh. A more lenient word, but still a patronizing word, would be "immature." But that implies innocence, imperfection, not evil. In the instances of social conflict someone is being the domineering and intimidating parent or the stubborn and petulant child. Someone is afraid to expose himself and his to betrayal, someone is afraid to trust. Someone wants a guarantee that excludes the need for trust. Such a guarantee produces a truce, not peace; it produces not a union among societies, but a juxtaposition of societies.

A microcosm of this can be found in the life of the corporation. The CEO and his vice-presidents or the general superintendent and his foremen meet to discuss a problem. The leader opens the meeting by outlining the problem and asking for discussion. Each proposal is rejected by the leader and some of the group or by the leader alone. Finally the leader suggests the solution and all agree to it. Anyone who has attended business meetings has seen this happen more than once. The leader is in a parent mode; the subordinates are his children, or worse, his slaves. And he is punished immediately for his behavior. As soon as the participants recognize what is going on, they hold back both information and insight. He and his company are deprived of resources that would improve performance; the whole group is deprived of trust and the fun of teamwork and growth toward the common good of that corporation.

A comparable situation exists when parental leaders and managers strive to make their subordinates "feel like they belong," "feel ownership of a decision or project." No person or company can make another feel anything. Human feelings are produced by the live human being coming in contact with reality. If the human being does belong, he will feel it; if he truly is part of the decision-making process or creating the project, he will experience his ownership. Those experiences cause trust and creative peace in any group. It is the experience of released competence achieving the common good that deepens trust, affection, loyalty and gives joy to the members. Their ordination toward individual and social good is completed by this experience. They are good. Their moral activity, their ethical activity, their good communication—all these are, in the words of Carl Rogers, "therapeutic," healthy.

POSITIVE LAW AS NORM

The purpose of positive law is to secure the inalienable rights of man and thereby effect the common good which is first of all the order of justice, the necessary condition for peace. Law is essentially a restriction of individuals or groups of individuals for the benefit of peace and the exercise by man of his unrestricted desire to know and create. This is the exercise of his right to pursue happiness. The definition of positive law is: Law is an ordination or directive of reason designed to achieve the common good. It is promulgated and sanctioned by those who have authority from and over the community (society). The essential elements of just law, therefore, are: reasonable, common good, promulgation and sanction by legitimate authority. Let us consider each of these essential elements.

First: Positive law is an ordination or directive of reason. It is based on the evidence of the real world. It asks what behavior does evidence show would be for the common good of members of this society. It then prescribes (prohibits) that behavior, e.g., paying taxes to cover the cost of roads, bridges, public education. Roads, bridges, education are for the peace and progress and growth of the community. It prohibits theft, rape, etc. because these inhibit the peaceful progress of the community.

Second: The common good, like any good, completes and perfects. In the matter of man, the common good completes him first as a collective, as a society. The society is just, at peace, and prospers. It completes him as an individual in that he shares in the justice, peace, and prosperity of that society and in that he personally grows because he actively contributes to the functions of his society. The common good is peace and prosperity, the dynamic life of trust that leaves men free and encourages them to learn, understand their own nature and the nature of their world so that they can adapt to it and to their fellow man more and more. Almost sixty years ago Walter Lippman gave a good description of a free society as dintinguished from those of Hitler, Stalin, and Mussolini: "Thus in a free society the state does not administer the affairs of men. It administers justice among men who conduct their own affairs."[4]

Lippman is profound in his specific yet broad description of the common good of the just society that should exist in this age of specialized labor, global industrialization and markets. Such a society will see to it that its markets are efficient and honest (221). Unearned income is unjust and the condtitions that lead to it must be corrected (226). Unearned income spent on consumable goods is sheer privilege (227). The way a free society "controls the economy is to police the markets, to provide in the broad-

---

4. Walter Lippman, *The Good Society*, George Allen and Unwin, Ltd., London, 1937, 267.

est sense honest weights and measures, to make bargains represent the exchange of true equivalents rather than the victory of superior strength, inside information, conspiracies, secret combinations, corruption, and legalized sharp practices" (237). That same just society will by law set limits to private property so that ". . . the land . . . the seas . . . the patrimony of generations to come . . . this natural inheritance will not be wasted or destroyed [but] on the contrary, be enriched" (213).

Third: Promulgated or published. The directive cannot be followed, cannot be obeyed if the community does not know it exists. If I must pay taxes, those who govern me must notify me and tell me how much to pay. One must know the law in order to obey it.

Fourth: Sanctioned. This means that proportionate punishment must exist so that reasonable persons will judge it a better thing to keep the law than to break it. They may not have occasion to use a particular bridge, they may be out of school, and so be inclined not to pay or to pay less taxes than those imposed on them. Taxation may seem unrewarding. But the fine or jail term persuades them to obey and to pay. Murder and rape may appear to be a good thing to some, but the penalty of death, imprisonment, or fine is such as to persuade members of society to refrain from those actions.

POSITIVE VS. NATURAL LAW SANCTIONS

We shall deal with positive law sanctions in great detail in the next chapter. For the present, suffice it to say that we have two difficulties inherent in our legal sanctions. First, the laws of society do not engender the same respect and awe as do the laws of nature. The reason is simple, man respects his fellow man and hopes to get along with him. There is the desire and reasonable expectation that the unlawful will once again become law abiding. Further there is the fear of punishing the innocent. And finally there is sympathy for one's fellow man who can suffer pain and lose his freedom. The second problem is the administration of sanctions is always delayed until long after the violation occurs. And the sanctions are almost always less than the maximum allowed.

Not so with the laws of nature. Being in order with nature is to be at peace with one's physical environment and to experience its goodness. Once one steps out of that order, he loses the good of the order. Privation takes place, and he experiences physical evil. This happens immediately, to everyone whether he leaves the order wittingly or not. The man and the baby die after the five hundred foot fall. The tidal wave drowns all who failed to evacuate. Nature is perfectly proportionate in her punishments; she does not hurt us so much after a three foot fall as she does after a thirty

foot fall; fifty volts is not as harmful as five thousand volts, etc. As the saying goes, "There are old sailors and bold sailors, but there are no old and
bold sailors." We have learned to respect the laws of nature because her
sanctions are prompt, indiscriminate, and perfectly proportionate to the
offense. Yet they do not force us to obey, nature allows us to be bold sailors
and die young.

If man expects his laws to command respect, he must devise sanctions
and administer them in a way that better imitates nature.

Fifth: By those who have authority over the community. This authority
is subdivided into legislative, judicial, executive. But it is given to those persons who have been chosen by the consent of the governed, the members
of that community. Public officials exercise that authority according to the
will of the governed. The manner of that authority can be regal, constitu-
tional, or other, as long as the governed consent to it, support it, and have
the power to change it. The community usually disagrees and works for a
change of those in authority when it becomes clear there is something
wrong with the exercise of authority, e.g., the laws are unreasonable, they
favor just a few, the sanctions are too severe or are not severe enough.

It is to be noted here that there are good, imperfect, and bad laws. The
good law has all the essential parts listed above and has them completely.
The bad law lacks or is deficient in one or several of those essential parts.
Laws supporting slavery and discrimination fail on the point of reasonableness (justice) for human beings. Other laws may not be enforced, i.e.,
actively and reasonably sanctioned. The written law may be well-intentioned, but if it is not adequately sanctioned it is fictional, not a real law.
Therefore law, the order of society, is a dynamic thing. Dynamic law is the
order, the reasonable structure and actual peace of a just society. Finally,
dynamic and enforced law acts as a moral not as an efficient cause. Law
persuades free men to make free choices. It does not and cannot coerce
behavior. Precisely because man is free is it true that a specific code of law
can neither contain man's malice (though it can confine or execute the
malicious man) nor completely promote the common good. The governed will always have to direct the governors to revise and develop law to
restrain man's malice and support his creativity.

NATURAL LAW AS NORM

Natural law can be understoood in two ways: First, as the definite structure
that defines all things and determines the way they operate as they pursue
their proper goals, ends, goods. Gold always "behaves" as gold, and never
can be mistaken for lead, tobacco "behaves" as tobacco, and never as cab-
bage, the lion never acts as the lamb, and the chimpanzee never uses arbi-

trary signs, language, nor does anything else that is proper to free and intelligent man. Second, natural law can be understood as the propositions man uses to articulate these constant patterns, "laws," which man discovers in nature. We generally refer to them as the laws of the natural sciences,e.g., physics, chemistry, biology, etc. And ordinarily we do not consider man as the proper object of the natural sciences. He is the object of the behavioral sciences. And we thereby seem to separate him from nature, and that is wrong. He is part of nature in the broad sense, and specifically has his own proper nature that determines the way he must act, e.g, as an animal that is free, intelligent, a decision maker that thereby transcends the animal cycle of mere survival and generation of his own kind. He must produce science (knowledge of causes) and art (the right way of making something, whether fine or useful) because this is the way he survives in and dominates his world and himself. His is not locked into the limitations of instinctive behavior but his nature locks him into freedom and rationality. The question then becomes: What does this free yet animal nature demand that he do in order to achieve the good of that nature? In other words what is the good that completes the nature of man. The actions that achieve that good become the norm, the natural law to which he is morally or freely obliged, not physically and necessarily forced or determined, to seek. There is a good that he must seek, but he is free not to seek it. Articulating that good, putting those normative actions into propositions or moral laws is not easy. We say that there are rights, that all men are equal, that they have the right to life, liberty, and the pursuit of happiness and that everyone must respect those rights in his neighbor. These propositions are the "natural law" in the second sense, somewhat like the laws of the physical sciences articulated from the observation of nature's phenomena.

These natural moral laws are sanctioned. The lie told to oneself disturbs the person; the lie lived, and therefore told to others, causes separation and loneliness. The lie acted out results in unjust acts such as theft, rape, murder, war, etc. There is immediate punishment in the person first, then in his personal relationships with others, and finally in his body when others defend themselves or retaliate against him. Finally, insofar as positive law protects natural rights through positve sanctions, there is the further sanction of public embarrassment, incarceration, fine, and even execution, the natural consequences of being discovered as unjust while living in a society.

Finally, if we contrast natural (moral) law with positive law it is immediately evident that natural law is far more detailed than positive law. Positive law is for the common good and must be enforced by those in authority. Those in authority cannot effectively carry their enforcement into the more private relationships of human life such as the home, office, school, etc. They cannot prohibit lying, cursing, insults, rejection, favoritism, humiliation, manipulation, and the hundred and one other manners in which we deal with one another. And yet all of these are against the moral law, all of these are unnatural acts, all of these deprive the agent of the goodness, union, peace, trust, affection, etc. for which his person was made. All of these bring disorder, disharmony and disturbance into the smooth functioning of the home, office, school, etc. In this sense, morality makes bad (positive) law. In this sense positive law can never prohibit and prescribe the proper behaviors of natural law. It has not the means to do so. The natural law as a moral norm is discovered by an analysis of the individual and social nature of the free person whose nature is not only free but also animal. What is it that brings him individual and social personal peace? Integrity, openness, justice.

Religion as Norm

Religion as a norm for the behavior of believers is found in the sacred books, traditions, and leaders of that particular belief. The sacredness of the leaders is found in such terms of respect as rabbi, father, reverend, mullah, minister, guru, bishop, pope, etc. One is said to be a good practitioner of the religion if he follows and adheres to those scriptures and traditions as communicated and interpreted by the leaders. Religion is like law in that it prescribes and prohibits behaviors through the authority of the leaders. It differs from law on the point of authority. The leaders demand obedience not because the prescriptions and prohibitions are reasonable and evident. Those characteristics are presumed to be present. Their ultimate authority, mediated by the books and leaders, is the divine. The credibility of the leaders is supported by their charismatic personalities usually accompanied by miracles and visions. There is always the possibility of conflict between religious authority and the authority arising from the consent of the governed. For God, by virtue of his supreme authority and power, can command anything regardless of its implications for civil authority. Implicitly, therefore, civil authority can be subjected to the authority of religion. Hence arise religious wars, battle cries such as "God wills it," witch hunts, religious persecutions, control of speech and writing (Galileo), etc.

Conscience as Norm

The above three norms for behavior—positive law, nature, and religion—apply to man as a member of a class, as someone who is indistinguishable

from all other members. Positive law binds him by virtue of his citizenship,natural law obliges him by virtue of his human nature, and religious
law binds him by virtue of his faith. But man is more than an indistinguishable member of a class as a fish is part of a school or a steer is part of
a herd. Man is unique and consequently, in a limited sense, a law unto
himself. The limitations are those of nature, society, and religion. All of
these allow the person to marry almost anyone, choose any career, change
occupations and location of his home, etc. But those decisions can bring
him either peace or misery. His unique obligation is to stay in order, to
maintain his personal peace. Only he can know what that is. And he
knows this by means of his conscience.

Conscience is not a voice, but an experience. It is knowledge with knowledge, from the Latin words *cum* meaning *with* and *scientia* meaning *knowledge*. By means of conscience I know *what* I am doing, that I am *the one
choosing to do it*, and *how* that choice fits in my person. The voice of conscience comes when I articulate that experience thus: "I should not do this
because it makes me feel bad." Or one says "I should do this because I just
feel it is the right thing to do." Those choices put me in or out of order
with myself. I gain or lose my personal peace and so am morally good or
bad, virtuous or guilty. Peace is the natural, immediate, and permanent
reward of chosen integrity. Guilt is the natural, immediate, and permanent
punishment for telling ourselves the lie, for rationalizing an action and saying to ourselves, "It's OK, no one will know, everyone does it, if I don't do
it or take it, someone else will."

There is a popular misconception that guilt is bad. We are psychologically mixed up if we feel guilt for something we are not responsible for. But
guilt is a naturally good thing. It is the personal experience of being personally out of order. Physical pain tells us where the physical damage is, it
directs our attention to the disorder, e.g., to the tooth, if it is a toothache;
to the head, if it is a headache; to the appendix, if it is a very painful side
ache. We quickly apply the remedy, remove the disorder, and the body is
at peace again, i.e., the pain is gone. If there were no pain, the physical
destruction would continue till we got worse and worse. Pain is a natural
phenomenon and necessary consequence of being alive, conscious, and
out of order. Disorder in the body we call physical pain. The experience of
disorder in the person is guilt and is contrasted to the pain of grief. Guilt
tells us that we have lost integrity and points us toward facing up to the reality of what we are and what we should now do. Grief is pathetic because we
are not responsible for the evil that has befallen us. Guilt is tragic because
we are responsible for what has been inflicted upon our person.

Man's conscience, therefore, not only makes him aware of how his
actions comply with the general laws of nature, society, and religion, but

also how his uniquely personal action fits him. He can deliberately marry the wrong person, choose the wrong career, stay too long in the same location and occupation, etc. The person knows this not by an interior voice that speaks to him in sentences, but by the experience of personal order, integrity, peace. We all have made choices like these and have been rewarded or punished in their consequences. If rewarded with personal peace, we probably stayed firm in them. If we were punished—had long experience of personal turmoil—we probably reversed that decision and hopefully made a better choice at the next opportunity.

Were we bad, immoral, when we made those choices that later had to be reversed? No, if our knowledge and psychological strength and support allowed no other. But "yes" the longer we stayed with the decision when the evidence of lost personal peace became ever more obvious, and "yes" we were immoral if we descended from the personal level to the human level or lower in attempt to silence the interior pain with the distraction of work or pleasure. But at some point of pain we said with Martin Luther, "Ich kann nicht anders!" I can't be otherwise, and we get out—or we stay. And slowly erode, stultify, and personally wither the most precious reality of our being, our person. We kill our freedom; we fail in fortitude, fail in justice to ourselves and probably follow some intemperate path to distraction, the height of imprudence.

The criterion, therefore, of the strictly individual ethic or the strictly individual morality is personal peace. Serious decisions are studied in terms of their anticipated consequences and in terms of past experience with that person, job, profession, way of life. When all seems to fit, the choice can be so obvious that any other choice is impossible. The choice can be just as obvious, but so demanding in its cost that great courage is required to say "yes." The ultimate reason for the "yes" is that I can't do otherwise. It wouldn't be honest. The great personal tragedy, of course, is letting others talk us out of what we know is right for us; or worse, for hope of success, power, riches, we rationalize ourselves out of the proper personal choice.

Some years ago Charles Kuralt, the CBS on the road reporter of American life, showed a family celebration. Perhaps it was a birthday party for one of the parents or their fiftieth wedding anniversary, I forget. These parents had had a very difficult life, limited finances, limited opportunities, the experience of discrimination. Their returning children were all amazingly successful—Ph.D.'s, master's degrees, managerial positions. I can still see the father seated at the piano with all the family around him as he played and they sang one of their favorite family songs. Watching that scene of the simple parents surrounded by the simple but highly educated and sophisticated children—that was a deeply touching experience.

I doubt those parents could make much sense out of this book and all its abstract concepts; but they know everything about the realities of openness, integrity, prudence, temperance, justice, and especially fortitude. How did they know those things? They always did what was for their peace. Did religion help? Undoubtedly. But at some point in their lives they had to say yes or no to religion, at some point in their lives they had to say yes to each other and say it again and again; and at some point in their lives they had to say courageously a long yes to the lives that had been dealt them. They could have done otherwise in each of those decisions, but they would have betrayed themselves.

Each honest personal decision is an experience of personal success. Success is learned, satisfying, and remembered. Thus there is in it the creation in man's spirit of an inclination or disposition to do that or similar acts again. I am building up my goodness, my *character*. Those who see me, and more importantly I myself, can and should *characterize* myself as good.

The same is true with the evil decision. But I leave the level of personal good and descend to the human. I choose the acquirement of money through deception. My cleverness is successful, learned, intellectually satisfying, and permanently in my memory. Thus there is created in my spirit the disposition to do that or something similar again. But I have also learned how to get away from the "hang-up" of integrity. That learning experience abides with me and makes the next evil decision easier than the last.

If conversion takes place, then the evil choice has been experienced as guilt, and that evidence leads to the admission, "I did what was wrong." The scar of personal failure remains in memory, but so too does the rejection of the evil decision. There is consequent peace and joy from rejecting the evil and deciding to do the good. The person now has two motives for similar good acts: the threat of personal pain and the promise of personal peace and satisfaction.

So there is a unique ethic binding each of us; there is a law that applies to us alone, and it is learned through the experience of peace caused by repeated honest decisions.

An individually binding ethic does not advocate or support the metaphorical statement: "I am completely unique." Rather, it is to affirm once again the complex reality that I am, namely common and unique. If I were absolutely unique, I would by definition have nothing in common with anybody. How could I communicate (common is at the root of this word) with something that had no eyes to see me nor ears to hear me. My uniqueness is relative, relative to my human nature. Nor am I "absolutely" common like the bird in the flock or the fish in the school; my freedom that transcends the limits of my body makes me different from all others who also have my nature. I am more than a number. I am not just a man as a lion is just a lion. I am unique, I have my own name.

Up to this point I have not used the term "sin" in reference to moral evil. I avoided the term out of deference to my fellow Americans who are atheists. I have no quarrel with people of various faiths using that theological term to describe unethical behavior as a sin against God. For certainly they hold that man and his world are God's creation, and that creation is an expression of His will. Therefore to violate the structure He intended is to violate His will and therefore offend Him.

How bad is bad? How good is good? When we look at the person who becomes good or bad by his moral act, what change has taken place in him and how long does it last? How long can we say of him that he is good or bad? As we have seen evil can exist in that which is good, as exemplified in the public figures of Magic Johnson and President Bush. The good person, as the good body can exist with some minor and major privations. He can be friendly and kind to family, friends, and neighbors. In a moment he can switch to disparaging talk and discriminatory actions towards "honkeys," "niggers," "spics," "kikes," "slant eyes," "round eyes," "micks," etc. He is both good and bad. This is judgmental, and the judgment truly expresses the objective reality of that person.

How measure it? You can count the number of *transitory* acts, but that is meaningless because the good and evil exist in the *permanent* and transcendent substance that man is. The human body is permanently all good, except at the point where the arm has been amputated. It is a physically bad and evil body in that respect, but not as bad as the body that has lost both arms and both legs. The body, being material, can be measured to some extent, I can count the missing members. But I can't measure the pain that person has. His inconvenience is constant; his memory of what he used to be and do only add to that pain. The pain is spiritual, inhering in his substantial freedom.

Moral evil inheres in the same substance. The evil (or goodness) can be understood, but it can't be sensed (seen or heard). Only its transitory manifestations or symbols, the transitory acts, are seen. They have meaning. They mean the person now using the disparaging ethnic epithet is bad now.

How bad? The epithet indicates he has separated himself from a particular group of humans. His degree of badness depends upon the degree of separation. It can be minor in that he avoids that group; it can be major—like the skinheads who go hunting for non-caucasians and gays and beat them to death. The epithet or murder is an act over in a minute or two, but the evil sprang from a permanent condition—the evil person.

This evil is two-fold in its nature and two-fold as it exists in the person. First, and most radically, it is a closing of his transcendent openness to the evidence that all human beings are equal and good. Second, it is a deliberate isolation from others. He deprives himself of the experience of trust and personal growth and fulfillment—good is being as perfecting and completing.

There are plenty of ethnic problems in America, and that is bad. But perhaps nowhere in the world is there the mingling in trust—from pals in school, to friends in business, to lovers in marriage—as there is in this country, and that is good. That good is rooted in nature and, fortunately for us, articulated in ". . . created equal . . . endowed with unalienable rights . . . life, liberty, and the pursuit of happiness." Evil exists in America, but she is constantly approaching the ideal and manifesting by her acts the radical and permanent goodness of her soul.

Conscience, therefore, is the norm of morality by which all other norms are measured. The individual can never escape the personal responsibility associated with every act of his civil and religious obedience. If following civil and religious dictates makes him personally uneasy, he is morally obliged to prudently consider the evidence and ultimately do what is for his peace. Some laws are bad; some divine experiences are misinterpreted in the writing or speech of the leader or in the hearing of the listener. As has been stated earlier, the divine is more intimate to us than we are to ourselves. The first word of God to man is what man is in his unique and vital structure. His first obligation, therefore, is to know himself as best he can. It is quite possible therefore that the dedicated atheistic scientist concerned with man and man's world is more dedicated to the will of God than the religious leader. For the scientist is concerned with what is really there, whereas the religious leader is constantly interpreting his scriptures and traditions in reference to the moral environment of man. His followers are docile because of his religious learning and rhetoric and their ignorance and inarticulateness. It is all the more necessary, therefore, that when they "feel" something is wrong with civil and/or religious law, that they examine the relevant data and do what is for their peace. That is the whole point of healthy self-respect and personal responsibility. Such responsibility is inalienable and therefore cannot be delegated to the state or to religion.

Often enough it is extremely difficult to let peace be the norm for behavior. Sometimes there is no physical or psychological survival outside of obedience to the civil or religious society. At that point one is forced to choose temporarily the lesser of two evils, i.e., survival and temporary loss of freedom. Sometimes the only choice is the affirmation of freedom and the acceptance of death.

7

Severe Sanctions:
A Break from American
Tradition

Pirsig's most valuable insight for me was the need for the intellectual to maintain those social patterns which contain and control the biological. He expressed this containment in a very forceful and graphic manner: There has to be a gun[1] in the hands of the police to enforce the Declaration, the Bill of Rights, and the Constitution. It is naive to expect everyone to cooperate with law. Law, to be law, must be effectively sanctioned. Clearly in almost everyone's opinion, the people of the jungle (biological level) are overwhelming the people of the city (social level). Violent crime is but the symbol of more profound crime, namely betrayal of the people by the professional (doctor, lawyer, educator, clergyman, entrepreneur, politician, etc.). Trust, the highest achievement among humans, has been destroyed again and again by individuals promising service and rendering exploitation. Homelessness, poverty, hopelessness are not merely the results of indolence. Our social order needs reformation[2] because though it does not justify, it does provoke to violent crime.

SANCTIONS

The word "sanction" needs to be distinguished in relation to several words frequently associated with it, e.g., just and unjust punishment, brutal and cruel punishment, vengeance, restitution. We shall try to do that now.

---

1. Pirsig, *Lila*, 310.
2. Walter Lippman's *The Good Society* greatly influenced Robert Bellah and associate authors in their works *Habits of the Heart*, Perennial Library, 1986 and *The Good Society*, Vantage Press, 1991. All three works give insights into the nature of the injustices in the social order and the need for reform of our social institutions. See our Chapter 9 "Business and Ethics" for examples. What we propose is the reform of only one of our social institutions: sanctions and their administration.

Strictly speaking justice and punishment have nothing in common. The proper notion of justice is that situation in which each has his due, each one's rights are respected. The just act is the act whereby one gives to his neighbor that which is due his neighbor. In an ideal world where perfect justice exists there would be no victims and no oppressors. Everyone, whether an individual person or a moral person (e.g. corporation, society), would receive his due and none would have more or less than is rightfully his. Injustice occurs when one is deprived of and the other thereby has more than his due. Restoring or reestablishing the order of justice means to take from the oppressor his ill-gotten good or benefit and and return it to the victim. This restoration is not punishment, it is restitution; and it can never be perfect. For example, if I steal my neighbor's car, I not only deprive him of his car but I also cause him inconvenience. Returning his car can never remove from him the inconvenience he experienced. I may and should try to compensate for that inconvenience, but no matter what I do I cannot make him not inconvenienced.

Punishment, on the other hand, has an entirely different purpose. It exists first as a threat to the would-be oppressor. As such a threat it promises some form of more or less serious inconvenience to follow upon the unjust act. That inconvenience is always in some form of loss of liberty, and may be extreme as in lifelong incarceration or death. In such cases society gives up trying to persuade and decides on the removal of the criminal from its community. The threat of punishment is designed to persuade the human being to be reasonable, to conform his behavior to the prescriptions and prohibitions of the law. Once he violates the law, the inconvenience follows. That punishment is arbitrary. There is no necessary connection between the illegal act and the specific punishment that follows upon it precisely because the establishment of law is a free act. The punishment can be anything the society freely determines as necessary for effective persuasion.

The punishment itself, no matter how slight, is essentially brutal for it is the deliberate use of force against a free human being. The criminal is forcibly subjected to the power of the officials of his society. The rational animal lawbreaker has refused to behave rationally, i.e., conform to the directive of reason that is an essential part of every law. The use of force, rather than persuasion, on a free being is by definition to treat him as an animal and not as a rational animal. Paradoxically, therefore, society acts brutally and inhumanely on the criminal in order to preserve and maintain a rational and humane way of life for those committed to the society and its common good. Consequently, to say that some punishment is inhumane and brutal is to say nothing. All punishment is inhumane and brutal. It must be, otherwise it would not be punishment.

"Just punishment" is a misnomer. One frequently hears after the execution of a famous murderer that justice is finally served. Execution does not serve justice; restitution does. The only way justice can be served is for the murdered to be brought back to the life of which they were unjustly deprived. Execution, punishment, serves law. By it society keeps its promised threat to brutalize the lawbreaker if he decides to be an outlaw, an oppressor. If society fails to punish, its sanction is an empty threat and therefore non-persuasive and inefficient. Law is thus deprived of one of its essential elements. But if law is a reasonable directive for the common good properly promulgated by those in authority and contains a real threat, then it is by definition a good law. But if it is deprived of effective sanction through faulty administration, then to that extent it is a bad law; it has been deprived of a due good, an essential element, namely, sanction. Properly administered sanction serves law; law serves justice. Good law is the necessary condition, not the cause, of justice. The cause of justice is human beings freely giving others their due. Good law effectively persuades humans to live justly. Law that is imperfect in the matter of sanction, will be imperfect in the matter of persuasion. As a consequence, there will be less justice. One cannot expect to live in a just society if its laws are not effective. "Just punishment" is a misnomer.

The proper expression is "effective punishment," which is distinguished from cruel and unusual punishment and insufficient punishment. Cruel punishment exceeds the purpose of punishment, namely persuasion. It goes beyond persuasion and becomes vengeance. The sufficiently punished can reasonably be expected to give up his criminal behavior, but the avenged is punished not to change him, but to satisfy the wishes of the victim seeking comparable pain and loss to match the pain and loss he has suffered. The victim has a right to restitution; and the victim has a right, but only as a member of society and not as a victim, to expect effective punishment. And this might, if society so deems, imitate the ancient formula of "an eye for an eye, and a tooth for a tooth." But the distinction between just restitution or compensation and effective punishment must be understood. Punishment tends to become ineffective if it is delayed again and again or frequently escaped altogether. The adage "justice delayed is justice denied" is to be interpreted as "restitution delayed is justice denied." Rather punishment delayed means that an essential element of law (sanction) is rendered inefficient exactly proportionate to the delay. Delay offers hope of escape and so weakens the real threat of punishment.

Discovering the mean between cruel and insufficient punishment and then arbitrarily specifying the punishment is an exercise of reason based on trial and error. It all depends upon how well society understands the evil of crime and how much it values social order versus disorder and progressive chaos. The society cannot, by definition, force free behavior. Therefore no threat of punishment can guarantee the observance of law. There will always be people willing to risk punishment to benefit from crime, to take more than their due. The question is: What kind of a sanction will it take to reduce their number? Discovering such sanctions will always be a matter for reflection and experiment. When society suffers enough from the disorder of crime, it will think, experiment, and develop new sanctions. Increased social pain always prompts the human social animal to make a change.[3] When it does so in the matter of legal sanction, it needs to know the differences among justice, restitution, punishment, brutality, vengeance, insufficient sanction. It should always be aware of applying any of these terms metaphorically. Therein lies theoretical confusion and real harm.

We have a model in nature to guide us in the development of sanctions. Most of us are extremely careful with fire, heights, electricity, poison, the sea and other natural forces, e.g., wild animals. When we or ours do not follow ("obey") the "laws" of nature, we suffer or die. Such experiences down through the centuries persuade us rational animals to stand in awe and reverence the "laws" of nature. And we do so. Parents "babyproof" their homes, manufacturers insulate wire, Edison companies build high tension towers, we put up danger signs near underground gas and electrical lines. These are the rational adjustments we make to live in harmony with our physical world. Nature's sanctions, therefore, are very efficient. That efficiency lies in the fact that the punishments are prompt, brutal, indiscriminate, always the same, allowing no exceptions or diminutions. We fear and stand in awe of the forces of nature. Yet nature does not coerce our behavior, we are free to be negligent, careless; free to act out of ignorance.

Do we want the laws of our society to receive comparable respect from the vast majority of the members of our society? The ultimate question regarding the establishment of sanctions is not whether they are *brutal* or not, nor whether they *guarantee* fulfillment of the law, nor whether they are *just* or not, but whether they are *efficient* in establishing the rule of law, social order, justice, peace, security—all the necessary conditions for the pursuit of happiness. The severity of those sanctions will depend upon to what extent the society values more or less social order, more or less justice, more or less security from the attacks of its irrational and more or less brutal members.

---

3. A recent example of widespread social change is that which has come about because of society's awareness of the dangers of smoking. The widespread awareness of violent criminal behavior is also producing changes, e.g., further restrictions on the sale of weapons and the enactment in various states of the "three strikes and you are out" law.

For example, how much graffiti is it willing to tolerate? How much corruption of its legislators, judges, and police will it tolerate? Are there such things as unspeakable crimes and therefore absolutely intolerable crimes, e.g., child abuse, sexual abuse, incest, rape, pedophilia, torture and murder? Is there an absolute hierarchy of crimes, and if so, what are the criteria that evaluate and order them? Finally, is there something which the society values more than its own peace, order, and security?

As we have said several times before, we know first by sense, then by reason. The visible, the sensations of the body, are immediately known. But the meaning of things only come to us by reflection; they are not sensed, not seen, not heard, not felt. The physical and sexual abuse of the child is unspeakable. It not only harms the child, but brings pain to all who know or even hear about the child.

But what about the betrayal by elected officials of their oath of office to serve the community? What about their deceptions that cost the people they serve not only money but also deprives them in more or less great degree of their rights to life, liberty, and the pursuit of happiness. Just as there is an unspeakable crime against an individual, there is also an unspeakable crime against the community. But often it is only seen as unspeakable after reflection upon a multitude of interrelated data. The data are not visibly seen and felt, but the meaning of them is only understood as monstrous after much disclosure, investigation, and study. Many can suffer and die in an unjust war; many can suffer and die because an unjust government official collaborates with an unjust entrepreneur in presenting a harmful or restricting a beneficial product or service. We understand this is monstrous and unspeakable; but it does not touch our whole being as does the sexual abuse and murder of one child. But it is a greater crime, just as the many is greater than the one.

If the purpose of punishment, therefore, is to be a real threat to the criminal and thereby persuade him to behave according to law, it must imitate the sanctions of nature Delay in actualization, delay in punishment, is to make the threat unreal. An unreal threat of punishment is, by definition, an inefficient sanction. It will not persuade the great multitude of rational animals to behave rationally; rather it will entice many of them to behave brutally. They will feel that crime pays.

Precisely because the rational animal learns first by sense, then by reflection on sense data, is it reasonable that all sanction contain some form of corporal punishment promptly and deliberately inflicted upon the law breaker. If he is to learn respect and awe of the law that in some manner matches his respect and awe of the power of physical nature, he must experience the physical power of society. Mere arrest, conviction, and confinement do not generate such awe and respect. Confinement can brutalize his spirit in the sense that imposed routine deprives him of that decision making that is essential for maturity. He is hurt, but he has no realization of the damage done to himself until he is released and has to fend for himself, support himself physically and socially in a law abiding manner. In many instances he finds he simply cannot do this. The world has not only passed him by technologically, it excludes him from many areas of gainful employment.

It makes much more sense to hurt the lawbreaker's body rather than hurt his soul, for the pain passes and the injury heals, but the memory of both is not soon forgotten. Nor does he easily forget why the pain and injury happened. This makes for a much more efficient sanction than confinement. And if the confinement is minimal, upon his release he is not out of step with the advancement of technology nor has he been psychologically damaged by years of dependence upon the solicitous care of his jailers who supply him with food, drink, shelter, medical care, even entertainment. If however the threat of actual corporal punishment and the actual administration of it do not successfully persuade him to conform to law, then society must remove him from its midst by execution or incarceration extended until the criminal is physically unable to harm society. Execution should be reserved for the unspeakable crimes of violence or betrayal. For in these matters there should be no question of allowing the criminal to learn by the experience of pain that he should not do the unspeakable. Rather he should be presumed to have learned from the deaths of other criminals that unspeakable crimes lead inexorably to death or permanent confinement.

One must beware of calling execution murder; that is to speak metaphorically. Execution is simply different but somewhat the same as murder. It is somewhat the same in that a defenseless and powerless person is overwhelmed by the power of the state. It is simply different in that murder is the unjust taking of *innocent* life. The criminal is not innocent, and the (prompt) taking of his life is justified by the essential need for an effective sanction, one in which society says to all its member: If you kill one of your own, we shall take your life. Our threat is real and that reality should persuade you to be one of us, law abiding and not an outlaw.

The purpose of society, government, is to protect and secure the citizens' exercise of freedom and inalienable rights as they pursue their common good. It fails in this if it is slow to detect, arrest, convict, and reasonably punish the lawbreakers. That punishment, because man learns first by sense and then by intellect, ought to be corporal. It must also be prompt, inexorable, allowing no diminution or exceptions.

The media have made it evident that our sanctions have none of these qualities. A man is convicted of murdering thirty young men, is sentenced to die, and then waits thirteen years on death row before being executed. During that time he and his lawyers search for evidence that has a shadow of probability to it, search for any legal technicality whereby the execution can be delayed, the conviction appealed, the conviction overturned, the sentence reduced. And they are somewhat successful. The delays render the punishment inefficient on the point of promptness. And so the would-be criminal has no certitude that his crime will lead inexorably to death. He not only has hope that he will not be detected and convicted, but has the reasonable hope that his punishment will be delayed indefinitely. The punishment is inefficient on the point of specific punishment. Circumstances of time and economy often dictate plea bargaining to a reduced punishment. The sanction is thus inefficient, the law is not feared, more crime is committed, and society is less and less secure in its pursuit of happiness.

If there is to be a decrease in the amount and severity of crime there must be a change in the way we punish and administer the punishment for breaking the law. We must admit that all punishment is brutal and that we are willing to be brutal. There has to be a gun in the hands of the police to enforce the Declaration, the Constitution, and the Bill of Rights. Society must be not only willing to use the gun, but also be willing to admit that using the brutal sanction is the responsible and moral thing to do.

PUNISHMENT AND TORTURE

One frequently hears that corporal punishment is torture. This is to speak metaphorically. They are simply different, but in on sense the same. They are the same in that they both inflict physical pain. But at that point the similarity ends. Punishment is specified by law and so is *limited*. The only limitation on torture is either the exhaustion point of the vengeance of the torturers or the confession or admission by the tortured of what the torturers want to hear. Consequently there is *no specified limit* to the pain that can be inflicted.

Punishment looks to the *past* and is the last element in the fulfillment of the law. It is the vindication of the law's promised threat and makes the threat real to would-be lawbreakers. Torture that is not simply vengeance looks to the *future*. It looks for change in the tortured, it hopes for a confession, a conversion, a revelation of secrets. Thus torture is in violation of man's freedom and seeks what is essentially contradictory. It supposes that the coerced statement is a human act, even though it cannot be so if it is not free. The confession is essentially a cry of pain and not a free statement of a fact. And no one can tell whether the statement is true or simply a statement of what the torturers want to hear.

Punishment does not look for a human reaction, and so does not violate the freedom of the punished. He is free to say anything he wants to say. Thus punishment seeks no information, no confession, no revelation of secrets because it does not need those things. For the guilt has been proven; punishment comes because all the relevant information is evident and is in. Punishment is simply a specific consequence of man's having deliberately violated the law.

The tragedy is that the exploited and victimized society lacks the courage to act. It does not want "to use the gun." It would rather rehabilitate than punish, and so it changes its penitentiaries into correctional institutions. It fails to think and develop rewards and punishments that adequately support the behaviors necessary to keep society in that state of peace necessary for the free pursuit of happiness, the acquirement of good, or as Pirsig would say, the achievement of Quality.

The word tragedy is very important here. We exploited Americans are tragic, not pathetic. Pathos is the result of victimhood. The victim suffers and dies through no fault of his own. For example, the immigrant who works so hard to bring his family to America, gets them and himself off to a successful start, clearly has a great future, then contracts a serious illness and dies before much of the dream is realized—that is pathetic, it is not tragic.

Tragedy is a matter of choice. It is self-inflicted suffering and ruin that proceeds out of the excess of some strength. The ruin did not have to happen. It did happen because a choice was made and maintained. Those observing the choice and see it made over and over again, they know where it is leading. They worry and fear and sometimes try to warn their friend or loved one; but he doesn't seem to realize or care. He can't or won't see. They pity him as suffering and ruin approach. The beautiful youths taking their first steps into the drug world are tragic figures. The competent professional making the first compromise with the standards of his profession is tragic. And the rest of us are tragic when we begin any pattern of behavior we know is wrong.

How is America tragic and not pathetic? She is an irresolute Hamlet. She sees the need for action, i.e., creating effective sanctions, sets up a committee, talks endlessly, but can't get by, can't think through and overcome the excess of one of her greatest virtues: Respect for the individual. That respect has taken two forms which block her on her evolutionary way to a higher pattern of quality of life. The first form is: America would rather have two hundred jungle people living in her midst (on the street, in government, in business, in the professions) than have one innocent person fined, jailed, or executed.

The second form is: America prefers delayed, mitigated, partial or completed commutation of sanctions. Her great concern in this matter and basic to mild application of sanction is to avoid "cruel and unusual punishment." This concern has led to the point where there is little reason for the intelligent exploiter not to become a savage living in the city.

This tragic dalliance, tragic procrastination, this inability to unite as a people and face the overwhelming savagery with effective physical and forceful control will fill anyone with pity and fear as he watches this great nation move closer and closer to chaos and its own ruin. There is a deliberate choice to hold back, to hold on to a traditional interpretation of respect for the individual and fear of cruel and unusual punishment that is the one of the major occasions for widespread exploitation and violent crime.

What would happen if more serious and prompt sanctions were put in place? Would there be miscarriages of justice, the innocent fined, jailed, and executed? Certainly. And that would be pathetic, not tragic. Pathetic because the punishment was unwittingly inflicted on the innocent. The pathetic effect came from the inadequacy of well-intentioned man to fully understand the meaning of the new process or to understand and control the malice of those who would abuse the new process. Just as the immigrant did not know of or understand how to protect himself from the virus, so in some cases with society. It makes mistakes out of ignorance as it learns how to accomplish a higher quality of life.

But that unjust "punishment" of the virus or execution is part of the territory when one becomes a pioneer into a new territory of an improved society. It is exactly like the pathos engendered in death by "friendly fire." Come to America, prosper in freedom, but you might be killed by polio three days before Sabin oral vaccine is developed. Join the service of your country, give your best, be ready to go anywhere to serve, but you might die in a jeep accident or by "friendly fire." The possibility of the pathetic is not justification for the decision to remain tragic. The immigrant fears, and so stays home and never lets the full potential of his talents and dreams come to fruition. And as he comes to the end of his stifled life and looks at the thirty years of seamy sameness, he dreams of what might have been for himself and his family. They are no better off now than he was thirty years ago.

A society at peace has the opportunity to think its way beyond random death by virus and beyond faulty application of sanction. It can grow from inferior to better technology, from inferior to better management, from inferior to better leadership, and from an inferior to a better legal system. But it can't think and grow if the savage is physically in society's midst and exploiting the people who are trying to do a little better. The exploitation is real and must be physically stopped. If it is not, the social pain will increase so much that there will be a return to vigilantism, anarchy, and then some sort of violent revolution. Who knows what will rise from the chaotic ruin and tragic end of so noble a concept—a people living as equals with inalienable rights in system of liberty and justice for all. What a tragedy that for lack of imagination and courage to develop and maintain an effective legal force so noble a concept died.

What might be more effective sanctions? Before suggesting them, some basic principles must be enunciated. For they are essential to any creative development. First, we have to believe in order to see. We must say there is a better way and we can find it. We really believe it can be found. If the question "How?" is always somewhere at hand, we won't miss the answer when, in research, we stumble upon it.

A second and correlative position has to do with the saying, "It can't be done, that will never work, etc." This should never be permitted as a first response to any suggestion, but only as a last. Then it must be supported by evidence; evidence that proves a negative is hard to come by. This principle is just as important as the first. For whenever anyone says "It can't be done," he has at that moment turned out the lights in his head, has stopped thinking and automatically excuses himself from the arena of thought and discussion. He becomes a complainer and an obstacle to progress. The question is destroyed, the answer will not be seen when it passes by.

The realization that present sanctions are ineffective and must be changed is the point of intelligent breaking through a traditional pattern that has lost its quality and is now harming rather than helping the freedom of Americans. They have to worry too much about survival to give sufficient attention to the unrestricted desire to know the world, know its possibilities, reduce those to actuals and so create more trust and benefits for themselves. They live in fear of physical force, physical power threatening their lives, their families and possessions. The very nature of this real situation is that it can only be stopped by physical force that is reasonable. Reasonable means that force supports and defends freedom and inalienable rights. Reasonable force means that hostile forces be stopped; better yet that they be anticipated and prevented. In terms of free agents of hostility, the only way a free person can be moved to a free choice is through understanding from experience that his choice really is good or bad for him now. The choice to engage in drive-by shootings or gun-point car jacking must terminate in enough terror and pain for the criminal that the very thought of such behavior is as repugnant as stepping off the 100th floor of the Empire State Building. Sanctions that imitate the promptness and thoroughness of physical laws must be created by intelligent man.

The fact that such creations will sometimes inadvertently result in a miscarriage of justice is pathetic. But that goes both with the territory of being imperfect and therefore a learning human being. That pathos is not justification for abandoning the necessary control of those elements that will necessarily destroy all the progress made for American humanity up to now. We must break through these two great limitations, namely, 1) the guilty should go free rather than one innocent person be unjustly punished, and 2) all physically inflicted pain is cruel. Physically inflicted pain is required by the manner in which man learns, i.e., first by sense or feeling and then by understanding. The risk of pathetic miscarriage of justice must be accepted if we are to advance to a new and more secure life.

It is more important that America think about principles and then apply them, than to think about examples of punishment a person might bring forth. The examples can easily be objected to and rejected out of hand. Therefore I'll call attention to some principles and offer two general examples of application.

First, there is a hierarchy of crime in society. The worst crime is the betrayal of trust. The highest level of that betrayal is in the political sphere, then the entrepreneurial, then the professional, then the individual (neighbor to neighbor). Consequently, the rewards and punishments should be proportionate to those levels of trust. Those who are chosen to govern should receive the highest rewards for their work. The reason is simple. They produce (are supposed to produce) the necessary condition for the successful performance of business and the other professions. Above all else business needs peace and freedom to think, research, create, engineer, manufacture, distribute products and services to an ever increasing multitude of consumers. Creation of wealth, not peace, is the proper object of business enterprise. Creation of peace is the proper object and duty of government.

Since these elected people are at the highest level of trust, since all else in society depends upon their successful work for the community, it follows that betrayal of that trust is the most far reaching and damaging to the society, truly monstrous.. Betrayal means that the powers of the governors are being used for personal (individual or special interest group) gain at the cost of great community loss. Betrayal attacks the mechanism of peace, puts the power of society as a whole at the service of an individual or group. It is a step away from the common good, the perverting of power to enslave the many to the interests of the few.

Since that is the highest of crimes, it should be threatened with the highest of sanctions. Those threats might be: 1) Loss of the rights of citizenship, deportation, 2) Life sentence, no parole, 3) Confiscation of all assets acquired during public service, 4) Confiscation of all assets shared with family, relatives, and friends of the public servant.

The same type of thinking should be applied to the business world. The great crime of business is the exploitation of the consumer. It is worse to exploit the government consumer than to exploit the business consumer, and worse to exploit the business consumer than the man on the street, unless of course the exploited man on the street is so numerous that his exploitation far surpasses the other exploitations' dollar value. Consequently, the sanction should be a serious threat to the well being of the responsible parties. Harming the government through fraud saps the power of government to promote and maintain peace and order. Defrauding another business will have widespread bad effects, but not as widespread as damage to the government. Thus leaders of business, who are paid to lead and manage, should be sanctioned differently. The sanctions should imitate to a lesser degree that which is applied to corrupt government officials. That is the principle. Its application is left to the creative thought of the reader.

So much for crimes of betrayal of trust. What about violent crime? First of all there is more reality in the moral order than in the physical. Therefore violence against the person is far more profound than damage to the physical order, damage to other living things. Consider the following for example.

A forest of oak, three generations old. One day a woodsman comes in and cuts an eight inch gap across the trunk. The gap is six inches deep. He is preparing the tree for harvest. For some reason he does not get to cut it down. The oak begins to heal. All that is left of the cut after a few years is a bark covered scar. Nothing happened to the other oaks living near this one.

Next consider a young married couple. After fifteen years they have three or four children ages 4 to 12. Their married brothers and sisters have children, and the grandparents are still alive. Over the years through many smiles and tears the family grows close. There are the Christmases, the Easters, the Thanksgivings, the birthday parties.

One evening this mother of fifteen years of marriage is leaving the store to get to her car parked in the distance. She is alone. She sees someone in a van parked next to her car. Didn't she see that van shortly before she entered the lot? A little apprehension. She hurries to get her keys. The van door opens. "Do you know the time, please?" Frightened, she glances at her watch. As she glances up, a heavy hand is across her mouth, a strong arm about her waist. Van door opens, she's thrust inside. Terror fills her, she is powerless. This can't be happening. What will happen to the kids if I die, to my husband? Will I be tortured, raped, and killed? Then the answers: beating, rape, unnatural sex acts, tied up, thrown onto the road, discovered, hospital, police report, then meeting the husband. Then return to the family, relatives, work associates, and neighbors. But let's specify just one of those relationships. The four year old daughter. She sees the bruised mother. What happened? Days later mother is alone and crying. She is not the same. Weeks later the child has caught the mother silently crying; she doesn't know why her mother has changed. Years later she learns the truth, and she too begins to know the possibility that rape may be waiting for her.

What realities have been damaged here? What qualities of life have been deprived of much of their goodness? Terror and trauma both actual and vicarious have permeated that three generation family of friends and acquaintances. Everyone who knew the victim has experienced according to his or her own level of maturity some violence to their relationship. How shall I talk to her? How can I help? What does she need from me? What does the son say? The husband? Her boss? The man next door? etc.

This forty-five minute or hour's worth of violent sexual release or gender retaliation has more than one victim. The violence affects more than one body. Life at the office and school and neighborhood and at the barbecue will not be the same for a long time.

The point: There is an infinite amount of reality in the moral world, far surpassing that of the physical world. One cut into the trunk of the oak tree stops there; one act of violent intercourse disturbs the peace and order of hundreds. A whole new set of relationships begin with that terrible act. Memories of peace remain to remind all of how bad the present is. New efforts struggle to get off to a new start to establish a new peace, a new joy, a new set of Thanksgivings, birthdays, etc.

The rapist, living at the level of sexual release neither sees nor values the good he is about to destroy. Nor is there any serious deterrent to persuade him to control his violent urge. On the contrary, if he is once successful in executing his planned violence, that very success is motivation to repeat. He has learned how to be the successful savage in the city.

Unfortunately the victim is seen by the rest of us as one person. "Thank God it didn't happen to me and my family." We are not even aware that we too are victims. But we identify with her. In a true sense she is part of us and we are part of her. We say, "*my* friend, *my* mother." She says, "*my* husband, *my* sister, etc." We don't even think of ourselves as having a right to be protected from such painful relationships with the victim. So what do we do? We think of mace, of karate, of lighted parking lots and neighborhood watches, of security guards, cooperating with police, reporting all suspicious activity. We do not think of rising above individual and neighborhood action to the level of participatory legislation. "What can I do," we say in helplessness that soon becomes mindless fatalism.

We are almost pathetic in our ignorance of what we really could do if we just thought and just got involved in the legislative process. But there is hope; we are becoming tragic. We know that something is terribly wrong, and suspect there is a way out. Tragically we decide to do nothing, to wait. Tomorrow our mother will be raped.

There is a reason why we are stuck at this level. First, we are ignorant. We are just beginning to appreciate, thanks to the media, the moral order. We see the widespread moral damage that comes from physical violence, e.g., rape, physical child abuse passed on from generation to generation, incest wrecking lives for years after the physical acts have stopped.

Second, the very composition of man as a body-person, who knows violence by sensation and morality by insight, is necessarily more focused on what he sees and physically experiences than on what he understands, but has difficulty articulating into resolutions. Further, it is easier to do something after the act—hunt, arrest, charge, jail—than to create an effective deterrent.

Third, man as physical (body) already is constrained by the physical laws of the universe. He is constrained by conscience—except that he can free himself from the moral experience of guilt by creating the more exciting experience of planning, organizing, and setting in motion the execution of the rape. He does not see himself about to fall off the ledge of a ten story building, because society has no ten story building from which he will certainly fall when he violates the woman.

Nature, physical man in physical world, threatens man with terrifying sanctions if he violates that good order. Moral man, free man, by the very definition of freedom must freely create moral sanctions that terrify him who would contemplate doing such violence to the widespread love, affection, trust, joy, friendship etc. that has been created by the acts of trust and love that have been going on for years. Control of man as a free being is a freely established control. It is not a given, as is the control put into the physical universe. What is given is the *moral necessity* to control; man is obligated by his free nature to create sanctions that are analogous to the sanctions in the universe. Just as man is superior to physical nature, so too should be his sanctions. Their superiority lies in their being freely established and successfully move the majority of free men.

Put another way, this given freedom from coerced good behavior is the necessary condition of his existence. There will be no sanctions in the social order unless he creates them. Further, he can create good, better and best sanctions. It all lies within his competence, resoluteness and courage. He can't prosper as a social individual without adequate sanctions protecting that society. Without sanctions his only alternative is survival, not prosperity. He returns to jungle existence, a member of a tribe juxtaposed to another in intermittent peace, truce, or war.

What might this terrifying sanction be and how might it be administered?

ADMINISTRATION

Corporal punishment could be administered in limited jurisdictions in limited states, e.g., in a few counties in the north, east, south and western states. It should be mechanically or roboticly administered and according to the body weight of the criminal. It should be publicized. The instrument should be seen in the media and vividly described on television. Demonstrations should be performed on dummies representing the differences of sex, age, size, etc. of the criminal. It should be limited to clear and obvious convictions, e.g., proved by witnesses and incontrovertible circumstantial evidence such as DNA, fingerprints, hair, clothing connecting the criminal to the victim at the time and in the place of the crime. Once evidence has been collected, it should be presented to a special court set up just for crimes such as these. There would be no appeal, no plea bargaining; all cases would be six person jury trials to determine guilt or innocence. The main concern would be was the evidence strong enough (jury) to prove responsibility beyond a reasonable doubt, and was the evidence properly gathered (*judge*). Conviction means mandatory sentencing at the time of conviction. Sanction to be administered within three days of conviction. The sanction should be administered at least twice, once to let the criminal experience it, a second or third time so that he experiences the terror of knowing that it is going to be inflicted again and soon. Finally it should be administered in groups, i.e., the criminal should see what is happening to his fellow criminal and become terrified at the thought that it is about to happen to him.

THE SANCTION ITSELF

The reader should use his or her own reasonable and creative intelligence to design the application of pain to the criminal who maimed or killed. The purpose that should guide that intelligence is this: the sanction should be brutal, designed to show (by his sense experience and intellection) the criminal become-brute what it means to leave civilization and return to the law of the jungle. It should become evident to him that it is better to stay a man than to become a brute. He should be able to see that the choice of jungle life for him is a terrifying and terrible choice. At present the rapist, the drunk driver, the drive by shooter, the car-jacker has all the benefits of civilization and no idea of the jungle he has chosen—we the city dwellers have let him enter our midst without bringing with him the laws of jungle survival that are proper to his mode of life. He doesn't have to look over his shoulder to see if we are coming to get him; we are not interested in taking his car or his money. He doesn't have to compete against us in the hunt for food and shelter, race to it and run off with it before we get to it, hide it and defend it. There is a different struggle going on within the peaceful society. The society at peace is trying to produce goods and services to make a better life available for more and more peace loving citizens. The brute of the jungle comes into this environment as a predator without natural enemies to control him. He is camouflaged. He looks just like one of us. His fur, fang, and tail are not easily recognizable. And he knows this. Time (8/9/93, Vol. 142, No. 6, p. 42) quotes one such criminal element (skinheads) thus: *"We are everywhere, and we are nowhere. You fail to see us, but we are here. . .We are the predators in your urban jungles. And our time to strike is fast approaching."*

Because we fail to philosophize, we fail to see that the savage man hurts himself before he hurts his victim. The first evil that is done in a rape or drunk driving maiming is to the rapist and drunk driver, not to the victims. He made an evil decision to become brutal, to step outside human self control. He is bad and brutal by choice. He now moves from *being* to *act*. The *being* is reinforced by the act and tends to become a habitual characteristic of the person and inclining him to more acts of the same. He *is* bad before he *does* bad. He brutalizes himself before he brutalizes his victim.

Consequently, the infliction of sanction is not an act of revenge. It is first and foremost punishment, and it is not cruel. It is the attempt of a free society to deal with the brute, who is radically free, in a manner that respects the brute's freedom. Society cannot coerce good behavior nor contain bad behavior. It can only persuade, demonstrate that it is more beneficial to the brute to change (*be* different) and consequently *act* differently, i.e., act as a human and not as a brute. Society can only act as a moral cause, not as an efficient cause in effecting free choice. Therefore creating and applying a brutal sanction is just the opposite of cruelty. It is a gift, an attempt to save the brute from the terrible consequences of being a brute and living brute life. We attempt first to save him from brutalizing himself, and indirectly thereby protect ourselves in the peaceful pursuit of happiness. For if the brute wins and destroys society, then he himself will live among the predators. Society will call them vigilantes. He will become prey as well as predator. He will find a host of natural enemies, and will be stuck in a survival mode rather in the mode of the pursuit of happiness.

What we are doing is choosing the proper order of being. That order is: A brute environment permanently attached to brutes, and a social environment permanently attached to those exercising equality and inalienable rights. Maintaining that attachment is a matter of free choice, and not a necessary result of the blind forces of nature. Society cannot abandon or delay that choice without slipping back down the evolutionary trail from which it has arisen at such great cost. Therefore we must take the breakthrough step: Apply brutal sanction to brutal behavior.

We have had successful experience in doing this. Brutal force has been vividly described, publicized nationally and internationally year after year. The result has been that those threatened with it have actually given up the brutal for the respect for freedom. The brutal force we have created as a deterrent to brutal action is the stockpiled atomic bomb.[4] The brutal system that suppressed individual freedom to the power of the state simply could not compete as a brutal force against a free force; it could not produce enough bread and bombs to stay even with the free world's standard of security and well-being. The absolute terror of retaliation was well-known and imagined both by governments and peoples. The thought of the brutal attempt to bury the West in atomic warfare, was the equivalent of standing on the 100th floor of the Empire State Building and seriously contemplating a jump into the abyss. The brutal government finally became rational. It made the free choice to return to the society of the free. It was morally forced. It was given a realistic choice between the peace of the social order and the absolute terror of the international jungle. It was persuaded.

If brute nations and governments can be terrorized into changing their behaviors, so too can brute individuals. If we believe it can be done, we shall find a way to get it done. We have taken the breakthrough step once. We must take it again. The individual brutes among us must be terrorized into freely changing their behaviors. If they don't change, then they must be removed from society permanently, either by execution or by lasting incarceration.

This theory of brutal sanctions attempts to make a point, namely that the present system of justice is ineffectual and that society must be protected from the violent criminal. Prompt brutal sanction is necessary. This is not the same as prompt detection, arrest, conviction, and imprisonment. Almost twenty-five years ago Karl Menninger cogently argued against the psychological brutality of our prison system[5] and for its replacement by an entirely different philosophy and practice of controlling the criminal element. I agree with all he says and support it. The simplicity of my position on brutal punishment is that it ignores the fact that the brutal criminal most probably has been brutalized himself, has not experienced love and hope, and needs to be treated with doses of both along with other remedies of the social and medical sciences. But this does not deny the need for

---

4. I do not say that dropping the bomb on Japan was justified. I only have wavering opinions. It was not justified because so many civilians were killed. It was justified to prevent further casualties, both civilian and military.

5. Karl Menninger, M.D., *The Crime of Punishment*, Viking Press, New York, 1968. See especially the cruelty of prison confinement on page 176, the need for prompt and more serious penalties on page 202, the need for diagnosis of the criminal on page 230, the conviction that the majority of criminals can be cured, just as mental illness can be cured, on pages 257 and 258; that the basis for such treatment is love and hope on pages 260,261, not vengeance, pages 190-218.

more severe, sure, and swift penalty in the treatment of some offenders. Menninger does not spell out how penalties are to be more severe.[6] He refers with approval to the severe penalties Scandinavian countries impose for the offense of drunk driving; whether he would agree to corporal punishment is questionable. One thing is certain: detention can be more inhumane than beating. "Detention in prison was supposed to be a mollification of pain infliction, but it is often more cruel and destructive than beating."[7] Corporal punishment with limited detention might be just the means to terrify would-be offenders from committing their crimes. But as was said at the outset, since man is free to resist all persuasion, no sanction can guarantee conformance to law. Therefore society will always be in an experimental mode[8] regarding sanction. It will always be looking for more effective means to create the awe and reverence for law that the physical world inspires in each of us. Some of these means will be in the form of legal sanctions; others will be the righting of social injustices such as discrimination and exploitation of the ignorant and weak by the rich and the powerful. But those are two distinct problems. Our concern here has been to deal with but one of them.

---

6. Ibid., 202.
7. Ibid., 203.
8. The American teenage vandal, Michael Fay, and the Singapore system of sanction received widespread publicity in the Spring of 1994. Many Americans, sick of rampant crime, favored the punishment of six strokes with a rattan cane. To those who recoiled at such a sanction the former Singapore prime minister, Lee Kuan Yew replied with irrefutable logic, "When a state of increasing disorder and defiance of authority cannot be checked by the rules then existing, new and somtimes drastic rules have to be forged to maintain order. The alternative is to surrender order to chaos and anarchy." *Los Angeles Times*, "Singapore: What Price Justice," 4/2/94, Sec. A, B. The *Times* headline is misleading. It should read "What Price Social Order." The price of restored justice is restitution. The price of order among free beings is law, which implies effective deterrence as one of its essential elements.

8

Animal Rights

This topic is given so much attention today that we, too, must consider it. We have to understand the differences and similarities between inalienable rights and animal rights.

Not only that, but we also want to know whether the use of animals for fur, food, and experimentation is moral or not.

Laurence Pringle in his *The Animal Rights Controversy*,[1] gives us a very thorough report on the state of the controversy today. He reports both instances of cruelty and legal concern toward animals. He presents both the extreme and very moderate views of the animal rights proponents. He also gives us the data on how many animals are used for experiemental purposes and shows us the dollar size of that business, $9 billion a year in the USA. (44) If he himself has a position in the controversy, he hides it well. He concludes his short and excellent report with "Do animals have rights? Are we morally obliged to insure their well being? To what extent can we use animals. . . . The answers should come from a careful and respectful study of the facts and opposing views in order to be fair to ourselves and to the animals." (90)

With an issue that is frequently discussed in hostility, anger, and shouting put-downs, Pringle is much like Tribe is on the abortion issue. What a welcome change these two scholars bring to the manner of discussing and debating sensitive issues.

The animal rights issue must be located within a larger issue, namely the environment. It is important here to mention all the aspects of that environment: biotic, physical, food chain, balance of nature, ecological succession and its climax, population, community, biome, and the six main parts of an ecosystem, i.e., sun, abiotic substances, primary producers, primary consumers, secondary consumers, and decomposers.

---

1. Laurence Pringle, *The Animal Rights Controversy*, Harcourt Brace Janovich, New York, 1989.

Both man and animal, since they come to life, live in the ecosystem, and then decompose within it, are involved in a necessary process, i.e., the system is just that, a repetition of the same process again and again. And yet, man, because of his freedom transcends the system. He can wreck it, repair it, conserve it, subject it to his immediate objectives or long range goals. He is not a just a passive victim, but can be a master. He can understand cycles, pollution, erosion, global warming, depletion of the ozone layer, etc., and is in a position to do something about each and all these things.

And yet he is locked into an ecosystem as a secondary consumer in the food chain and a producer of wastes for the decomposers. He experiences necessity and freedom. In order to have an accurate understanding of the term *right* when speaking of man and animals, it is helpful to observe how the two pursue their well-being.

The animal does it by physical power; man does it by both physical and moral power (free choice, communication in trust).

The animal lives, survives and dies in the relative comfort of the wild and the jungle. It does this by anticipating and fleeing danger, by grazing or attacking its prey. It has no interest in cause and effect, population control, erosion, destruction of forage, balance of nature. If there is to be any balancing, it will not be by choice of the animal, but by the "chance" of nature. For example, the Isle Royal in Lake Superior achieved a balance whereby 3,000 moose starving for forage became, with the advent of the wolf, a stable ecosystem of 600 moose, 20 wolves, and enough forage to support the moose.[2]

Man, on the other hand, as an animal must do exactly as his fellow animals: consume, produce waste, and decompose. But unlike the animals he is the unrestricted desire to know and create, to control both himself and his manner of being an animal. The lion will never start a zebra ranch, the eagle will never start a trout pond, and the praying mantis will never start an insect farm. But man will organize resources and capital to produce food, clothing, shelter, and time saving devices so that he can have more freedom to transcend the limitations of his physical environment. He does this by his moral power, his ability to understand and choose. This moral power dominates his physical power. He understands growth, animal husbandry, the wheel, the lever and with this understanding joined to his physical power he pursues his good. He can do more than anticipate danger, flee from it, forage, attack, and kill. The use of moral power in the pursuit of his highest good—trust, love—makes it possible for him to respect the independence, equality, the rights of others. Through moral power, man

2. Richard S. Miller, "Ecology," *The World Book Encyclopedia*, VI, World Book, Inc., 1982, 38.

is essentially a persuader. He moves his fellow man, not by force, but by evidence. His listener, if a person of integrity, can hear, see, and understand the evidence. He agrees, as he must, and the result is peace and union, not victory of predator over prey.

Note that this communication process is not manipulation or the technique of selling; rather in its purest form it is the rational adult dealing with another rational adult as both seek a clear elucidation of the facts of the issue under discussion. The result is a double victory, a win-win situation where both speaker and listener come to share the same truth.

The animal can't do that because it has only physical power. The zebra can't say to the lion, "Get off my back. I'm just as much an animal as you are. Repect my independence, let me graze in peace." Nor can the trout or salmon say to the bald eagle, "Don't swoop down on me and snatch me from my home with your strong feet and sharp talons. Repect my privacy and independence." If the zebra runs fast enough, it lives and the lion dies of starvation; if it doesn't, it dies; so, too, with the trout and the eagle. In the wild and in the jungle might makes right. There is no justice. There are no rights.

Man, as animal, is part of this wild and jungle, a superior part. As *part*, he is a primary (vegetation) and secondary (animals) consumer. He kills and consumes as all animals kill and consume; the killing is more or less violent, more or less "cruel."

Pringle reports that strong proponents of vegetarianism and animal rights have the T-shirt and bumper sticker battle cry of "Meat is Murder." (43) Is this true for all the animal world, or just for man? Do animals have rights regarding man, but no rights regarding their other fellow animals? Using the "meat is murder" analogy, one could say that the 3,000 moose of Isle Royal were practicing genocide on the vegetation of their habitat until the wolf came and effected a holocaust of 80% of them. We do not need rhetoric and metaphor confusing logic and proper language.

As a *superior part* existing in the wild and the jungle, man is intelligent. This same term is applied to the animal. Whatever it means, and however it is to be distinguished—if at all—from instinct, one thing is clear. Animal intelligence is *simply different* from human intelligence, yet in some sense *like* it. Put another way, to say the animal is intelligent is to speak metaphorically, not properly. Properly speaking the animal is not intelligent. It cannot abstract, cannot count, does not see that too many of its species are inhabiting too much of the land, does not problem solve, cannot use arbitrary signs, and is not free from the limitations of its sense faculties. Being in the wrong place at the right time is unrecognizeable to it. It will die, not because of its ignorance, but because it cannot but be ignorant—being unintelligent.

Thus the animal is subordinate to man in the strictest sense of that term. Subordinate means that the animal is of a lower order of being, and by nature (by what it is and by what man is) controllable by man. Animals are not free of him as he is free of them. He can use them to better his life. They have neither the physical nor moral power to do the same. The most they can do is to escape his control is to anticipate, flee, attack. They cannot assert independence and discuss.

The moral question for man is: How will he exercise control over them? What happens to him when he is cruel, kind, slaughtering, experimenting[3] with them? Pringle's book details many harsh treatments of animals: broiler chickens, layers, breed sows, calves, beef cattle, rabbits (28-40), monkeys. (57) He also notes legislation in the European Economic Community and Sweden[4] where animals must be treated more humanely. What is the moral and political difference between the Swedes and Americans *in this matter* of animal treatment? Are the Swedes better?

The animal rights question can be put more poignantly in the matter of the rhesus monkey and the testing of polio (71) vaccine, or the heart transplant from the baboon to the human infant. Both primates are close to us in physical, emotional, and social structure. We violate all of that when we use them for our lives and well-being. Do such ends justify the means, namely death to the infant baboon and death to the rhesus monkey for the benefit of safe polio vaccine the saving of infant human life?

It would seem so, for two reasons. First, the animal has no rights, as we have seen, existing between itself and other animals. There is no justice in the wild or in the jungle. Second, the animal is not transcendent or free, and therefore is neither person nor incorruptible (immortal), and therefore cannot exist as an equal to man but only as a subordinate being to man. Therefore man's *might* (intelligence) makes *right* over the animal. But that might must be used according the intelligent nature of man. He can recognize suffering and pain in the animal. He must have a legitimate reason for causing or permitting this evil (privation of a due good) to occur during the use of the animal either for food or experimentation. What is the point of permitting pain, e.g., locking infant chimpanzees (59), who

---

3. Ibid., 62. Pringle notes that efforts at more humane experimentation are succeeding. ". . .significant progress has been made in developing alternate ways of conducting product tests and other biomedical research." The ways are designed to ". . . *replace* the use of laboratory animals, *reduce* the number needed, or *refine* a reasearch procedure so that stress or other harm to animals is reduced."

4. Ibid., 43. "In 1988, intensive factory farming was outlawed in Sweden. Cows were given grazing rights. Pigs could no longer be tied up and had to be given separate bedding and feeding places. Chickens could not be kept in cramped cages. And no drugs or hormones could be given to farm animals except to actually treat diseases."

have comparable social and emotional needs as human infants, in cramped and isolating cages that irritate to insanity? Reduce cost, make profit, save time. What else does it do for the captor or experimentor? He can recognize the pain. He can watch it. He can tolerate it. He can ignore it; yes, and perversely, he can enjoy it. Are these behaviors good for his person? How many dollars is it worth to watch an animal suffer and know that the suffering is under man's control? It may be worth a lot, if man's need for food right now desperately depends upon that animal's suffering and death. It may be worth even more, if man's protection from disease can be shown to be directly dependent upon that suffering and death. But on the face of it, for man to tolerate needless pain in the animal is not rational, and therefore beneath man's dignity as a free and rational being.

Strictly speaking, man owes it to himself, not to any right held by the animal, to respect the life and well-being of the animal. Man's moral obligation—which will affect the well-being of the animal—is to understand as fully as possible the order of subordination that exists between himself and animal world and respect it. Observing that order, of which he is a part, means being a good man; ignoring and or deliberately violating that order is to be out of his own proper order, being bad, and therefore losing the good of that order, e.g., the extinction or near extinction of plants and animals that can give him a greater understanding of himself and his world.

If one wants to speak of animal rights, one can do so, but only metaphorically, not properly. They have *restricted* rights, not *absolute* rights, as man has. The restriction is that their lives and well-being are subordinate to the intelligent lives and well-being of men. Except for this restriction, they are free and independent enough to use their physical powers to live, survive, propagate and die in the relative comfort of the wild and of the jungle devoid of all moral power and of all justice. Strictly speaking, animals, insects, and vegetation have no rights.

9

Business and Ethics

Up to this point we have developed from the nature of man's freedom his inalienable rights, his obligations proceeding from the structures of his person and his nature. We have seen how that person is obliged to stay open and does so in communicating with his fellow man. This communication is designed to terminate in trust, the union of friendship and love. Such trust is not only the goal or object of the individual person, but is also the goal of human society in general and the particular societies of family business, city, state, national governments. Trust is another word for human peace, the tranquility of dynamic human order. The common nature of man—we are equal in our humanity—is social because its proper action is to reach out to its fellow human in the natural and arbitrary signs of body and verbal language. He can get to the moon, but not alone. And getting to the moon is the natural expression of his unrestricted desire to know and create. He gets there by speaking to and working in a relationship of trust with his fellow man.

We saw, too, that this was good for man and, conversely, that isolation, separation, distrust was bad for him. Insofar as he is responsible for such conditions, he is morally bad. He is evil if he deliberately closes himself off from the experience of trust. In a word such behavior is unethical.

In order to better himself he engages in business. The question now is: What is the nature of business and how does it relate to the nature of man? If it is a natural phenomenon, a natural expression of what man needs to do to perfect himself, to be good, then such business activity will always be either in accord with nature or against nature. It will be ethical or unethical.

But if business has nothing to do with nature, is no more necessary for man than tying his shoes or combing his hair, then it will be much like a game. He creates the game, determines its purpose, sets its rules, then proceeds to play to win. The game is only remotely associated with moral or ethical behavior, i.e., it has little to do with making him a better or worse person. So we ask the question: Business, what has it to do with ethics? Everything or nothing.

Milton Friedman in 1970 said, and rightly so, that responsibility lies with people, and in terms of business, responsibility lies with the corporate executive. He is directly responsible to his employers. He is to achieve their wishes "which generally will be to make as much money as possible while conforming to the basic rules of society, both those embodied in law and ethical custom."[1]

Friedman's remarks are in the context of a debate about the social responsibilities of a corporation. His position is that the corporate executive is not supposed to use the corporation's resources to correct social ills, but to earn profit and return on investment: ". . . the key point is that . . . manager is the agent of the individuals who own the corporation. . . and his primary responsibility is to them."[2]

According to Friedman it is "pure rhetoric" to say that the business executive has a social responsibility

> to refrain from increasing the price of a product in order to contribute to the social objective of preventing inflation, even though a price increase would be in the best interests of the corporation . . . or that at the expense of corporate profits, he is to hire "hard core" unemployed instead of better qualified available workmen to contribute to the social objective of reducing poverty.[3]

Another very clear, very plausible, and very cogent article by Albert Z. Carr makes much the same point. Business is like poker, it is a game with its own set of rules. Businessmen " . . . in their office lives . . . cease to be private citizens; they become game players who must be guided by a somewhat different set of ethical standards."[4] According to Carr the business man has no obligation to consider who is going to get hurt. If the law says it is OK, that is all the justification he needs.[5] The golden rule is not a feasible guide for business. Violations of ethical ideals are not necessary violations of business principles.[6] As long as business men comply with the letter of the law, they are within their rights to operate the business as they see fit.[7] Without grave psychological strain, the businessman cannot allow himself to be torn between a decision based on business considerations

---

1. *Essentials of Business Ethics, A Collection of Articles by Top Social Thinkers*, edited by Peter Madsen, and Jay M. Shafrtiz, New York, 1990, Milton Friedman, "The Social Responsibility of Business Is to Increase Its Profits," 275.
2. Ibid.
3. Ibid, 278.
4. *Essentials*, Albert Z. Carr, "Is Business Bluffing Ethical?" 68.
5. Ibid.
6. Ibid., 71.
7. Ibid., 70

and one based on his private ethical code.[8] Business considerations may
require him to

> deny a raise to a man who deserves it, to fire an employee of long stand-
> ing, to prepare advertising he believes to be misleading, to conceal facts
> that he feels customers are entitled to know, to cheapen the quality of
> materials used in the manufacture of an established product, to sell as
> new a product that he knows to be rebuilt, to exaggerate the curative
> powers of a medicinal preparation, or to coerce dealers.[9]

"The major tests of every move in business, as in all games of strategy, are
legality and profit."[10]

> In the last third of the twentieth century even children are aware that if
> a man has become prosperous in business, he has sometimes departed
> from the strict truth in order overcome obstacles or has practiced the
> more subtle deceptions of the half-truth or the misleading omission.
> Whatever form of bluff, it is an integral part of the game, and the exec-
> utive who does not master its techniques is not likely accumulate much
> money or power.[11]

From what we have seen of Carr's opinions, several things are clear. The
purpose of business is to make a profit. Its ethic is different from the non-
business aspects of life, i.e., private life. It is like poker. In fact it would be
good to see now how far he carries that comparison.

> Poker's own brand of ethics is different from the ethical ideals of civi-
> lized relationships. The game calls for distrust of the other fellow. It
> ignores the claim of friendship. Cunning deception and concealment of
> one's strength and intentions, not kindness and openheartedness, are
> vital in poker. No one thinks any the worse of poker on that account.
> And no one should think any the worse of the game of business because
> its standards of right and wrong differ from the prevailing traditions of
> morality in our society.[12]

Finally Carr sees that the purpose of business for the individual is the
accumulation of "money and power"—a totally different view from that of
Lawrence Miller[13] which we saw in Chapter 4.

---

8. Ibid., 74. "If an executive allows himself to be torn between a decision based on business
considerations and one based on his private ethical code, he exposes himself to grave psychological strain."
9. Ibid., 74, 73.
10. Ibid., 75.
11. Ibid., 78.
12. Ibid., 67, 68
13. Miller, *The American Spirit*, 37.

Carr's opinions have some very interesting implications. The rules of poker that apply to Toyota, GM, Ford, Honda, and Chrysler as they sit around the table of automobile manufacturing also apply to the other poker games going on in each of their many offices. If the goal of every executive and each of his subordinates is the accumulation of money and power, then there is not only competition among the manufacturers but also within the groups that are trying to manufacture. "Sauce for the goose is sauce for the gander." If we can bluff and deceive GM, then I can do the same to you, and you the same to me. Money and power, not trust, not sacred honor are the governing principles.

Those two articles were written in 1968 (Carr) and 1970 (Friedman). Things have not changed much in twenty years. Control Data's Bill Norris in an interview said,

> One of the appalling things that has happened is the lack of responsibility of banks for business. Twenty years ago, you could go to an investment banker, you could talk to a commercial banker with absolute confidence that it was confidential. You can't do that today. Hell, they'll put you into play if they see an opportunity. No compunction about it at all.[14]

That was in 1988. In the same year Myron Magnet writes

> Formerly circumspect investment bankers now routinely trade confidential information, hoping to glean tips leading to new business. Information seeps out to other clients, too.

> But in many instances investment bankers haven't scrupled to work against their clients by putting them in play when that looked more profitable than working for them. A veteran of one august firm says of his colleagues: "When they speak of ethics, you'd think they've worn white gloves all their lives. But these days they'll sell their clients out for a couple of million bucks in fees." Typically says this veteran, you look over your client list, picking out a company that appears vulnerable. Somebody's going to put him in play, you sigh philosophically, so we'd better do it first—and accordingly you shop his company around behind his back.

> Turn over one stone and out crawls Boesky's tipster, investment banker Dennis Levine, dirt clinging to his $12.6 million insider trading profits. Turn over another and there's a wriggling tangle of the same slimy creatures, from minute grubs like the Yuppie Gang to plump granddads like jailed Deputy Defense Secretary Paul Thayer. A shovel plunged into the ground above General Electric recently disclosed a bustling colony industriously faking time sheets to overcharge the government on

---

14. *Essentials,* "Corporate Do-gooder: Control Data's Bill Norris," 295.

defense contracts. Almost everywhere you look in the business world today, from the E.F. Hutton check-kiting scheme to the Bank of Boston money laundering scandal you glimpse something loathsome scuttling away out of the corner of your eye.[15]

The object, of course, is to win; and winning means money and power for the players. The players are the corporations and the individuals of the corporations. And what happens to the players? They do get rich, some of them get caught in illegal acts, and their consciences begin to hurt because business life does not support conscience as Carr noted.

"Conscience is a fragile thing," says Dr. Abraham Zalenik, a psychoanalyst and Harvard Business School professor. "It needs support from institutions, and that support is weakening"

"Clinically speaking," adds Zalenik, "these people [inside traders] are fighting off major depressions stemming from the fear of being unloved, unlovable, and worthless."[16]

The non-professional observation of Carr about the psychological strain of living out a private ethic while trying to follow the rules of a business ethic is now professionally confirmed. The "strain" is very clearly and professionally specified. We are now back to our definition of evil, the privation of a due good. We are not now dealing with a toothache, a side ache, a pain from a bruised muscle; we are talking about personal pain, disorder, privation of good owed to the structure of the person. We are not talking about pathos, the loss of a good—which loss stems from something beyond our control. That pain in the person would be the pain of grief. We are talking about tragic pain, the pain that comes from self-inflicted, self-chosen disorder, the lie, the betrayal. Since the disorder is in the personal and, therefore, conscious part of their being, it is totally different from a toothache, etc. and demands a totally different cure. Since choice inflicted the pain, and since choice remains, i.e. they stay in business and function according to its "rules" day after day, the disorder and therefore the pain continues. It will continue until the choice is revoked. We said earlier that a good or bad conscience is first of all an experience, then the experience is articulated. In the case of these men that articulation is "Nobody loves me, I am unlovable, I am worthless." The articulation of these feelings and experiences are correct. None of his business customers like him, he really is unlikable, he is worthless to them. If he spends eight or more hours a day in business activities that totally absorb his powers as they pro-

---

15. *Essentials*, Myron Magnet, "The Decline and Fall of Business Ethics," 137,136.
16. Ibid., 140, 141

ceed from his radically personal decision to be like a poker player, that doesn't leave him much time or energy for telling the truth to his wife and children, his neighbor, the people of his private world. In fact it is more than likely that, having become a skilled deceiver, manipulator, and games player, these skills will be applied to the relationships of his private world. He then will have even more evidence for the judgments of himself: "People outside the business world don't like me either. I am unlovable even for them. I am worthless to them, too." And those judgments are correct, too, insofar as he has applied his business skills to his private world.

The principles of self-fulling prophecy are at work here. Any person whom he sees as an object to be fooled, manipulated, conquered etc. will pick up that attitude, especially, if that object-person has caught him in the slightest deception. Then the customer looks upon him as an object not to be trusted with the whole truth, as one who must be manipulated and, if business and profit demand, deceived. Put another way the customer is actually sending messages of "I don't like you, you really are unlikable and, quite frankly, as a person you are worthless. I wouldn't want to spend five minutes with you outside a business relationship." Those messages are heard. The result is that this insider-trader, this businessman, now has two sets of evidence of his worthlessness, namely what he knows himself to be, and what his customer or his poker-playing business associate is telling him.

We are structured. There is a structure to our person, and a structure to our human nature. If we act according to those structures, we are at peace. If we don't, we will experience pain. Pain is a certain sign of disorder, the privation of a due good. It is all ineluctable, we just can't escape reality, especially when that conscious reality is ourselves.

Both Friedman and Carr are fundamentally wrong in their conception of the nature of business. Since it is impossible to start any business without creating a product or service that is desired by my fellow man, it therefore follows that profit can only come if the business creates that product or service and can demand a return that exceeds the cost of production. The desire for profit will stimulate the creation of product. But profit can never be directly intended; it can only follow invention and creation of product. Business is essentially altruistic.

Miller, referred to above, has the correct notion. His words should be repeated here:

> [There is a] social justification for the existence of the corporation. This justification is a creative one. The purpose of the corporation is the creation of wealth, those goods and services that enhance our standards of living. When the corporation increases its productivity, it produces more goods and services at lower cost and thereby increases that which is available for consumption. This is an increase in the aggregate wealth of society.

Wealth is not money. Wealth is that which may be bought with money.

This [the creation of wealth] is the social purpose, the noble purpose, of our business institutions.[17]

Miller has more on the nobility of business and its natural function of creating wealth. I quote him at length for he says in a different manner and so well what we have been leading up to in this chapter.

An organization is much like a living organism. Its function and structure are much like the body's. Its action may be either intelligent or stupid. Its adherence to a consistent set of beliefs, a "good," higher in scope and priority than any short-term decision or action, which exerts overriding influence on all actions, is its soul. In our secular society we have segmented our lives into matters concerned with material pursuit and matters of the spirit. We have even looked upon the pursuit of material gain as inherently counter to the attainment of spiritual values. The poor and those who reject our wealth-producing institutions for ideological reasons are viewed as claimants to a more noble spirit. This is a false delusion. On the contrary, it is those who bear the burden of production, who are responsible for the creation of wealth and permit the leisure and education our society allows, these are the ones who are making the noble contribution.[18]

That is high praise for business; but it is not high enough. The creation of wealth is not simply an ideal that one is free to choose or not choose. Man is morally obliged to strive for this objective. That is the nature of being in business, creating products and services that our fellow man wants and will pay for, and that are ever more and more available to more and more people at ever lower costs. The alternative is to work for money and power. And so such mottoes as "Caveat emptor" and "Price according to what the market will bear" become such a businessman's techniques of making more money from the customer. If the market in its ignorance will pay the price, charge it. If the buyer isn't careful, take advantage of his carelessness. If you don't, someone else will. In today's climate of corruption, "Caveat emptor" might well be expanded to "quia vendor latro est." Let the buyer beware because the vendor is a bandit. Really, does any business person, who is also a good person, want his buyer to beware?

In 1989 Rogene A. Bucholz concluded an article by asking:

Does not business have more of an obligation to society than is evident in the self-serving attempts to manipulate the political environment for its own advantage? Does not business have a moral obligation that goes

---

17. Lawrence Miller, *The American Spirit*, 37.
18. Ibid., 184.

beyond obeying the law and complying with government regulations. If business does have social and political responsibilities as well as economic responsibilities, what is the moral basis of these responsibilities?[19]

The moral basis for those relationships of responsibility is the human nature of man that must have private property to complete himself, that must be social, that must create and manufacture if he is to do more than survive, that must therefore seek the common good as the necessary way of accomplishing his individual good. This is the moral law, which will always be prior to and more specific than positive law. Put another way, the moral basis for social responsibility, is the social nature of man. That nature dictates and proposes for the free choice of man all the actions that necessarily flow from his nature. Those actions are living, exercising freedom, owning property, working with others to create products that mutually benefit one another and lead to a better life. Better life means less work, time to think and create and improve and trust and love. Business is not a game invented by man, it is the natural and necessary expression of man's freedom, of his transcendent spirit. Man is whole. When man chooses to be what he is by structure, he has integrity. This is what he must have in all his acts. This is especially true for his business actions, for business is the beautiful blossom and sweet fruit of man's unrestricted desire to know, to see relationships, to create, and to execute in an environment of mutual dependence and trust. All mankind went to the moon with Neil Armstrong;[20] all mankind did it through freedom and business.

---

19. *Essentials of Business Ethics*, "The Evolution of Corporate Social Responsibility," Rogene A. Bucholz, 310.
20. "That's one small step for a man, one giant leap for mankind." Neil Armstrong on stepping on the moon, July 20, 1969. *Bartlett's Familiar Quotations*, 15th Edition, Little, Brown & Co., Boston, 1980, 910. Note that Armstrong did not take a narrow and provincial view and say "one giant leap for America."

10

Sexual Morality

The first thing to note about human sex is that it is a physical and moral union, a union of rational animals, a union of persons who are not only transcendent, but also animal.

The sexual organs are comparable to other organs of the vegetative part of man, e.g., the kidneys, liver, pancreas, etc. But with two major differences, a) they are incomplete and correlative in individuals, and b) they are somewhat under the control of the individual. The individual's human nature is vitally designed toward that of another individual as male to female and female to male. This animal design means that each is correlative to the other, each is the sexual object of the other, each subordiante to the other. Granted that subordiantion in the past and somewhat less so in the present has been of female to male. That abuse is not to be corrected by another abuse—the personal independence of one from the other. Children born out of family (wedlock), exemplify this personal independence and abuse. The human animals use each other for their own individual purposes. The female gets a living doll to nurture, love, and be loved by. The male is sexually gratified and free to "service" other females. His aggressive nature is not subordinated, controlled, civilized, nor elevated by the restraints of love for wife and child proved by physical and moral support. He gets no doll to love, nurture, and to love him. He roams among his fellow human animals unattached and alone. This use of his sexuality tends to make him a predator, more animal than rational, and the female tends to become his victim, or he hers when she seduces him. The personal equality of the two and their biological uniqueness are never harmoniously united. They therefore tend to perpetuate a group of individuals that are more animal than human, a group that is more a jungle than a civilization. And so they are morally bad persons, for they have deliberately chosen to be this way.

If the personal sexual action is allowed to accomplish all that it can, the result will be union, conception, gestation, birth, nurture, communication between parent and child, familial society, clan or tribe, state, nation, etc.

A whole series of trusting relationships can result. These relationships are so strong that, when broken by death, extreme grief touches widow/widower, the parents and siblings of the deceased son or daughter, and often enough the friend and neighbor. And if the person is famous and loved because he has communicated across nations and cultures, e.g., J. F. Kennedy, the grief can touch those nations. Thus the purpose of sex is not just the production of another member of the animal genus, but the production of a being that is transcendent and can generate trust and love that transcends the limits of space and time. For the trust and love of the spouses is a commitment that endures beyond the birth and raising of the child. The trust and love of the children for the parents and siblings endures throughout their lives. Human sex produces a human family in the broadest sense, so that there actually is a concern that is international, i.e., a concern for the rights of the weak and the responsibilities of the strong that transcends all boundaries, customs and cultures. That all this actually occurs at all is an indication of what sexual morality should be even though in most instances that morality is neither known nor observed. The point is that that is what sex is designed to do because it actually does it. Therefore the choice to be sexual, to do sexual things, should be embraced, chosen for what it was meant to do. That it is almost always chosen for only a part of its total design is irrelevant to its real purpose and therefore to the fullness of the goodness of the moral choice. But the criterion of the full moral goodness of the sexual act is the choice to become a part of the continuation process of the family of man living in peace, love, and trust. This purpose of human sex is the norm and criterion that is to guide the human when he freely decides to engage in sexual activity.

Obviously there are and have been many departures that sex can take from this direction. Some directions are wrong, immoral, unethical. Wrong here means bad for the individual exercising his sexual faculty. Bad means a privation of a good that should be present and is not. Since sex is essentially a communication as well as a physical union between two, the morality of sex can be judged on whether it accomplishes a union of trust between two individuals or not. What good or privation of good occurs when one deliberately "speaks" to another sexually? That can be seen by analyzing different sexual activities. The good that can occur from the sexual act is clear from what has been said about the human family. The moral evil may be obvious, but not explained as to how it affects the one performing the immoral sexual act.

That is our concern here. For though there are many victims of sexual abuse, what happens to the perpetrator of that sexual abuse? What precisely is his moral badness? It is not the visible act that, if done publicly, would embarrass us and probably shame him. It is the privation of the good that should be in the person. Thus moral evil can and does exist in the most secret acts. The evil of a sexual act does not depend on whether others are hurt by it or not. We shall discuss a few such evil acts that may provoke disgust in the reader. But the excusing reason for doing so is to let one see how the transcendence of the human being and his innate desire for attachment to another is actually harmed by such acts. Bestiality is one such act.

Cats, dogs, horses, birds, etc. are loved by many humans. When one of those persons begins and completes sexual activity with an animal, it is clear that the sexual action cannot unite human with human nor produce anything like family. There may be increased attachment, but there certainly is no trust present because the communication is between non-equals. It is not even a communication between master and slave. Thus the meaning of the human engaging in sex with an animal is a talking to oneself: "I am going to use the animal to gratify myself, to produce orgasm in me and perhaps in it." But talking to oneself and self-gratification are not the only results. Another result is that the human finds it easy to engage in bestiality and is now inclined to accomplish that same gratification again. Thus his human sexuality is being directed to the animal as well as to or instead of to a human. This is to pervert human sexuality on three counts: 1) Human sex is exercised but does not produce trust; 2) Its exercise tends to build up a habitual disposition in the person toward an animal instead of to the human; 3) It is exercised and can never produce a parent child relationship. So the question must be asked: "What is the person doing to himself when he attempts to communicate sexually with an animal?" And the answer is : orgasm for the sake of orgasm and without the relation to the purpose and full meaning of orgasm. Bestiality creates an addiction to the practice and diverts him from his higher potential of understanding, creating, experiencing acquaintances and friendships, and involvement in the opportunities and problems of society. The practice is isolating and a closing or narrowing of his transcendence into a confining practice. His person is damaged and so he is morally bad.

Incest is another sexual activity generally considered morally bad. It is a human activity, not merely animal. It occurs within a group in which there already are personal relationships of trust based upon dependence that has been supported by independents. The infant, toddler, child, pubescent, adolescent, and young adult have trusted the parent or older sibling to help it survive, adapt, and achieve more and more independence. Unless the infant, toddler, or child experiences pain, it can hardly be expected to distrust the one who is sexually abusing it. The abusive union can occur orally, anally, or by natural copulation. And it all occurs within a situation of familial relationships. In such a context there is no expectation that any courtship be initiated nor any exclusive and marital relationship be pursued. Thus it would come as a surprise to the pubescent, adolescent, and young adult if anyone of the familial group would approach it sexually. Further, any such approach would almost always be in secret because the meaning of sex, i.e., leading to another union and family, is redundant in this familial situation and would suppose an agreement in trust among the other members that this new proposed union is acceptable to them. This implies that they would know what is going on and accept it. The new union would mean a coexistence of a relationship of dependence alongside a new relation of equality. Son and mother becoming man and wife, uncle and sister, etc. Such relationships are not mere names, but have foundations in human acts and human blood. All of this is inconsistent with any promise of exclusive commitment made between parents and reiterated in word and deed as familial life advanced. The question, therefore, must be repeated: "What is one saying to his offspring or sibling infant, toddler, child, etc. when he approaches it sexually?" To hug or cuddle, or kiss that person says one thing, namely, I love you, care for you, want good things for you, want you to be happy. But the sexual approach? Its full meaning is family, its proximate meaning is the aggressor's sexual stimulation, orgasm, pleasure occasioned by using the infant, toddler, child, etc. The minor relative can only be a physically and morally defenseless object. It is not strong enough to resist; it does not understand enough to distrust, or if there is a flicker of distrust it is not mature enough to articulate its defense. And so it usually ends up trusting the deceptive adult. There can be no communication between a person and an object, and there is no communication in trust here, no matter what the incestuous person says to its family member. Consequently the first violation occurs in the incestuous person and then in the victim of the act. The incestuous person violates his openness. He closes himself to the possibility of an honest message of care or love, and narrows his concern to his own sexual pleasure. He is deliberately alone even though he is in the physical presence of his relative.

We are not here concerned with the damaging effect of incestuous behavior on the victim. Nor first and foremost with the moral evil of the person who is willing to do such damage. The media, especially television, have demonstrated this evil again and again. Our main concern is what is sexually immoral for the person engaging in incest. The fact that he does not care about the betrayal of trust nor the psychological damage he can inflict only increases his radical selfishness and radical isolation that is in the first incestuous act. The incestuous person deprives himself of moral union with his family. He really separates himself from those he knows and could love best. This separation is his badness, his moral evil.

Another aspect of incestuous behavior is its secretiveness. The spousal, parental, and sibling relationships are open for all to see day in and day out. A routine is established and expected to be followed. One does not expect a "pursuit," a "courtship," or an "affair" to be taking place. Consequently when one maintains the routine while secretly establishing another that conflicts with the supportive relationships of family, a lie is being lived. One shuts down his openness and candor, presents himself as something he is not, and so violates the trustful communication that all think is still being maintained.

Pedophilia is comparable to parental incest; an adult sexually victimizes a child. The child is treated as an object and is either seduced or overpowered to satisfy the sexual desire of the adult. It is clear what the adult is trying to say as he or she approaches the child: "I want to use you." Thus there is no communication even though one person comes in contact with another. The result is the same: selfishness and isolation and frequently followed by psychological damage to the child or murder of the child. But the radical moral fault is the failure to communicate in an openness that respects the freedom and trustfulness of the physically and morally defenseless child. The adult is so damaged that it is almost impossible that he could ever receive the trust of that person when he or she became an adult.

Sexual behavior among consenting adolescents and adults can be morally good or bad. It is good if the parties are capable of free consent and know to what they are consenting. That is the theory. Practically speaking it is hard to determine when adolescents are mature enough to validly enter into a marital commitment. And society has arbitrarily set age requirements. But valid legality is always trying to be validly moral. Whether an illegal consent is also a morally invalid consent can only be determined by the consenting individuals, usually sometime after life has been lived a while.

But the sexual activity among consenting parties can also be morally bad. Again the criterion is "What are they saying to one another and does what they say effect personal union? For example, "I would like to use your body, and it is all right with me if you want to use mine. As for children and commitment, well, I am not ready for that. Commitment? Maybe. We'll see whether that works out. Exclusive commitment? Well, no promises for now. Let's just enjoy each other." Do such statements make the consenting adults morally better, indifferent, or bad?

Birth control and abortion make it possible for the parties to enjoy sex without having to accept conception, birth, nurture, and the personal relationships that deepen and multiply with the fullness of the sex act. Is there anything harmful to the persons who exercise sex in this way?

The human sex act is not only physically intimate, it is personally intimate and exclusive. It involves trust at the outset that matures into trusting affection and finally trusting affectionate union. Any attempt to remove communication so that there is nothing more than a "This is fun" and "Let's do it again sometime" are statements that have the effect of leaving the partners free not only from the physical results of sex, but also from the moral results that the physical act symbolizes, namely a permanent exclusive union. One can become accustomed to that kind of sex to the point where many different partners are had and the possibility of developing a permanent relationship of exclusive love and family is for all practical purposes an impossibility. "I could never be satisfied by one woman (by one man)" indicates a damaged person incapable of exclusive love. In place of this capability is the habit of attraction to almost anyone of the opposite sex for a physical union and a minimal personal relationship. This habitual attraction deepened by frequent sexual success leaves the person at a lower level of moral development. He does not rise to the level of paternal/maternal love nor to the faithful love of a spouse. He never has had the experience of making and trying to keep an exclusive commitment to another person. And the result is loneliness, no one to communicate with on a familial level, no intimate "you" to share life with. Friends, even sons and daughters, ease but do not fill the emptiness that can only be filled by the intimate other. Thus frequent and different physical intimacies are imperfect. They neither demand nor give what man can receive (the other) and what he wants to give (himself). This willed disposition of emptiness and self-withholding in the person is caused by the partial giving and receiving present in promiscuous sex. The moral evil is in the incomplete communication, a refusal to give all that can be given and a refusal to be open to the unknown that life can bring with the total acceptance of the sex partner. It is an essential refusal to trust while performing an act that by the fullness of its nature demands trust. Thus it is essentially a refusal to be open and therefore a closing of one's transcendence. It is a refusal to believe that life is worthwhile and an affirmation that I alone am the measure of all value.

Within the marriage union itself all sorts of sex acts are possible. The marriage commitment does not make all of them morally good, that is, they do not necessarily make the persons better persons. It may strike the reader that the ideal proposed throughout this section is severe and unreal, that too much attention is focused on the evil or good that happens to the person who engages in certain sex acts. But it must be remembered that we learn slowly through experience. For years the Romans unwittingly poisoned themselves by storing their wine in leaden vessels. For years asbestos was common insulation in homes and businesses, for years people worked in noisy factories without ear protection, for years people have lived and worked near toxic fumes, and for years they have used tobacco without being aware of its harmful effects. These are physical evils we have discovered over time. The harm that comes to the moral development of the person from his choices are more difficult to discover. But just because they are not discovered does not mean that they are not harmful to the person and his society. Xenophobia (racism) and homophobia are two such moral evils or immaturities that are gradually being recognized as such. The radical criterion of personal goodness is in the act of communication in trust and mutual respect. Sex is a means of communication. Any exercise of that power that is essentially selfish, that uses the other person as an object is harmful first to the user and then to the object who becomes the abused person. Thus within the trustful relationship of marriage where the adult and child ego states function in intimate fun, trust, and affection, the question must be asked, "What am I saying when I speak, touch, engage in oral, anal, vaginal copulation?" There is a fine distinction between needing a person to communicate with and wanting a pseudo-communication. In the first I look for and find personal satisfaction; in the second I want a person to give me some form of satisfaction without my giving that person any real trust and honest respect. The message of the human sex act must be love, trust, genuine affection and commitment if both partners are to be made better and more mature persons by such acts.

Finally, there is the private sex act performed on oneself. What does this do to the person who habitually masturbates? Deborah Laake[1] in her book gives us some insight into this kind of sex. The book records an impressive personal victory. She describes a personal struggle in which she tried to find herself in a life filled with total submission to religious teaching. The struggle included losing her first love to the call of religion, then entering two loveless marriages, having two affairs, and failing in a third marriage. Sandwiched in among these sufferings were an attempted suicide and hospitalization for a nervous breakdown. She overcame all that to find personal peace and become an award winning journalist. She has this to say about masturbation. "Suddenly I grasped sickeningly that false measures of resuscitation like masturbation weren't going to even come close anymore to filling the emptiness I'd been trying so desperately to ignore." (132) This realization came after ". . . the act of masturbation had been the thing that revealed me to myself. It now became the thing that hid me. I masturbated constantly; I became an orgasm machine." (121) Clearly she was using sex to accomplish something it was not made to accomplish,

---

1. Deborah Laake, *Secret Ceremonies, A Mormon Woman's Intimate Diary of Marriage and Beyond,* William Morrow and Company Inc., New York, 1993.

namely satisfy herself as a person. It was a "false measure of resuscitation" that did not resuscitate. What was the harm done to her person by that practice? The same harm that comes to anyone who delays facing a real problem and surrenders to work, alcohol, drugs and other diversions. The diversions distract and satisfy some appetite other than the personal one. The diversions satisfy and the satisfaction entices to more of the same diversions. And the possibility of addiction occurs, making the facing of the original problem ever more difficult. As a personal act, masturbation is fruitless. There is no personal communication, on the contrary there is the addictive desire to be alone (123, 124). In the case of Laake, this frustrating act was a symptom of a deeper frustration. Yet the symptom itself was harmful, for it delayed confrontation with the real problem. The practice is not an indifferent act like tying one's shoe or combing one's hair. It promotes isolation and self-satisfaction and escaping from socializing with others. The criterion here, as with all other sexual activity, is communication in trust. One cannot simply say there's no harm done because no one else is affected. Others are not the ones in whom the act occurs or to whom the act is done. The question has to be what does this personal act mean in itself and what does it do to this person and not simply to his body. In itself it is a pointless personal act, the effect of which is to isolate him who needs to communicate.

Birth control and divorce need to be considered here because they must be reconciled with what we have already said about the full choice of sex that includes establishing a family and the attempt to give oneself exclusively and totally to another. The only reason divorce is really possible is because the nature of the transcendent person is such that he cannot comprehend nor grasp and therefore cannot dispose of himself totally. The reason he cannot grasp himself is because he is more than a thing, more than a finite object. He is a person, transcendent, and therefore in some sense infinite, boundless, free. He transcends concepts and images. They cannot contain him and make him disposable and understandable as, for example, a fact, formula or process or animate or inanimate thing is disposable and understandable. As a victim he can be disposed of, but as a free being he cannot be disposed of either by himself or by another who respects his freedom. He can dispose of his lung or kidney to benefit his child or sibling, but he cannot dispose of himself. The most he can do is communicate himself in word (promise) and the physical sex act, the personal intimacy of which is to concretize the meaning of the promise. The two are not only physically one, but that oneness is destined to bind them physically (sharing times and places) and bind them morally. The moral unity is the day after day choosing of life together. Life means human life, i.e., family, growth, aging, etc.

If man could give himself irrevocably, divorce would be impossible. It is because he is always transcendent and therefore always free that divorce is not only possible, but even in some instances necessary and therefore morally good, in spite of the immediate suffering that may come to children and to relatives. The moral goodness is that all the family honestly face the fact that the partners do not love each other. They cannot honestly say to one another "I love you."

There are many reasons why the promise of fidelity has to be retracted. One or other may have known from the outset that this union was just not right for him or her, but went ahead with the marriage anyway. That act was a lie to himself and a deception of the partner. Perhaps the person hoped to avoid immediate embarrassment of a sudden cancellation of the ceremony, and thought he could make things work out later on. Or one or both became selfish, even violent, and refused to communicate in honesty, or something else happened that simply made it a fact that they now do not love one another. There may be obstacles to their love which, if removed through fortunate insight or insight through counseling, would now permit the original love and commitment to grow and mature. But whatever the cause of the absence of love, they really do not love each other, find each other incommunicable and a burden, and so are not really, though legally, man and wife. Marriage is a human union first and only subsequently a legal one. Its real dissolution occurs before the legal one, and the legal one should follow the real dissolution. The fact that the divorce rate is higher than it was in the past does not necessarily mean that in the past all those apparently enduring marriages really were enduring unions of love. It is possible that many were hypocritical unions. Perhaps the high divorce rate will lead the human sciences to discover insights that will lead people to prepare themselves better before they carefully enter that relationship that is designed to lead to familial love and maturity.

Sex in such circumstances is simply an abuse of one another; a release, but no communication, no giving and no receiving, no deepening of trust and love. It is simply the practice in the use of a person as a sexual object. The aggressor becomes the petulant child, the permitter becomes a patronizer. Neither should submit himself to such an indignity, for there is no equality, and therefore no self-respect possible, in such a communication. Lest this appear too severe, let it be said that sometimes the child needs the patronizing parent to help it become an adult.

Birth control at its best has the partners saying to each other, "In spite of our love and commitment to life, we do not want a child now, but we do want this intimate act of love." Considered in its best light, the partners of birth control sex would accept the conceived child if the birth control technique failed. At its worst, birth control is simply using one another for sexual pleasure; if a child were to result, the male would either deny it was his or persuade to abortion. The female would terminate the pregnancy whether the male wanted it or not. This is birth control sex at its worst. The selfishness is apparent, obvious. In the best scenario the partners are radically open to the direction or tendency of human life, because they will accept the child if it comes. But there is an essentially closing aspect of this act, a refusal, as far as one can, to be open to the child now. And like any other act of any other appetite, the presence of pleasure incites to performing the closed act again and again. The worst result can be that the biological clock has at last stopped ticking and there can be no choice of family. The disordered practice has produced the fullness of its privation, barrenness.

On the other hand, once children have come and the couple have mutually decided they wish no more, then the birth control act becomes at best an act of intimacy that repeats their trust and dedication to one another. At its worst it contains the problem of using one another as sex objects. And if one can use one's spouse as an object, it becomes easy to use someone else as an object. This acquired disposition of the person to use another is the harm that can (not must) come to the person practicing birth control sex.

Sexual activity, therefore, must be seen and chosen for what it is: A moral union of free persons expressed physically and that terminates in family. These persons must respect one another's freedom and individuality, otherwise there is no union of free persons. Using another is first of all a privation of the experience of self-giving and trust that one needs to mature. And second it is the privation or suppression of the freedom of another. In some sense or other it turns a free person into a slave. This harms not only the victim, but it violates the victor and makes him either a physical or moral monster, depending upon whether force or seduction is used to conquer the victim. The basic American doctrine that all men are equal and entitled to justice, life, liberty, and the pursuit of happiness should be the spirit and soul out of which human sexual communication should proceed. That tendency to communicate honestly will always tend to bypass bestiality, masturbation, incest, pedophilia, adultery, fornication, and rape because the goal it seeks is exclusive commitment to another in the fullness of human life, i.e., the trust and openness that comes with family, relatives, friends, neighbors.

11

Homosexuality and Morality

The concern here is not with the morals of the homosexual, but rather with our morality as we live and deal with homosexuals.

Like so many of us I have learned about homosexuals through the media of newspapers and television and have heard about their coming out of the closet and seemingly thereby enjoying a better life. On a personal level I have known six homosexuals.

The first I met on a transatlantic trip from New York to Le Havre. I don't remember much about our conversation except for a point of resignation toward the difficulty of his life. His own family had rejected him. The second homosexual was a 19 year old ROTC student who came to me just once for counseling while I was at John Carroll University. I don't remember what I suggested he do; we parted amicably enough. I especially remember the agony and tears as he tried to talk about and deal with the confusion he felt about himself. I was under the impression that he had had no direct homosexual contact up to that time. The third person, and his lover, were both alcoholics who finally got control over their alcoholism when they admitted and accepted their gayness.

The fifth and sixth were lesbian lovers, one of whom is my ex-wife and the mother of my four children. We have been amicably divorced for years now. The divorce had to be because to continue the marriage would have been to live a lie, i.e., to say to neighbors and friends that we were married, when there really was no marriage beneath the legal marriage.

Obviously, I learned a few things first hand of what it means for a homosexual to struggle with coming out of the closet. And one thing that seems most apparent to me is, that once this done, the homosexual is at peace with himself and seems better off than ever before.

Biologically speaking, which is to speak narrowly since it prescinds from considering the person who informs and acts through his biology, homosexuality is a biological perversion. The homosexual use of the generative powers makes as much sense as using a Mercedes-Benz as an anchor for an expensive yacht. The M-B will work as an anchor and hold the yacht in place, if there is some proportion between the size of the yacht and the weight of the M-B. But clearly, such use of the M-B is a violation of the intention and execution of the designer and manufacturer. So it is with anal and oral copulation in homosexual activity. The actions "work," they produce orgasm. But the goal of the orgasm is never fully accepted for what it was designed to do.[1] The totality of sex, i.e., conception, gestation, birth, nurturing, parenting, etc., can never be achieved. The biology of it all is perverted, i.e., the power is used against the intention of the "designer" and "manufacturer," against nature. There will never be more than two at the annual homosexual family Thanksgiving and Christmas dinners. And Mercedes-Benz, whenever it is a manufacturer of anchors, will have to change its slogan to "engineered like no other anchor in the world."

Some people, who see the Bible as the inspired and infallible word of God, see homosexual activity as an abomination. Sodom and Gomorrah come to mind; and so does St. Paul in his letter to the Romans, I, 22-27. There he speaks condemningly of both male and female homosexual activity. These words are very troubling to us who both love God and want to love our fellow man. And a saying has been discovered which helps us through the difficulty, namely: "We love the sinner but hate the sin."

But, as we saw earlier the necessary being, God, is in intimate contact with us. This contact is beautifully expressed by St. Augustine, "God is more intimate to us than we are to ourselves." Thus we can see that there is another word of God, other than the ones we read in the scriptures (Bible, Talmud, Koran, Mormon, etc.) we accept. That other word is His creative and conservative power working in us all the time.

If I want to know what God has in mind for me, I ought to read all his messages, particularly the ones that come to me on a regular basis. It would be well for me to look at the structures that I am, and I am more than biological. I am a person working in and through a biological structure. And even that biological structure is not totally known and understood. There is some evidence suggesting that homosexuality among males is genetically determined.[2] This possibility raises troubling questions. First,

---

1. JoAnn Loulan, *Lesbian Sex,* Spinsters Ink, Minneapolis, 1984 and the gay clinical psychologist, Don Clark, Ph. D., *Loving Someone Gay,* Celestial Arts, Berkeley, 1977, rev. 1987 both look upon sex as a means of communication without any connection to reproduction. Clark speaks of recreational sex (164); Loulan describes a multitude of techniques for sexaul pleasure and since "Lesbian sex is not connected to reproduction, we don't have to worry about whether we can have sex while we're ovulating." (59)
2. There is some evidence suggesting that homosexuality among males is genetically determined. See *Science,* "Evidence for Homosexuality Gene," 7/16/93, Vol. 261, pp.291,292. Dean Hamer and his team of geneticists at the National Cancer Institute "...report linking some instances of male homosexualtiy to a small stretch of DNA on the X chromosome." 291.

there is the evidence that homosexuality is a biological defect, i.e., physical structure correlative to the opposite sex, but the human and physical attraction is to the same sex. Man's unrestricted desire to know wants to understand the total causality of this conflict between structure and tendency, just as he wants to know the total genetic causality and remedy for Down's syndrome, Alzheimer's disease, and cystic fibrosis. Secondly, supposing the cause is genetic and its correction or control is discovered, how should the correction be applied while still respecting the freedom of the homosexual? Perhaps it should not be applied at all, as was suggested by Jonathan Tolins. "Can you remove that which makes a person gay and maintain that unique sensibility that has played a disproportionate role in the world's art and history?. . . Science is giving us the knowledge and tools that Hitler's medical staff only dreamed of . . . was Hitler wrong about the Jews but right about the homosexuals?"[3]

Further, structures in man are not only the first and immediate word of God to him, they are also his proper way of speaking to man. "Proper" means his native language, as it were, for no one else can "speak" the creative word, and no one else can "speak" the conservative word. Only God can bring into being (create) and only God can keep in being (conserve). Assuming that God has intervened in human history, His second language are the scriptures; and He uses human instruments to write them. These instruments, as we saw when we discussed causality, reveal their limitations. The limitations are not chalk and ink, but rather the limitations of language, style, culture, world view, etc.

The homosexual clearly experiences a contradiction between the two "words" of God. If he pays attention to what he is, he is at peace. Peace, as we have seen is a sign of good order and well being. But if the homosexual reads the Bible and accepts the words of Paul, he is condemned.

When the homosexual confronts us with whom he really is, he challenges us as we rarely are challenged. He, in all honesty, comes to us and says, "Believe me, I am gay." And what do we say to that? Are we open? Do we trust him? Do we accept the message? What happens to us if we do trust him and are deceived? Suppose his gayness is not what he really is, but rather is an acquired personal perversion. What have we lost by believing him? Later on we may discover, through his words or another's, that he actually lied to us. So we now see we have not the friend we thought we had, and that is sad. But what else have we lost? Are we worse for the trust we gave? Or are we better for having taken the risk, having been open and understanding, and are now courageous and still have hope as we suffer

---

3. *Time*, 7/26/93, 39.

the betrayal? Recall, betrayal is only possible if one trusts. If one does not trust, not only is betrayal impossible, but so also is all communication, and therefore all true communication, affection, friendship, love,—these are all impossible without that first act of trust.

So what choice do we have? Some sincere people say "Love the sinner, but hate the sin." But what does that saying really mean? By saying that to the homosexual, I say "I really don't believe you when you reveal to me the most important aspect of yourself. You are not gay as you say you are. Somehow or other you are deceived about yourself. Really, with the help of God's word, I know more about you than you know about yourself. I care about you, I want to be your friend; yes, I trust you. I'll lend or give you some of my possessions and trust you to return them to me. But I hope you change. I fear God's punishment for you."

"I love the sinner, but hate the sin," is clearly correct grammar; but the correct grammar has nothing to do at all with the real world it tries to express. The homosexual's gift of self to the non-homosexual is rejected. A request for trust is made; the request is denied.

Now we come to something that is truly frightening. The non-homosexual, as all human beings are, is made to be open, transcendent. When he rejects the homosexual and refuses to believe him, he closes his openness. And what kind of perversion is that when compared to a biological perversion? Which perversion is worse? Abuse of the generative faculty or abuse of the very core of one's humanity?

For most "straight people" the abuse of the generative faculty is very easy to judge an abomination, for we have either seen pornography or imagined it from verbal descriptions. It is not an abstraction rather it is physical, an object of the senses that is understood to be a frustration of the generative faculty, and therefore easy to hate. Unfortunately, since we know first by sense, and then by intellect, it is not easy to imagine or depict the perversion of an immaterial reality. The radical evil of the lie is not easily appreciated, and even less do we appreciate the radical evil of turning away from and rejecting the unproved and unproveable statement of one's fellow man. We do not appreciate what we do to ourselves when we shut down our openness and refuse to trust and believe.

Fortunately for us, here is often a case where our actions belie our words, speak louder than our words. The family is often more "sad" about the homosexual family member than "rejecting." The homosexual is still welcome at home, the lover comes to meals, too; holidays are shared, people learn to live with it because the instinctive human goodness of the straight persons is more powerful than their allegiance to religion. As it should, conscience again triumphs over creed.

a theological and philosophical

Here again we come back to the question of my own integrity. What is my state of mind? Certitude? Opinion? Doubt? Ignorance? Contradiction, a proved negative? The first evidence I have is that my fellow human being asks me to believe him/her. The second is the two words of God that seem to be in conflict, namely the Scriptures and what God makes my fellow man to be—if I trust his statement about himself. If these confuse me, then certainly I have no certitude about the sinfulness of my fellow man. I am in a state of opinion at best, and more likely in a state of doubt. That being the case, can I condemn him/her? Perhaps the better position is, "It is not for me to judge you; I must admit I don't quite understand, but I trust you, I believe you. I accept your gayness."

Such a statement would preserve our integrity perfectly. We would accept the other just as he gives himself to us, and we would be giving ourselves to him just as we are, somewhat confused, doubtful, accepting, and totally honest. The ball is in his court; it is his turn to accept us as we are, i.e., not understanding but believing.

12

Morality and Abortion

Abortion is clearly a moral issue,[1] but more profoundly the discussion of abortion is a moral issue. The pro-life and pro-choice people are constantly challenged to be open, to respect their own transcendence, face and accept the evidence and meaning of the evidence. The greatest concern is not whether the liberty of the woman is saved nor that the life of the unborn is protected. The greatest fear is that one group or the other become comfortable with ignorance, or error, or, worst of all, with the lie told to oneself and then deepened in the psyche through the clever and loud battle cry. All human progress is stalled at the point of ignorance, stopped at the point of error, and morally wrong at the point of the lie. The lie leaves us tragic in some form of self destruction. We are only pathetic, but still have hope, when we are ignorant or in error.

Abortion: The Clash of Absolutes, by Laurence H. Tribe,[2] is a moral book in the fullest sense of the term. It is eminently honest in its learned and thorough presentation of literally hundreds of aspects of the freedom to choose and the right to life issues. It is a model of respectful dialogue, and thereby teaches us how we should behave and so avoid harmful and polarizing confrontations. His last topic, "How We See and Talk to One Another" is profound in its insight, sympathetic to both parties, and encourages and persuades by example to honesty toward ourselves and to those with whom we discuss (134).

---

1. It is also a legal issue. Should the law protect the life of the fetus? Supposing, for the sake of argument, that the fetus is a person, what can the law do to protect it? Neither the person nor the moral person of the state is obliged to do the impossible. Is the state capable of preventing a mother from chemically aborting her fetus in the privacy of her home? Probably not. Can the state criminalize abortionists and abortion clinics? Probably so. Suppose a woman suffering from a bungled abortion comes to a doctor or hospital for aid, should she be prosecuted for aborting her child? Clearly the hospital and doctor should not be prosecuted for helping her. The legal question, therefore, is: What can the state do or not do by means of sanction to effect the common good in the case of the human fetus?
2. Laurence H. Tribe, *Abortion, The Clash of Absolutes*, W. H. Norton & Co., New York, 1990.

I hope to follow his lead and imitate as best I can the model of integrity he so thoroughly sets before his readers.

Basic to our discussion is what I have stressed throughout this essay, namely that we know by sense and understand meaning from what we observe. Each of us is a metaphysician because we are concerned with freedom, equality, rights, person, etc., none of which we see, but all of which we understand as being in him whom we do see, namely our fellow human being.

THE UNIVERSALITY OF HUMAN NATURE

Specifically I refer to the unenumerated rights that are affirmed by the Ninth Amendment of the Constitution, "The enumeration in the Constitution, of certain rights, shall not be construed to deny or disparage others retained by the people." The jurist discovers those unenumerated rights when he sees fundamental liberty about to be abridged without compelling reason (Tribe, 111, 114) Tribe refers to four such rights recently articulated: right to procreate, right to family in a broad sense, right to educate, right to send children to non-public schools (Skinner v. Oklahoma, Moore v. City of East Cleveland, Meyer v. Nebraska, Pierce v. Society of Sisters.)

The point of all this is that the unchanging human nature is the source of those rights protected by the Ninth Amendment. In other words "natural law" philosophy is at the heart of American positive law. When Tribe quotes Woodrow Wilson that the constitution is a living document that must be nicely adjusted and determined by the new exigencies and new aspects of "life itself," that life is the one and the same substantial human life, the homo sapiens of the caves, igloos, hogans, cottages, palaces the world over. He is the one we have in mind when we speak to South Africa, South America, Korea, China and the others about improving their concern for human rights. That one human substance can and does go through many accidental changes for better or worse down through the millennia. In particular civilizations or cultures certain values ruled absolutely, but were contingent upon the group from whence they arose (27). Man is the absolute, the constant whose advances and declines are accidental or contingent to his substantial nature.

On the same page Tribe speaks of "our fundamental beliefs about the way people should live . . . are historically created and dependent upon particular experiences and modes of understanding." It is true that a multitude of experience and insight preceded the Declaration's statement about liberty and inalienable rights. But to say that there were different modes of understanding is to suggest that human nature operated essentially differently at different times and different cultures. Understanding is an essential characteristic, an essential action of man. It is what his nature does because of what his nature is. Man has but one mode of understanding: application of the senses to phenomena, then understanding meaning in the phenomena sensed. If there are other modes of understanding than this one, they must be asserted and proved. A different mode of understanding is first hard to imagine; and second would imply a different nature and therefore—whatever sort of being it is imagined to be—would not be a human nature. There is but one constant nature of man,[3] and one constant mode of knowledge. In my opinion, Tribe is speaking inadequately when he says man has different particular modes of understanding. He might better have said that man has different languages and cultures that shape his world view. But the manner of understanding is exactly the same for all, i.e., the application of the senses to phenomena to form ideas and judgments.

THE FETUS: A PART OF THE WOMAN?

Science detests figurative language. It wants to know *what* and *why* and cannot rest with the information that something is *like* something else. It goes beyond to find out what it is. Therefore, in the matter of abortion it is metaphorical to say that the fetus is a part of the mother. "[T]he fetus . . . begins as a *living part of the woman's body* . . . It is not a lodger or prisoner or guest, nor is its mother a mere home or incubator. The fetus is, after all her "flesh and blood" (102). "But if a woman's protected liberty includes a right to decide that her body will not be used to incubate and give birth to another, and if a woman is entitled to choose not to develop a *part of herself* into a separate human being . . ." (114).

Relevant terms in this matter are ovum, fertilized ovum, embryo, and fetus. Only the ovum can be considered a part of the female reproductive system. Strictly speaking it is a product of the ovaries, not a part of them or a part of anything else. The fertilized ovum is a *unit* of sperm and ovum. It is not a part of the mother, nor is it exclusively her "flesh and blood."

There is no question about the great dependence existing between the woman and the fertilized ovum. But it is one of *environment*, and not of *part to whole*. The fetus is not an integral part of the woman's body, as the arm or leg is to the torso. Nor is the fetus an essential part of the woman's nature. If either of these were the case, obviously all women would always be pregnant. Well, what then is the meaning behind the metaphor? The

---

3. Wilson, *Moral Sense*, 26. Wilson, as does Tribe here, casts doubt on the uniformity of human nature. The proof for uniformity, and therefore the freedom and transcendence of all men, is their use of arbitrary signs (language) to communicate ideas and insights. See below, Ch. 13, 144.

fetus is *simply not a part* of the woman's body, but it is *like a part* in that it is in the woman's body and *dependent* for its life and activity upon the *supporting environment* which that body supplies. A comparable environment is that of the earth in reference to the plant or tree. Both will die without attachment to the ground. Further, it is *from the woman's* flesh and *from the father's* flesh, but is *its own flesh.* It is autonomous, following its own law of development.

Consequently, the woman's control over this "part" is not at all like her control over the true parts of her body. There is no question that she is free to have cosmetic surgery, free to have her appendix removed or not removed when her gall bladder is removed. But she does not enjoy that same autonomy over the fetus, for the fetus is not a part of her, though it is in her. Everything that Tribe has to say about the right of the woman regarding behavior toward the fetus is severely limited by the fact that the fetus is a whole and independent being existing in itself and for itself within the supportive environment of the woman's body. If Tribe wishes to say something else, then he needs a clear definition of a part as distinguished from a whole, and a clear description of the proper versus metaphorical use of the term.

WOMEN: SUBORDINATE THROUGH A BIOLOGICAL ACCIDENT?

The entire thrust of Tribe's book proceeds from his concern for freedom and equality of the woman. It is clear that he feels she has not as much freedom and equality as the man, and points to the great inconveniences, yes, dangers, associated with pregnancy. On page 27 he speaks of "women's bondage," and on pages 103 and 104 lists these in great detail. Many of the details are mentioned in other places. Though he shows great sensitivity for the feelings of the mother toward the child she carries and brings to term, and is very much aware of the mother-child ideal (every child a wanted and loved child), the preponderance of his concern is for the difficulties of motherhood. As a father of four children over a five year period I would be the last one to minimize the inconveniences and dangers of motherhood or maximize its goodness. In spite of three Lamaze trips and six years of diaper changing, I know I was always remote from motherhood. But that experience and seeing other families both poor and well off showed me that Tribe's presentation is not the whole picture. I see a somewhat unflattering bias against the demands of motherhood. And as I shall indicate shortly, these complaints against the demands of motherhood are demeaning to the woman.

Tribe sees that restricting her access to abortion "deprive[s] her of the very core of her liberty and privacy . . . reduces women to mere instrumentalities of the state." He concludes the passage from page 104 with another metaphor. He analyzes what it means for the state to restrict a woman's access to abortion. He says: "Pregnancy is a burden that cannot be imposed by the state without the most serious justification." To make a very strong point: The state can't get anyone pregnant. And refusing to permit abortion, the state is leaving the women to the instrumentality of her female nature, and not to the instrumentality of the state. That is the fact. It is a pure figure of speech to say the state by doing nothing positive (omitting to enact a law permitting abortion or repealing a permissive law) is actually changing a woman into the instrument of the state. The state is indifferent to whether the woman wishes to become or not become sexually active. Once she decides to do so, there are natural consequences. The "laws" of reproduction are as constant as any other laws of the physical universe. Step on the ledge of a ten story building, and you have something to be concerned about. Become sexually active, and you might become pregnant. Obviously therefore, there is responsible and irresponsible sex. Let us not deprive her of the opportunity to be responsible in so serious a matter and give her the escape "Oh, let's do it. If anything happens (a euphemistic dodge for the reality "If I conceive a child") I can always get rid of it with an abortion."

I am aware that this seems very harsh and insensitive to the many cases like Sherri Finkbine (37), Cano and Abel (5,6), Becky Bell and Spring Adams (203), and the mother of four (158). I fully agree with Tribe that as we must not ignore "the silent scream" that is supposed to occur in the abortion, so we should not anesthetize ourselves to the sufferings of the thousands represented by these few symbols.[4] My position is: For the sake of open and problem solving dialogue, let us drop the metaphors and euphemisms and use proper language.

For me, the most serious weakness in Tribe's attempt to gain freedom and equality for the pregnant woman is his theory that she is in a position of subservience through a biological accident. "Yet a ban on abortion imposes truly burdensome duties only on women. Such a ban thus places women, *by accident of their biology*, in a permanently and irrevocably subordinate position to men," (132). "In addition, equality for women must

---

4. Sherri Finkbine learned that her fetus was seriously impaired by the drug thalidomide. Sandra Race Cano could not get an abortion in Georgia and so gave birth to a daughter, Abel, and put her up for adoption. The two now are human representatives of the clash of absolutes. Becky Bell, aged seventeen, was afraid to ask her parents consent to an abortion and tried a home remedy, and died. Spring Adams, aged thirteen, was shot and killed by her own father when he learned she was pregnant with his child. The "mother of four" was single, on welfare, and wouldn't be able to provide diapers and milk for another baby.

mean the same ability to express human sexuality without the burden of pregnancy and childbirth that has always been, *by accident of biology,* available to men." (212) His great concern is that they be equal, equal, therefore, by law since they are not equal by nature. To deprive them by law of this equality is to discriminate against them and deny them equal protection of the law (105). This not only burdens them disproportionately, it burdens "women alone." (105)

But the accident of biology also has negative effects for the father of that new life that is properly his. He cannot constantly care for the new life of his son or daughter as the mother can. He cannot directly protect it from drugs, alcohol, or tobacco. He cannot directly nurture it with proper diet and prenatal care. He cannot begin bonding with it through tender singing and talking to it in its womb life; and he is never alone with his embryonic child. A mere accident of biology prevents him from doing these things, for he is unequal to the woman he has made pregnant. It is obviously unreasonable to use law to remedy this so called "inequality." We are not dealing with realities that are comparable and can be described as equal or to what degree they are unequal. They are essentially different and therefore incomparable.

Thus it must be said that in the matter of *gender,* not the matter of *humanity* nor in the matter of *person,* men and women are correlative. They are not the same. They cannot be compared because they are different in precisely the point of comparison. There is no similarity. Just as the boat is correlative to the sea, the door to the door jamb, the basketball to the basket, the nut to the bolt, and thus simply different and incomparable, so male and female make no sense considered in themselves, but only in relation to one another. And in that relationship (sexuality, not nature, not person) they differ from each other completely. To wish them to be equal is to destroy their correlativity; it is to destroy what they are: male and female. They are not equal, they cannot be compared, and consequently there can be no real sense in which one can be said to be better than the other, superior to or subservient to the other or unequal to the other. For travel, is the boat better than the sea? Is the door better than the door jamb? Is the basket better than the basketball? Is the nut better than the bolt? What is subservient to what in a correlative relationship? What is unequal to what ? On the other hand, male and female are equal as responsible persons. As embezzlers, murderers, or victims of racial injustice they stand equal before the bar of justice. As performers of equal work they deserve equal pay because in their humanity one is no more nor less human than the other. In their humanity and their responsibility they are identically equal. Not so in their sexuality. They are totally different. It behooves us to understand the meaning and purpose of those differences.

This means that the female will never be in the Canton, Ohio Hall of Fame alongside Jim Thorpe and Dick Butkus. It also means that no one on the Green Bay Packers will conceive, carry, and bear a child. The problem here is not one of establishing liberty through abortion. The problem is one of understanding as profoundly as possible the full purpose of their correlativity, and adapting to those realities as much as possible. There is no doubt that the male, simply because of his physical strength and the early needs for survival of the species, has physically and psychologically dominated the female. As a "depression kid" I saw plenty of intelligent mothers locked into Monday wash days, Tuesday sprinkle the clothes for ironing, Wednesday ironing days, housekeeping forever, plus canning all day long come August and September. That they could do executive work as well was proved by their sisters who became nuns and established hospitals and women's colleges across the land. More recently it is evident in the work place that they are just as good and just as bad in their own female way as are their male counterparts in their male way.

Some attempt to adapt is already taking place in Europe. "Western European countries almost uniformly provide maternity leaves and benefits, as well as child care, cash grants and tax benefits to women with dependent children. . . preventing pregnancy works. In Sweden, where the law providing for abortion upon request was coupled with a program expanding education about and access to contraception, rates of both teenage abortion and pregnancy have fallen" (72,73).

There is good reason for another adaptation to the "biological accident." One can consider women as being victims of the accident, but that "accident" has hurt men, too, especially in the development of their personal maturity. Is it really good for them as persons to think and feel and act superior to women? Are we as human beings really better off that there have been so few women in business and politics, so few Golda Meir's and Margaret Thatcher's? Perhaps if we could imitate Tribe's and Carl Rogers's spirit and method of thinking about and talking to one another, perhaps then we would begin to appreciate and adapt to the great possibilities of the correlative differences of the genders. Perhaps it would be wiser to exploit those realities rather than take the easy way out, namely abortion on demand, to free women from the "demeaning" role as instrumentalities of nature. Perhaps such an instrumentality is ennobling both for her and the father of her child. Perhaps the real degradation for both male and female is to deliberately run from the meaning of their correlative genders. There seems no question at all that the male domination of the female is harmful to both—perhaps far more harmful to the male than he realizes. An abortion on demand system, not only frees the woman; it grants even more freedom to the man. It is another tool to make easy sex easier for the male and to delay his growth to full maturity—whatever that means.

As was suggested in Chapter 9 concerning effective sanction of the brute element in society, those ideas are especially relevant to the brutality of incest and rape. The very thought of rape and incest should *terrify* (because of a very painful physical sanction) the would-be incestuous and rapist person. The sanctions should be so terrible that the overwhelming majority of men would fear them as nations fear nuclear war. Unfortunately, we have not matured as a society to develop such sanctions. Clearly, that is the path to the future—if we are to have more society and less jungle.

PERSON

When does she or he come to be? This question is not as difficult to answer as one might think. It has little to do with the multiple and various phenomena of embryonic and fetal development. It is essentially a matter of determining when the fertilized ovum begins its stable activities. By stable activities I mean at that moment when the unit no longer can split into twins, etc. and no longer can combine with an another embryo[5] to form a single unit. At that moment it is united in itself and divided from all all others. It fulfills the definition of a substantial being, i.e., it exists in and by and for itself; it does not exist in another as an accidental characteristic in a substance (white, black, running, breathing existing in a human being). Its independent existence in the mother is environmental and local existence, not integral existence, e.g., as the arm to her torso.

Why should this independent being be called a person? This is easier to understand if we keep in mind two familiar ideas we have experienced before, namely, integration and disintegration. We have all seen what happens to living things when they die. The unifying life is gone, and the many parts begin to disintegrate. Just the opposite happens when we look at the various stages of human development. We look at our pictures as a 7 pound new born, then a 70 pound youngster, then a 117 pound teenager. Over the years we, one and the same substantial being, have taken nutrients into ourselves and changed them into these three different forms through the substantial act of living and metabolizing. We speak of different stages of development. We do not speak of three different persons. That would contradict both our memory experience for the second and third stage, and the words of our parents for the first stage: "That's the way you looked the day you were born." Our name is the same, no matter what the weight or size.

If we go back further in the development to the stage of independently developing embryo, to fetus, to viable fetus, to fully developed child about

---

5. Charles A. Gardner, "Is an Embryo a Person?" *Nation*, 11/13/89, 557-559.

to be pushed through the birth canal, we are again looking at one living reality repeatedly expressing itself ever more in accord with a definite design through time. Each stage, which appears significantly different, is still the one life changing nutrients into a more highly developed form. We do not have a series of differing independent beings, but one being developing through different stages of greater self-actualization. The human substance is metabolizing and organizing the nutrients into tools so that the substance can do ever more and more. The one *being* is acting, *developing* tools so that the one being can do more with more tools than it can do with less tools. The point must again be made. *Being* precedes action, and the *nature of the being* determines the nature of the action. If thought or intelligence ever comes out of this embryonic independent substance, it was always there ready to come out. All it needed was to make the tools (senses, brain, etc.) Clearly, it can make the tools.

Many people would want to say that the person does not exist until there is some evidence of personal activity. Two things should be noted. First, there are many instances in which we have no personal activity yet, we in those periods of time are clearly persons, e.g., sleep, unconscious through accident, coma. Thus absence of personal activity is no proof of absence of person. Second, we need to ask what is the high point of this one substance's activity? The high point is thought, understanding, trust, love, the expression of its freedom. The activity of personal behavior is the expression of what the substance is. The characteristic of an action proceeds from the characteristic of specific nature of the being expressing itself. Since that action is personal, the nature of the being, no matter what stage of development, always was personal, even at the very lowest manifestation of its developmental process. What it *is* now is exactly what it *was* as it started to *act*. *Being* always precedes *act*. Specific nature determines specific action or operation

What is the nature of the human being? It is *substantial freedom* waiting through its controlled process of development to accomplish the *free act*. That is the meaning behind two facts: 1) the independence and unity of the developing embryo, and 2) the free and intelligent act that later comes from that now highly developed independent substance. Man is a person at the first moment of his stable independent developmental process. I, the person, live and metabolize in order to grow. I grow in order to sense. I sense in order to understand. I understand in order to choose, communicate, and trust. I, the one complex life with many powers, was present from the moment of my life's first independent movement of metabolization and growth.

Spontaneous abortion means death from unknown causes and is essentially pathetic. The person is killed by force or dies because of some form of system or nutritional failure. If the abortion is not spontaneous, but induced deliberately by the mother and/or the attending physician, then we have the taking of innocent personal life. This is the reasoning that supports the pro-lifers position: Deliberate abortion is murder because the substantial free human being has its freedom violated unto death. Such a death is also pathetic. There is nothing this free human being can do to protect itself.

We now have arrived at a very emotional point of our discussion. It is the point where many pro-lifers justify their strong and even physical opposition to abortion clinics. Sometimes they justify their intervention in the name of God and religion. Tribe makes a very telling point here (123, 124). Embryology experts estimate that fully two-thirds of fertilized ova fail to implant in the uterus. If those ova have independent substantial existence we have been talking about, that means that almost 7 out of 10 persons die before reaching the most limited maturity. We have here something that is repeated in other forms of life, e.g., the fruit tree. Thousands of blossoms are fertilized and begin the development of fruit. One can see the green pea-like orange is on its way to becoming large and mature fruit. But within a few days or weeks, the ground is littered with thousands of these incipient fruit lives.

Even granting in the case of human implantation failure that the number is half the estimate of the experts, this loss of human life is amazing. But what does that say about the author of human life and the value He places on the lives he has just created? Those lives are just as pathetically lost as those in spontaneous and induced abortions. Tribe makes a very valid point: Why don't the pro-lifers raise a hew and cry to save the fertilized ova? They would rightly say: The threatened life is easier to find, and easier to save. We can do something about it; there is little we could do about the fertilized ova. Childless couples will probably spur research to discover just how to do that more effectively.

In the meantime, Operation Rescue might well take itself less seriously in its crusade to save human life and realize that it can't stop all the evil (pathos) in the world, and that if the Almighty can tolerate such tremendous loss of human life, so they, who have less power than He might be just as physically tolerant as he is.

Such a position is no way is meant to approve deliberate abortion or abortion on demand. Nor is it meant as a recommendation to cease opposition to deliberate abortion. As Tribe has so well stated, in a democracy all we have is the vote and persuasion (240) through reasoned discussion. He might well have added: We have civil disobedience, too. But that hopefully will be the pure kind of King and Gandhi, not the violence of harassment of both the pregnant and the medical profession, the violence of the hateful shouts, and blows, and fire bombs. A democratic society under law must still provide adequate sanction against such civil disobedience and keep the peace until it sees, as with separation of races, that its laws are unjust and must be changed. Bombing, persecution, violence cannot be tolerated. To adopt these means is to return to the jungle.

YOUR STATE OF MIND AND CHOICE

A very important moral question arises here. After considering the reasoning above that points to the existence of the person from the first moment of its stable and unified pursuit of human development to its arrival at personal action, what is your state of mind?

Do you say, "The reasoning is correct. The independent fetus is a person." If you do, you have certitude, the assent of the mind without fear of error. But suppose you say, "The reasoning makes a lot of sense; it probably is a person, but I wouldn't say so for sure." Then your state of mind is one of opinion. You incline to one side of the proposition rather than to the other ("It is not a person"). The question then is: why do you hesitate? What evidence is missing that would convince you? Recall, we are dealing with metaphysical reality. It has been abstracted from sensible phenomena. We can't be looking for sensible evidence when the only evidence that matters in a metaphysical question is the testimony of the intellect, the meaning of substance, accidents, natures, specific being leading to specific action, etc. So what is the metaphysical evidence for my reluctance to move from opinion to certitude?

But consider another mental position. "I see the reasoning. It really doesn't convince, nor does it move me to a favorable opinion. I really doubt the independent fetus is a person. It may be for all I know, but I doubt it." Again, what is the evidence or motive for the doubt. Again, caution, we can't look for phenomenological evidence and the certitude that comes from measuring, weighing, and counting. We are in a different realm of knowledge, science. The only evidence that is relevant is the meanings derived from the phenomena, i.e., cause, effect, nature, accident, substance.

One state of mind that is impossible in the face of the above reasoning is the state of ignorance. We can't say, "I don't know anything at all about the fetus-person question." We do know something, we have seen some evidence, and that evidence produces certitude, opinion, or doubt, but clearly not ignorance.

Finally, there is another state of mind in this question, i.e., contradiction or "The fetus is certainly not a person." That statement needs evidence, too. Contradictory evidence, evidence that excludes the possibility of the fetus being a person. Negatives are very hard to prove. The only way I can prove I was not in Chicago on July 4, 1991 is to show (have positive evidence) that I was somewhere else at that time and that date. What evidence is there that the stable and independently operating embryonic substance is not in its *being* personal as it begins to develop the tools needed to *express* that personal substance in *acts* of intelligence and freedom. Recall that the law of the mind is the law of being. We are not discussing democracy of thought, here. Nor of freedom of speech. We agree to listen to anybody express his or her opinion. But if they have no evidence for their position, they do not deserve our attention. Put very forcefully and necessarily: No one has a right to any opinion that is not supported by evidence. To have such opinions is to create them independent of the realities given us by our senses and intellect. It is to wish and to dream.

These states of mind are extremely important for the moral act of deliberately aborting the independent fetus.

If I am certain the fetus is a person, then my abortion means I am willing to take an innocent life. If I am of the opinion that it is a person or if I am in a state of doubt, I must resolve the doubt before taking threatening action against the fetus. Failure to resolve the doubt means that I really don't care whether I kill a person or not. " If it is a person, too bad. If it isn't, no harm done."

Thus the basic moral question is not what happens to the fetus, but what happens to me. What do I become when I abort, perform the abortion, assist at the performance of the abortion?

PRIVACY

In light of what has been said about the fetus, independent from the mother and existing not as a part of her but existing in and for itself, Tribe's great concern for the privacy of the mother takes on a new and very limited meaning. With approval he cites Justice Louis Brandeis ". . . the right to be left alone—the most comprehensive of rights and the right most valued by civilized men" (92).

The reason Brandeis is correct is because privacy is a consequence of man's transcendent substance, his freedom, his independence. He has a right to be left alone because he is alone. That is what substantial independence is; that is the meaning of substantial transcendence or substantial freedom. His right to be left alone is another way of saying that others have the duty to respect his freedom and his rights to life, liberty, and the pursuit of happiness. But it is simply incorrect to say that the pregnant woman has a right to complete privacy, the right to be left completely alone regarding the life living within her for she did not conceive it by herself and in complete privacy.

Privacy, like so many other terms, can be used either properly or analogously. Properly speaking it applies to an individual alone. As soon as that individual deals with another or others, privacy ends and the social or public begins. The others become witnesses to the individual's acts, willing or unwilling participants in the acts. From that point onward the "privacy" of consenting adults, the "privacy" of the family, the "privacy" of the sorority, fraternity, boardroom, union meeting, yes, even the internal (private) affairs of independent nations are examples of privacy by analogy only. They are simply different from proper privacy, but in some sense the same. They are similar to, but not identical with, privacy in the proper sense.

The act of intercourse is not strictly, or properly speaking, a private matter no matter how well concealed by the home or other "private" place. Marital rape is not a private matter; neither is incest, nor is marital love. A woman's claim to privacy regarding her embryo is an unjust claim. She is responsible for that human being, but that responsibility is not private, for she did not conceive it in private but rather in union with another. She has rights regarding that human being; but she is not the only one who has rights and responsibilities toward it. Consequently, when she claims that all jurisdiction ends at the point of her body, when she claims that she is the sole determinant of what happens to that independent life that is living within her life, she is incorrect.

Physically speaking, she can end that life just as she can physically commit suicide. Ultimately, no one can respect the freedom of others and physically prevent their acts of suicide. And no one can prevent the pregnant woman from attempting and accomplishing a miscarriage or abortion. As technology improves she will probably be able to accomplish that effect whenever and wherever she is able to be in strict privacy. But that does not mean that she is performing a morally good act, an act that makes her a better person, an act that respects the rights of the father and the rights of the person living its embryonic life. Obviously the termination of human life is a serious matter. It is not a morally indifferent act such as tying one's shoe or putting on a hat. The question that she and others must ask is this: "Does her terminating of human life make her a better person, one who respects the rights of others and duties to herself?" It is a distracting irrelevancy to ask the leading question, "After all it is a matter of the woman's privacy, isn't it?" Abortion has nothing at all to do with a woman's strict privacy.

If it is reasonable to say the fetus is a person or probably is a person, then the right to privacy belongs to the independent fetus, too. It, by virtue of its independence, has a right to be left alone to pursue the full flower of its independent life. The privacy of the mother is limited to all and only what she is. She has no right over the life of the fetus, simply because she is not the fetus and the fetus is not she.

But what about the fantastic inconvenience and human suffering of cases like Sherri Finkbine, Becky Bell, and Spring Adams? Why did those situations occur? Because we in our ignorance could not prevent them. Because they are the instances of the pathos in human life. We didn't know what thalidomide could do, we didn't know how to have parenting that could insure communication between teenager and parent, and we didn't know how to have a sanction that could literally terrify an incestuous parent into social rather than jungle behavior. And so we suffer, and will suffer until we learn to anticipate and prevent. Ignorance will always hurt and kill, and that is pathetic.

Is it moral to put an end to a pathetic situation by killing the fetus of incest or rape? It certainly is convenient, especially for the rapist or incestuous father. It certainly is economical for just about everybody concerned. And clearly it is most convenient for the child-mother or rape victim and family. But convenience is one thing, morality is another. What happens to the persons of those who choose to abort or assist in abortion? Nothing? What happens to their persons when they choose all that it implies to let the child live?

What is the alternative? The quick solution is to put off learning and abort now. The easy way is to put aside some of the solutions of Western Europe, wherein education and child support make birth control and child support more attractive than abortion on demand. Unfortunately for us we have already learned how easy it is to abort and thereby escape dealing with the retarded and defective birth, escape dealing with teenage pregnancy, and escape dealing with the further discovery of the meaning of correlative genders. In the name of freedom from the *female biological accident,* we put off learning more about the correlative meaning of the human male and female. We delay our adaptation to and benefiting from those differences. Thus we delay our intellectual and moral maturity.

Abortion on demand is so technologically easy. Lasting support of the life of the human fetus is so demanding of thought, of creativity, of expense, of personal sacrifice, of courage, and of execution of social reform—it is no wonder at all that we see the female as the *victim* of a biological accident. It is very hard to accept that that is her radical meaning as correlative to the male. There is something positive in the meaning of this correlative relationship that is yet to be discovered and articulated. What is it?[6]

---

6. Dr. Bernardine Healy, a former director of the National Institutes of Health, has called attention to the unique needs of women and the knowledge gaps in gender differences in health care. *See ABC News This Week with David Brinkley,* May 22, 1994, Transcript #656, p. 5. For a start in answering this question of gender differences see Wilson, *Moral Sense,* "Gender," 165-190, esp. 185.

13

Wilson's
The Moral Sense

The origin of Wilson's[1] book is comparable to mine, namely the felt need for the clarification and justification of traditional common sense morality. We both feel that the present day skepticism (viii) can and should be refuted. He especially wants to help people recover the confidence with which they once spoke of virtue and morality, and he wants to show that mankind has a moral nature (vii). Our methods differ. He "scavenges" (26) through the sciences to find details vindicating the "moral sense." I start with the fact of man's freedom and analyze its meaning. His method is scientific, mine is metaphysical. He is inductive, I am deductive. But he, along with all natural scientists, uses metaphysical principles all along the way. He regularly speaks of human nature and mankind (218), metaphysical concepts. The principle of causality is ever present, for he asks "why" and answers "because." He asks "how" and offers explanations that give sufficient reasons to justify a particular effect. He compares studies and rejects one (15) because of insufficient evidence. Thus, as all men must, he accepts the principle of cause and proportionate effect and the principle of contradiction. Implicitly he admits that he, too, is guided by science and logic (viii). But that logic is really the logic of sufficient reason, and thus causality, and thus metaphysics. I think these logical and metaphysical principles that underpin the scientific method need to be enunciated, lest the science of metaphysics be denigrated. Thus it must be remembered that science is an analogous term. Science, that is knowledge of causes, applies to phenomena, number, free beings, and being, thus natural science, math, behavioral or social science, and metaphysics.

Wilson's scholarship, organization and argument are evident and compelling. He gives plenty of evidence for the existence of a moral sense and, to his mind, its four predominant aspects of sympathy, fairness, self-control,

---

1. James Q. Wilson, *The Moral Sense*, The Free Press, Macmillan, New York, 1993.

and duty (xiii). He defines that moral sense thus: ". . .an intuitive or directly felt belief about how one ought to act when one is free to act voluntarily
(that is, not under duress). By "ought" I mean an obligation binding on all
people similarly situated" (xii). The moral sense is natural and innate
(229). Wilson comes to this conclusion by induction, that is by citing untold
examples of human behavior, especially of parent-child relationships that
illustrate what he calls a prosocial tendency (127). This moral sense is supported by the facts that 1) Man feels obliged to justify his acts (230), 2) man
rejects murder or attempts to justify it (226), 3) man prohibits incest (17),
and especially 4) man cares for his children (18). These widespread behaviors lead Wilson to reject the notion that the human person is morally indifferent and infinitely malleable (130, 143, 251). Implicitly, therefore, there
are criteria for judging behavior as barbaric and cruel (ix).

There is a tone of caution throughout Wilson's book. This seems to be
rooted in the scientific method of scavenging through the data, as if there
just might not be enough to validate his moral sense. This caution militates
against the confidence he wants to establish in discussion of virtue and
morality. This caution appears in its strongest form at the end of his first
chapter when he says:

> Before the reader repeats the well-known criticisms of the idea of a
> moral sense, let me acknowledge that I know of them also: If there is a
> moral sense, what is the sensory organ? If sincere people disagree about
> what is right and wrong, how can there be a moral sense. If a moral sense
> is supposed to emerge naturally, what evidence is there that human
> nature is sufficiently uniform so that this sense will emerge among most
> people in more or less the same way?

> I do not think one can easily give general answers to these important
> questions. The truth, if it exists, is in the details. This book is about the
> details; it is the result of scavenging through science in order to illumi-
> nate everyday life.

> I suspect we will encounter uniformities; and by revealing uniformities, I
> think that we can better appreciate what is general,nonarbitrary, and
> emotionally compelling about human nature.(26)

Even though I agree with Wilson's position that morality and a moral
sense are natural and innate, there are important differences. The above
paragraph is a good place to begin such a critique. His comment "The
truth, if it exists, is in the details" may be the statement of the modest
scholar. Whether modest or not, it does not promote the confidence Wilson wants us to have when discussing virtue and morality. That confidence
is further weakened when we learn that it is difficult to name the organ for
the moral sense, that it is somewhere in the details, and that there is a con-

cern whether there is sufficient evidence to validate a uniform human nature.

The details will show the sensory organ. I think they show there has to be one, but they do not show what it is in human nature. A quick answer can be found in in his own definition of a moral sense. The key words are "intuition," "felt," and "belief." Recall that we are talking about the complex unity that is man, not a compound of juxtaposed disparate realities. He is a body-person, intellectual, sensory, vegetative all in one. The question about a moral sense organ prejudices research so that it looks for something like an eye, ear, or nerve endings in nose, tongue, hand or parts of the brain. We are dealing with more than animality. We are dealing with rationality that uses its animal life as a necessary condition, not cause, for its acts of transcendence (intelligence and volition). So the "organ" will not be found in the body; it will be found in the transcendence, the substantial freedom that is an essential part of the human essence. The organ of intuition is the intellect. The intuition is felt in the one body-person, much as any insight is felt in the "Oh, I see." The belief is the same as the insight or conviction, but it is supported by the feeling concomitant with the insight.

The question "What evidence is there that human nature is uniform" is a peculiar question. If there were any evidence that human nature as human nature were not uniform, we would call that different thing something other than human nature precisely because of the different evidence observed. Our present observations show us that man is an animal, but with one specifying difference—he is rational. This difference is an essential part of his nature. Recall that the term nature is used to indicate a principle of action, that essence is used to indicate what that nature is, and that substance is used to indicate that the nature exists in itself and not in another. All three of these terms are the result of the mind distinguishing a reality that is metaphysical, understood from the phenomena observed by the senses. Animal as such, human nature as such, are universal concepts abstracted from phenomena. One cannot use the term and then wonder whether it is uniform. If one perceives the reality human nature and then notes that in this particular human there is an activity emerging that is not found in other humans, then that new activity proves that this "human" is essentially different, deserving of another specifying name. It may be like humans, as apes are like humans, but the activity emerging from the nature indicates that it is a simply different nature. It is well at this point to recall the distinction between substance and accident, proper or necessary accidents and contingent accidents. The human nature of our experience is substantially the same throughout the world. Its proper accidents are intellection, volition, and extension. Every human nature has these as necessary characteristics or properties. Some characteristics are contingent to the human nature. The one human nature can be differentiated by race, color, size. The essential parts, shared by all those we call human, are animality and rationality. The evidence for those parts are: a) animality—sensation, local motion, metabolism, quadruped or biped, sexual union, gestation, birth, etc. b) rationality—ideas, judgments, insight, inference, conclusion, arbitrary signs (language), friendship, love, arbitrary laws for social groups. To raise the question whether human nature, or any nature for that matter, could possibly be non-uniform in particular individuals having that nature is to ask a grammatically correct question that has no meaning. Any faculty can be misapplied or abused. And yet we should be grateful that Wilson posed these questions and suggested answers that might not be true ("if it [truth] exists"). For he keeps us alert for more convincing evidence that will strengthen our confidence in the existence of virtue and morality.

Assuming that it is evident to all that man is an animal, language is the evidence that human nature is uniform and that there is a moral sense in everyone and that it will emerge in more or less the same way. For language is the arbitrary and even capricious use of physical symbols to distinguish one from another among the different realities of life. Language proves freedom and the substantial transcendence of the human essence. Language shows an understanding of relationships and manifests abstraction, inference, insight, etc. But above all else it illustrates the tendency or appetite for personal union. It goes beyond the natural signs of the smile, the stare, the caress, the blow. And since it occurs among male, female, and child it indicates the natural freedom and equality of each.

Implicitly, therefore, each is able to speak the truth or lie, seek to manipulate or to earn and give trust. Once those faculties begin to exercise within the particular physical and social environment, those faculties will be shaped for better or worse by repetition. But radically the transcendent, the openness to objects and to other equal persons is always present. That is what the substantial freedom of the uniform human nature means. Language implies it all.

Wilson is right when he rejects the notion that the human person is morally indifferent, infinitely malleable (130, 143, 251). There is no such thing as an indefinite reality. Everything is limited or defined in some way. Therefore there is a good (being as perfecting) in every reality and the possibility of evil (privation of the good that ought to be present) for every reality. Since man is definite, some things complete him and others can deprive him of what he should have. Morally speaking (in the realm of free choice), therefore, he can make choices that complete him, make him good, and there are others that will make him bad or evil, for they will deprive him of what he should have, personal peace. When Skinner (143) says that morality is a conditioned response to rewards and punishments, he was not totally wrong. There is a moral choice and it is rewarding; there is an immoral choice and it is punishing. This is necessarily, metaphysically, so because being is definite. If it is a vital being, then it maintains and acquires its good through acts proper to its nature. If it is free and autonomous, it can act to attain its good or act to deprive itself of any good on any level (vegetative, sensory, intellectual, personal) of its being. Because being is definite, some things are always bad for it and some things are always good for it. Everything depends upon its definite structure. The goodness or badness of conscious beings is an experience. The experience is called pleasure or pain.

When a person makes a choice to act, he does so based on what he perceives. If those actions deal exclusively with objects, they bring him pleasure or pain, satisfaction or dissatisfaction for one or more of his appetites. But when he deals with persons, attempts to communicate with or to answer the communication attempts of another, he is dealing with a completely different kind of appetite or tendency. The tendency to communicate is an attempt to accomplish a moral, not a physical union. It is an attempt to be with and to stop being alone as a person. That being with is a matter of degree, all the way from being in the presence of to being understood, being liked, and being respected by the other. In all these degrees of union there is a type of peace, tranquility of order, and therefore no cause for disturbance or alarm. This peace is experienced by the person and because of the substantial union with the body, has its overflow into the body and is experienced. The glands, muscles, neurons, heart beat, lungs are also at peace. Most people, psychopaths excepted, undergo bodily changes when they lie (106). These disturbances are what the polygraph records. The lie as well as the honest communication overflows into the body. The tendency to union is interrupted and broken off; the person is separated from the one with whom he is now only verbally, not personally, communicating. This is the result of being conscious of the self, the other, and the honest or dishonest self communication. Wilson seeks the organ that produces the intuitive and directly felt belief of how one ought to act. The intuition and feeling are produced by the intellect of the body-person as it reflects upon the experience of its own peace or disturbance, the experience of integrity or duplicity anticipated in the potential choice or actualized in the actual choice. When the child cries, when it looks at either parent, a communication is sent out that expects a response. That communication is heard and there is a personal tendency to respond. The animal instinctively does respond. The rational animal has a choice, he can close himself off or answer and unite. If he closes, he is alone and that is a privation and therefore morally evil and unnatural. If he answers, he unites, and completes his natural tendency and experiences goodness (good is being as perfecting, completing). The organ of the moral sense is the intellect of the body person, but the object sensed is the good or bad person conscious of its real goodness or badness. Almost seventy years ago H. G. Stoker[2] clearly presented this distinction.

> If the phenomenon of conscience is to be present, the deeper experiential level is essentially necessary; only where the reality of being bad is experienced is there a bad conscience.
>
> Neither the images of thought, nor conclusions, nor a judgment can be the primary cause of a disturbed conscience, only the reality itself can be the cause . . . and real moral guilt can bring the greatest confusion and desperation. . . . The one who is plagued by his conscience flees not from his judgments, is ashamed not of the concepts of his guilt, does not regret his conclusions and thought processes, but only the objective guilt which these judgments indirectly reproduce. . . . The bad conscience is directly concerned with objective reality. (78, 79)

Everyone at one time or another has seen in the media the record of someone getting rid of the lived lie and unburdening his personal evil because being conscious of it was just too painful to live with. A rather famous example of this is that of Alonzo Mann, who seventy years after the fact, provided testimony[3] that cleared the lynched Leo Max Frank of the 1913 murder of Mary Phagan. More recently Katherine Ann Power, an anti-Viet Nam war radical and fugitive of 23 years, surrendered to police and pleaded guilty to past crimes. Her words are quite appropos of all that we have been saying about openness. "Leaving my son, my husband and my friends to enter prison is not easy. But I know that I must answer this accusation from the past in order to live with full authenticity in the present. . . . I am now learning to live with openness and truth, rather than shame and hiddenness."[4]

The objective reality of guilt is the personal decision to close oneself from the other, to fail to give in trust when one is asked for an honest response. The natural inclination or tendency is to give the honest answer, because as Wilson says both the animal and the rational animal have an inclination for attachment (105). And it is this desire for attachment that is the underlying mechanism of human moral conduct (127).

It is at this point that I feel Wilson and I say substantially the same thing. The desire for attachment is essentially the necessary tendency of the tran-

---

2. H. G. Stoker, *Das Gewissen, Erscheinungsformen und Theorien*, Friedrich Cohen, Bonn, 1925.
3. Robert Seitz Frey and Nancy Thompson Frey, *The Silent and the Damned, The Murder of Mary Phagan and the Lynching of Leo Frank*, Madison Books, New York, 1988, 156.
4. *Los Angeles Times*, 9/16/93, A12. See a similar comment by her husband in *Time*, 9/27/93, 62.

scendent being to be one with another transcendent being. Wilson's "desire for attachment" is essentially the need to communicate, the need to reach out to the other and be united with that person through an answer. It is not a purely animal need or the need for an object, but a need for a person. How do we know this? Because the parent brings the child peace now and more and more so later on as the child matures into lingually expressing both its need and its satisfaction. We are not dealing here with a vegetable (fetus) that becomes an animal (infant) and then a person (one who speaks). We are dealing with a transcendent substance, one human being, that is maturing from fetal to articulate and creative adult life. This vital mechanism, this vital desire for attachment is nothing else but an appetite, a teleology, an innate tendency different from all other appetites and tendencies in the human. Its object, the good thing that completes it and satisfies it, is the mutual experience of the question and answer that occurs when two people communicate as persons. This experience of satisfaction upon successfully doing what the two persons were designed to do is radical morality, a radical instance of virtue being its own reward.

This appetite is a necessary emergence from the nature, a proper—not contingent— characteristic or accident of the nature. It emerges from the transcendence of the nature. It is necessary because nature must act according to what it specifically is. Inoperative vital nature is an impossibility. Human nature is vitally open not only to objects, but to persons. It can comprehend and take to itself objects that complete its vegetative, sensory, intellectual, and personal tendencies or appetites. But each of these appetites operates differently: vegetation by intussuception and metabolism, sensation by external objects contacting the sense organs, intellection by deriving meaning from objects sensed, and personal union and attachment in trust by honest communication. These are the goods that complete and must complete these appetites. When completed they have achieved good, physical well being for the body, truth for the mind and moral goodness for the person. Absence of these goods is a frustration of the appetites, they seek and cannot find, they are deprived of their natural objects, and that is bad. This means starvation for the vegetative tendency, darkness, silence, etc. for the sensitive appetites, ignorance for the mind, and isolation and detachment for the person. If isolation is inflicted, i.e., if there is no answer to the communication sent, the person is pathetic; if isolation is chosen by means of the lie, or manipulation, or rejection of the person, the person is tragic, morally bad, deliberately alone. The only cure for this is the cure of Alonzo Mann and Katherine Ann Power: get rid of the lie, admit the truth and accept the consequences.

Wilson sees limitations of this "mechanism for attachment." He says that " . . . the moral sense for most people remains particularistic; for some it aspires to be universal" (226). He exemplifies this when he contrasts American and Japanese cultures. American culture gives high priority to sympathy and fair play. This encourages a deference to universalistic standards of justice. The Japanese culture tends to limit personal loyalty to the immediate group, the family and workplace. And these tend to keep the moral sense particularistic (154, 155).

It is a fact that culture with all its factors of gender, religion, geography, climate, etc. can and do have an influence upon the man's openness to person or mechanism for attachment. But it is simply wrong to say that in some instances this mechanism aspires only to be particularistic. It is much more accurate to say that it always aspires to be universal, but in most instances culture prevents it from doing so. We are looking at a natural and universal appetite that has grown stronger with social evolution. We have a United Nations where leaders of peoples have to talk to each other, and at least live in peace in the United Nations building. There is a growing awareness of such things as crimes against humanity, human atrocities, human rights. We have American high school classrooms where ethnic diversity is the norm and the students are friends and sometimes even more. A booklet of prom pictures will show ethnically mixed couples. None of this would be possible if some people had a mechanism for attachment that was incapable of tending beyond its own cultural group.

The Apache (194), the Japanese (154), the Arab (200), the Christian vs. Muslim are cultural manifestations that stifled this universal tendency to respect those outside the religion, family, tribe, clan, etc. Since this universal mechanism for attachment is violated to some extent by these cultures, to that extent the culture is bad. Recall: evil inheres in good. We are not saying that the entire culture is bad, but just that part of it has been deprived of what would be good for it. This must be said if we are to hold that cultural relativism (moral values are solely the product of culture [xii]) is invalid and morality is objective and radically independent of culture. Thus there is a criterion by which not only every person, but every person's culture, is to be measured and judged. That criterion is whether the person or the culture supports or inhibits the natural, innate tendency to attachment and openness to the other equal person, no matter who or how many he may be.

The point to be made here is that just about any culture can spring up around this need and obligation to communicate. The Japanese culture, for example, stresses an attachment to the group which manifests itself in mutual dependency and family obligation. This leads to a sense of duty to the group. Dutiful behavior is reinforced by shame and honor. The individual is subject to control by the group and therefore is more inclined to self-control rather than self-expression. On the other hand, the American culture, which is rooted in the tradition of individual rights being protected from oppression by the group, e.g., England and then the Constitution that had to be amended by the Bill of Rights, that culture favored individualism and contact with people outside the family. This culture promoted sympathy for the other and a sense of fairness in dealing with him (154, 155). The result is that this culture allowed the need for attachment to do what it could do, to do what it was intended to do, i.e., to reach out to, to respect, to sympathize and become attached to any human being, and not just to members of its own familial group. Any culture can inhibit this universal disposition to be open to and receive the other. The tendency to stay within the group can at best keep the group in a state of truce rather than a state of peaceful cooperation with its different neighbor. The "Omne ignotum pro magnifico est" (The unknown is always exaggerated) of Tacitus is the occasion for developing an isolating xenophobia and changing a global economy into an economic war instead of a global economy of cooperation and peace.

But different people can get along with each other, as American culture proves. Ethnic differences do exist and function well in government, business, entertainment, religion, sports, and family. These facts of peaceful life indicate what should be when this undefined aspiration for union is permitted and supported by its culture.

On the other hand, this openness and respect for the liberty can be excessive and at the expense of the good of the group. The right to privacy can conceal child and spouse abuse. The right to bear arms can occasion the proliferation of guns to such an extent that citizens must be constantly be aware of the violent criminal and the peace officer must fear that he is outgunned by the criminal. The right to freedom of speech and press have been extended to protect almost any kind of individual expression so much so that decency, obscenity, and pornography cannot be defined. The same is true with the right to private property. Our history of individualism has resulted in the abuses of the environment, discrimination in employment, monopoly, child labor, etc.

But both the concern for the group and the concern for the individual are rooted in the same natural tendency to be united with the other person. This openness implies sympathy because communication among equal human beings is not merely intellectual and known, but it is also experienced and felt in the whole complex being called human. Fairness is another aspect of this communication precisely because the other is known as an equal and has reached me by his sent out communication and my need to respond. Duty is present because if I do not respond I am alone and experience the pain of loneliness. The response is a good that is due me as well as to him who spoke to me. Deliberate isolation is bad and therefore I am morally evil, experience that evil as guilt. That real guilt is the reality I express in the sentence "I should have answered him." And self-control is also present in this tendency to communicate. For the absence of self-control is the positive presence of seeking objects for myself and ignoring the need to be united to others in the actual observing of their rights. Lack of self-control is to be out order, out of the community of friend, family, neighbor, etc. Communication and attachment cannot exist where there is no self-control.

Wilson's book is admirable in the scholarly support it gives for the universal mechanism of desire for attachment underlying moral conduct. I see it as identified with the substantial transcendence of the human being. As transcendent the human is conscious of itself as being completed (good) or deprived (evil) by its choices to be open or closed, attached or detached, to the other personal being. This consciousness is the objective reality intuited by the intellect and felt by the body-person. The felt intuition is "I ought not to have done that" or "I ought to do this now." I believe this need for attachment always aspires to union with any and all persons, regardless of cultural differences, and that any culture can assist or inhibit this aspiration. As man grows in an understanding of himself and his history, there is reason to believe that the impediments will be reduced and the supports will increase.

14

Pirsig's *Lila*:
An Inquiry into Morals

In the first chapter I refer briefly to *Lila*. From those references it is evident that I disagree to some extent with Pirsig. Before discussing in detail the points of disagreement, let it be said at the outset that I found *Lila* an intellectually exciting book. The author is learned, brilliant, and he can write. It is rare that a volume manifests so much science, philosophy, and insights into their relationships. Pirsig's first book, *Zen and the Art of Motorcycle Maintenance,* moved me deeply, as it did many others. Lila is different. It is metaphysics and moral philosophy carried by the story of one human being trying to understand his philosophy of life and what he is to think and do regarding the troubled woman who has entered his life.

That being said, let's get on to the discussion of our points of agreement and disagreement.

My concern regarding morality is the person. Pirsig's is society. My concern has been to show the obligating nature of the human being's substantial transcendence. The human person must choose to be open because that is what the structure of his transcendence demands. I am concerned with the corruption of the individual. Pirsig's emphasis is on the problem of the deterioration and corruption of society, ". . .a reversion to rule by terror, violence and gang death—the old biological might-makes-right morality of prehistoric brigandage that primitive societies were set up to overcome." (304) My solution is the metaphysics of substantial transcendence; his solution is the metaphysics of Quality. Both are theoretical and persuasive, i.e., they hope to effect change by persuading the reader through logical argument. Pirsig is hostile to Aristotle (105), particularly towards the concepts of substance (104) and causality (103). Quantum mechanics invalidates both notions (139). I favor Aristotle and agree with those physicists who "question the universal validity of quantum mechanics."[1] My position is that both substance and causality are valid concepts representing what is in the real world. As do I, Pirsig accepts evolution, but not in a mechanistic and deterministic sense. Atoms evolve into chemistry professors because

> something in nature does not like the laws of equilibrium or the law of gravity or the laws of thermodynamics or any other law that restricts the molecule's freedom. They only go along with laws of any kind because they have to, preferring an existence that does not follow any laws whatsoever.

> This would explain why patterns of life do not change solely in accord with causative "mechanisms" or "programs" or blind operations of physical laws. They do not change valuelessly. They change in ways that evade, override and circumvent these laws. The patterns of life are constantly evolving in response to something "better" than that which these laws have to offer. (143, 144)

Pirsig's model of evolution is: 1) Inorganic evolves from chaotic, 2) Biologic evolves from inorganic, 3) Social evolves from biologic, and 4) Intellectual evolves from social. The driving force behind this evolutionary process is Dynamic Quality. Each stage is a code of ethics. (301) The entire process is ethical because Dynamic Quality is always striving for the better. Pirsig says "that not just life, but everything is an ethical activity. It is nothing else. When inorganic patterns of reality create life the Metaphysics of Quality postulates that they've done so because it is "better" and that this definition of "betterness"—this beginning response to Dynamic Quality—is an elementary unit of ethics upon which all right and wrong can be based." (157) The ultimate good is freedom from domination by any static pattern, "but that freedom does not have to be obtained by the destruction of the patterns themselves." (157) To illustrate: Society has imposed patterns of law on the biological (jungle) stage of evolution. When intellect discovers some of the social patterns are unreasonable (Galileo vs. Church, post WW I vs. Victorianism) it must remove them, but it should not remove the reasonable restrictive patterns. Present day America's intellectualism has looked upon the present social system as the enemy (309) and has come down on the side of the individual's freedom against the

---

1. Paul Davies, *The Cosmic Blueprint,* Touchstone Book, Simon and Schuster, 1989, 171. Roger Penrose is mentioned here: "There is something deeply unsatisfactory about the present conventional formulation of quantum mechanics..." David Bohm's position is found on 156. Pirsig would substitute "preference" for "causality" (104); iron filings prefer to move toward the magnet. The magnet does not cause this movement. Apropos to that statement is the statement of Davies rejecting Kenneth Denbigh's uncaused emergence of a new level of reality. "To say that this orderly unidirectional progression is uncaused, but just happens to be that way seems to me like saying that objects are not caused to fall by the force of gravity—they just happen to move that way. Such a point of view can never be called scientific, for it is the purpose of science to provide rational universal principles for the explanation of all natural regularities." Davies, 141,142.

legitimate restrictions of the social system. "Intellectuals must find biological behavior, no matter what its ethnic connection, and limit or destroy destructive biological patterns [law of the jungle, might-makes-right] with complete moral ruthlessness, the way a doctor destroys germs, before those biological patterns destroy civilization itself." (311)

Really, our theories of morality have much in common. Most important of all we agree that freedom is the ultimate norm of objective morality. For Pirsig Dynamic Quality is essentially freedom and the cause of the above mentioned codes of morality. For me freedom, though restricted to the substantial transcendence of the human being, still is the structure that must be obeyed, i.e., the inescapable moral obligation for the individual is to remain open to all evidence and to chose to conform by action to the particular truths that evidence supports. Pirsig's freedom is not license. It supposes that some of the static patterns Dynamic Quality has created through evolution are permanently valid. There can be no regression from the social back to the biological level. I hold the same thing. Some static patterns of behavior, e.g., the rule of law, will remain valid no matter what the advances made by man's unrestricted desire to know and create. In other words insight into evidence might show that some traditional static patterns are no longer valid, e.g., Puritanism, Victorianism, slavery, racial discrimination, the Vietnam war, child labor, either side of the abortion controversy, free trade or protectionism. Each of these convictions represent a static position of human beings. These patterns can only and should only be broken (or maintained) by insight into reality that shows they are wrong (or correct).

Morality is both objective and subjective. Objective (i.e., independent of my thought) because reality (e.g., Pirsig's phases of evolution as codes of morality) is definite, structured, specifically progressive because of both Dynamic and Static quality and as such is an object of man's understanding. Morality is also subjective, that is, as obliging reality known and understood by the individual human being.

Right here, where we distinguish between objective and subjective morality, is the place to distinguish the word "truth," especially objective and subjective truth. Pirsig is wrong when he says, "Truth is a species of good . . . a static intellectual pattern within a larger entity called Quality." (364) Truth is not a species of anything. It is a transcendental concept. Along with the other transcendental concepts of being, good, one, beautiful, it is applied (predicated) differently to different realities, but in some sense the same. A being is objectively *true* if it exists or is made or created in accord with the specifications of its exemplar or design. For example the vertical corner line of a brick building is said to be "true" or "out of true" depending on whether it conforms to the mason's perpendicular plumb line. The same corner line is said to be or have *being* because it exists. It is said to be *one* because it exists in its own way and can be distinguished from other types of beings. It is also said to be *good* because it is complete, it has the being or perfection it should have. And finally it can be said to be *beautiful* because its goodness, unity, and truth, once perceived, pleases the beholder. In a word, being is the object or material from which the knowing subject apprehends the real existence (being), unity, goodness, truth and beauty of any particular thing—from the Necessary Being down to the being of the tiniest sub-atomic particle. The Necessary Being is the prime analogate, the fullness of being, unity, goodness, truth, and beauty. Contingent beings are simply different from it, but in some sense like it, i.e., their existence, unity, goodness, truth, and beauty are contingent on the free act of the creative and conservative power of the Necessary Being.

Finally regarding truth. It is objective. It is also subjective. This latter occurs when the mind is conformed to the real world by means of a judgment or proposition, e.g., "It really is raining outside." Thus truth is essentially a relation of *conformity*. In objective truth the existent or created or manufactured reality is *conformed* to its proper exemplar or design. In subjective truth the mind by means of a proposition is *conformed* to the object it knows. Pirsig must be speaking of subjective or logical truth (not objective truth) when he calls it an "intellectual pattern."

The major differences between the two theories of morality go back to the notion of substance and the physical scientists' narrow view of science. Science or knowledge is the perception or understanding of causes. Those causes can be phenomenological activities, mathematical, or metaphysical. The physical scientist, though he uses principles of metaphysics day in and day out, e.g., the principle of contradiction, the principle of causality— every effect has its proper and proportionate cause, is afraid to rise above phenomena to the metaphysical world. This is especially true when confronted with the fact of life, and especially the fact of personal intellectual life. Fortunately there is some evidence that "dynamic quality" is about to make a breakthrough in this freedom restricting static pattern. Paul Davies[2] approvingly quotes the physical chemist Michael Polanyi as saying ". . . there is no reason for suspending recognition to the obvious fact that consciousness is a principle that fundamentally transcends not only physics and chemistry but also the mechanistic principles of living beings." And John Boslough[3] shows Stephen Hawking opening the door to the metaphysical world just a tab. "The odds against a universe like ours emerging

---

2. Paul Davies, *The Cosmic Blueprint*, A Touchstone Book, Simon & Schuster, New York, 1989, 194.

out of something like the Big Bang are enormous," he told me. "I think there are clearly religious implications whenever you start to discuss the origins of the universe. There must be religious overtones. But I think most scientists prefer to shy away from the religious side of it."

Because of his great respect for the scientific method and hostility toward Aristotle,[4] Pirsig is forced to collectivize and substanialize activities and properties (characteristics) into a thing he calls Dynamic Quality. He has many synonyms for it: Value (107), perfection (141), primary reality of the world (97), indefinable (107), best (104), principle of "rightness" (383), source of all things (143) pre-intellectual cutting edge of all reality (143), freedom (103) is its only perceived good and its perceived evil is any pattern of one-sided fixed values that tries to contain and kill the ongoing free force of life. (115) He makes a permanent and abiding thing out of characteristics and metaphors for characteristics. In this he is much like natural scientists who will not take the metaphysical leap from activities they see and measure to affirm the one living substance their minds tell them underlies and unifies those activities. They look at the ant, the fish, the bird, the dog, the man and see different characteristics in different individuals and refer to each as different things, but they will not take the next step and say there is a permanent principle or cause that makes the "I" of the man or the "Fido" of the dog, etc. No wonder the man of common sense becomes irate with the scientist and says "when I say to my wife 'I love you' that is nothing but one meaningless mound of atoms interacting with another meaningless mound of atoms."[5]

When I criticize the natural scientist for not taking the metaphysical leap, I am not implying that physics and philosophy are identical. They are similar. Simply different, but in some sense the same. Both have the unrestricted desire to know the causes of their objects of study—phenomena for the physicist, being for the philosopher. But what is identical is the man who is essentially capable of both research and philosophy. Stephen Hawking is an illustration of this identity when he philosophizes thus:

> Even if there is only one possible unified theory, it is just a set of rules and equations. What is it that breathes fire into the equations and makes

---

3. John Boslough, *Stephen Hawking's Universe*, Avon Books, New York, 1989, 109.
4. Davies, *Cosmic Blueprint*. Some scientists favor Aristotle. The geneticist Giuseppe Montalenti is quoted as saying, "This is the main reason why in the competition of Aristotelian and Democritean interpretations [of the origin of life] the former has been the winner, from the beginning to our days." 100. See also 159 where Davies sees current thinking as leading to the restoration of "the old Aristotelian classes of causation, even leaving room for the notion of final causes."
5. Davies, 198.

a universe for them to describe? The usual approach of science constructing a mathematical model cannot answer the questions of why there should be a universe for the model to describe. Why does the universe go to all the bother of existing? Is the unified theory so compelling that it brings about its own existence? Or does it need a creator, and if so, does he have to have any other effect on the universe? And who created him?[6]

There is no reason why his colleague, Roger Penrose, could not object, "Steve, why do you suggest the need for a creator? And aren't you involved in an infinite series when you ask, 'And who created him'? Are you suggesting the universe has a choice of either bothering to come into existence or not bothering? Is such a choice conceivable?" There is no reason why one and the same man cannot and should not be both physicist and philosopher, even though the objects of his unrestricted desire to know are different. That is what makes the brilliant Pirsig so admirable, interesting, and helpful to us all. He is not afraid to move from anthropology, to physics, to history, to language, to biology, to culture, to literature, to chemistry, to philosophy. There is no question that today's physicist and other natural scientists are brilliant persons, capable of philosophizing and speaking in English as well as in math. Their fear of the metaphysical and teleological as being some sort of mysticism is irrational. They can and do think metaphysically and teleologically all the time, for all their study is purposeful, consistent, and concerned with cause. It is time for the natural scientists to break out of the "static pattern" of focusing on phenomena and its mathematical expression and give free reign to their natural desire and ability to think and talk metaphysics. Both we and they will benefit from that growth, just as we benefit from the thought of Pirsig.

There is good reason why Pirsig should feel forced to make quality a thing rather than simply a characteristic and activity existing independent of a subject. He has rejected the notion of substance. There is no "place" to put Dynamic Quality, so just affirm that it is. Fine. If it is the source of all reality, is it the eternal and necessary being that is the rational explanation for contingent being? Since it is the explanation of the evolutionary process, is it the singularity totally identical with the material of the Big Bang? Or did it exist prior to that material, brought that material from pure possible existence into actual existence, and then ignited it? If Pirsig is not speaking metaphorically when he attributes *perception* of good and evil to Dynamic Quality (115) and sees it as the source of intellect evolving from the social phase of evolution, then is not that intellectual activity also

6. Hawking, *A Brief History of Time*, 174.

conscious of itself as both knowing and known? And since nothing exists before this source of all reality goes into action, does it look upon itself as the model and exemplar of the lesser beings it brings into reality? If it is the source of personhood in this universe is it not also personal? And finally, supposing Dynamic Quality is identical with the firecracker before its change into the Big Bang, how does one explain the act that is free from the matter that exhausts the reality of the firecracker. The act of understanding, as the arbitrariness of language proves, is essentially independent of matter. Whence transcendence, since it is not identified with the materiality existing prior to the Big Bang?

Dynamic Quality, therefore, is another example of poetic or metaphorical language. Etymologically, *quality* comes from the Latin adjective *qualis* meaning what sort of, what kind of. The notion of *kind or sort* is derived from specific nature or specific substance or specific essence. Specific natures or substances have essential characteristics that qualify them as members of that kind, sort, class, substance, nature, etc. Pirsig labors to make Dynamic Quality a permanent thing, a collective noun and almost a personification, without letting it become an independent substantial being. He would have been better served had he stayed with one of his synonyms for Dynamic Quality, namely, perfection. Had he used that in an absolute sense, namely the fullness of being, he would have arrived at the concepts of Necessary Being and Contingent Being. Then his descriptive terms of "source of all reality," "best," "indefinable," "ability to perceive," etc., would be proper characteristics of the substantial fullness of being. Then his theory of evolution, initiated and maintained by the Necessary Being's creative and conserving activity, would hold until the point of created freedom, created transcendence, i.e., the evolution of the free human being. At that point there would have had to be some form of creative intervention by the Necessary Being, for an immaterial effect cannot arise from a strictly material evolutionary cause. Such an intervention is readily understandable when one sees the necessity of the conservative action of this Necessary Being. The Necessary Being is present to all contingent being by its conserving power. Such presence makes possible the further creative act that produces life from its lowest form—metabolism, growth, reproduction—to its highest form—transcendence, trust, free society.

Further his notion that all reality is ethical or moral would also hold true in both a proper and metaphorical sense. Man is obliged to be rational, obliged to be open and prevent irrational social customs from suppressing the freedom of his intellect, obliged to restrain the license of individual freedom from overcoming the valid patterns of society (the laws providing for the common good). Insofar as there are structures in reality, structures in the evolutionary process, these can be considered moral in a metaphorical sense, i.e., the structures become the "norms" for the way things should be and according to which man is morally obliged to adapt. If he chooses not to adapt to evidence, he closes his openness and is, therefore, immoral.

The "law" of being is the "law" of mind. Man understands and is forced to create according to possible being. The same is true of the Necessary Being. It cannot create that which is intrinsically contradictory, for that would be to make a non-being—which is nonsense. Rather the Necessary Being understands its fullness and the manner in which that fullness can be imitated in a limited way, e.g., makes the firecracker for the Big Bang. It then chooses some of those imitations and by its unlimited power brings them into being and keeps them in being according to its purpose(s) for creating. This is the only sense in which non-personal creation can be described as ethical or moral. Non-personal reality is the structure that man is obliged to be open to, respect, and act in accord with. In a word it is the evidence around which he must build his life. To speak of the non-personal world as ethical is to use the metaphor of synecdoche—cause for effect, accepting particular structured reality causes this particular choice to be moral or ethical.

For me the most valuable contribution Pirsig makes in moral philosophy is the insight that "We must understand that when a society undermines intellectual freedom for its own purposes it is absolutely morally bad, but when it represses biological freedom for its own purposes it is absolutely morally good. These goods are not just 'customs.' They are as real as rocks and trees." (309) That is a good contrast between the metaphysical real and the phenomenological real.

The peace of American society today is threatened with deterioriation and destruction because it is paralyzed. The paralysis comes from what Pirsig calls a confusion between social codes and intellectual codes of morality. (307) The individual rights issue, which is essentially a concern for the individual against the power of society, has brought us to a state of boderline anarchy, as is evidenced by rampant violent crime, frequent riots, and slowness with which the courts and the penal system re-establish justice. As Pirsig says, we haven't got ". . . a single moral principle that distinguishes a Galileo fighting social repression from a common criminal fighting social repression." Our amoral objectivity has been "the champion of both. That's the root of the problem." (306)

"Society can handle biology alone by means of prisons and guns and police and the military. But when intellectuals in control of society take biology's side against society then society is caught in a cross-fire from which it has no protection." (300)

And what is Pirsig's solution? "Intellect can support static patterns of society without fear of domination by carefully distinguishing those moral issues that are social-biological from those that are intellectual-social and making sure there is no encroachment either way." (300)

Pirsig is advocating, as do I, the creation of a moral philosophy. I find fault with his creation because Dynamic Quality is essentially a metaphor, dependent upon numerous synonyms, which does not succinctly deal with the objection "Don't tell me what Dynamic Quality is like, tell me what it is. Define it clearly, so that I can see what it is and how it is distinct from all other things that are."

In my opinion, this one nation of diverse individuals and groups ("E pluribus unum") must develop a natural law philosophy based on the transcendent nature of man—the freedom and equality of all existing in a society and government designed to protect that freedom and equality from the criminal element that arises in our midst. Such a philosophy will guide our actions in creating peace. Such a condition of peace will then make it possible for individuals and groups of individuals to go about the business of satisfying their unrestricted desire to know, to trust, and thus create a better life for themselves and others. Integrity, accepting the evidence revealed by our transcendence, is the first principle of such a natural law morality and philosophy.

15

Singer's
Practical Ethics

Peter Singer's revised second edition of *Practical Ethics*[1] must be considered here because it is recent, has had wide publication, is learned, and significantly differs from or is in conflict with many of the ideas of this book. I found his style to be very fair, neither polemical nor rhetorical when opposing other theories of ethical positions. I found his arguments in favor of active and passive euthanasia, the more humane treatment of animals, and respect for the inanimate environment quite convincing. On the other hand, there is much that is inadequate, philosophically wrong, and in one instance, arbitrary with his explanations of the data on which he bases his ethical theory.

Essentially his philosophy of ethics is the utilitarianism of Bentham and Mill. He would go beyond their criterion of the ethical (increase pleasure reduce pain) to furthering the interests of all those affected by the human action. He is not certain that this criterion was not included in theirs (14). The principle of equality of interests must guide our ethical decisions. Interests are interests, no matter whose they are (21). Following Bentham he extends equality beyond the human species to animals. The criterion for equality is not whether other species can reason or talk, but whether they can suffer (56, 57). Since they have an interest in avoiding pain and an interest living, the right attitude [our ethical disposition?] is to avoid killing them for food (287) unless killing them is necessary for survival (134). The concept of person is any being that is self-conscious, rational (87), and aware of itself as a distinct entity existing over time with a past and a future (111). The fact that an orangutan, an ape, a chimpanzee, and a gorilla have learned some sign language, have shown a concern for past and future events, and indicate the ability to plan is proof that they are persons, though not of our species (110-117). Conversely, those beings that

---

1. Peter Singer, *Practical Ethics*, Second Edition, Cambridge University Press, New York, 1993.

cannot do these things are not persons. That would include not only the human embryo and fetus, but also the human infant. None of those things, or stages of human development, has the right to life (183). They are subordinate to other interests, e.g., abortion, embryonic and limited fetal experimentation (165), passive and active euthanasia(213), infanticide (173), which is not morally worse than abortion (190). His other ethical positions are: the rich, those living in absolute affluence, ought to give a tenth of their income to those living in absolute poverty (246), politicians have the moral and geopolitical obligation to take in refugees (262) and the number is to be determined by the basic utilitarian method, i.e., measuring the pleasure/pain, counting the consequences, balancing the benefits. Anything that is harmful to the environment is ethically dubious and anything that is unnecessarily harmful is plainly wrong. Extravagance and unnecessary consumption are vices; conservation and recycling are virtues (285). Terrorist violence is unethical, but not all violence is necessarily wrong, e.g., violence done to a laboratory to liberate animals from painful experimentation would have to be judged according to utilitarian criteria, i.e., consequences, balance of benefits (313).

The critique of Singer's work will show that it is arbirary, shallow, founded in a contradiction, and, based on his own premise, can have little meaning. It will then consider particular statements that we think are erroneous. I realize that this general statement, though clear, is extremely harsh, particularly in the light of the evident learning and research incorporated in his work. No disrespect or ridicule will be stated or implied. But the evidence seems to justify the critique.

SINGER'S ETHIC IS ARBITRARY

Singer says that "Ethics requires us to go beyond the "I" and "you" to the universal law, the universalisable judgment, the standpoint of the impartial spectator or ideal observer, or whatever we choose to call it." (12) It must go beyond the individual and his particular culture. (4) Yet in another passage he doubts ". . . that there is any morally significant property that all humans possess equally." (19) Put another way there is no basis found in all men for a universal ethic. Yet he acts as if there were, for he appeals to something common in all men, their intelligence, by writing books, having them tranlated into several languages and obviously hopes that people will understand him and change their behavior. On the other hand he says there are ". . . ethical ideals—like individual rights, the sanctity of life, justice, purity, and so on—that are universal in the required sense." (14) It is not clear that Singer identifies ethical ideal with ethical obligation. I assume he does so. But whether he does or not, he offers no explanation or proof of the universality of ethics. The most he can offer is that other ethicians, who differ on many counts, agree on one thing: ethics must be universal. (11) He does not give their arguments. This makes his position suspect. Further, towards the very end of his book he undermines his position on universality by saying " 'Why act morally?' cannot be given an answer that will provide everyone with overwhelming [convincing?] reasons for acting morally." (335)

The basic problem with a universal ethic is a philosophical one, namely is the reality in any universal idea such as man, animal, fish, insect, etc. really found fully and equally in the individual from which it is abstracted and to which it is predicated. We are back to the first chapter, back to the question of whether the testimony of the intellect can be trusted. Singer must be listed along with Pirsig, Pringle, Tribe, and Wilson as one who wonders whether there is such a thing as a human nature, human substance, human essence that has essential properties of intelligence and free will and has other properties that are not essential to it, such as color, size, gender, talents and inclinations. Implicitly rejecting the notion of a universal human nature, Singer has to look elsewhere for a basis of a universal ethic. This leads him and other utilitarians to the impossible task of counting consequences, measuring pleasure, balancing benefits of the greatest number. And since psychopaths look like the rest of human beings, but find pleasure in moral and immoral behavior, Singer must find some way of excluding them from the universality of ethical behavior. (328-332) Like Wilson, Singer is afraid he might find a human being who isn't human. No problem. Give whatever you find a new name based on the essential difference discovered, but don't deny the obvious. Those beings that think, abstract, use arbitray signs, make progress to transcend the cycle of survival and species generation, communicate in trust are all equally human because they have the same nature that can do these things. The psychopath may be human, but we recognize him as a sick human and consequently cannot be expected to act as he should, humanly. He has been deprived, by whatever cause, of something that ought to be present. Consequently, whether he experiences pleasure or not when he functions is irrelevant because his functioning is impaired. We know this because the term psychopath fits him. We validly abstracted this characteristic from the phenomena he offers us, just as we abstracted normal from the phenomena of normal men. In a word Singer arbitrarily postulates universality when he need only analyze his own behavior, namely he writes and has translated books for beings that are intelligent, can understand, and ought to make the right choices based on evidence. The behavior implies that there is out there in the real world   a constant, permanent substance, nature, essence that is equally reduplicated again and again with different languages, different races, different genders, sizes, weights, talents, inclinations. That reality is the human being, that reality is the basis for a universal ethic, for a moral way of living that is absolute and not relative to particular circumstances or cultures. Human nature and its good is the criterion whereby all cultures and all behaviors are to be judged as ethical or unethical, moral or immoral.

SHALLOWNESS

Singer's criterion for the morally good or bad act is shallow. An action is right ". . . if it produces as much or more of the increase in the happiness of all affected by it than any alternative action, and wrong if it does not." (3) It stops at the point of phenomena, i.e., measuring pleasure, counting consequences, balancing benefits to see which acts promote the happiness, pleasure of the most. It could and should go further to the nature, essence, substance of the human and see what is good, what completes that substance. What is first and foremost good for that substance is the free act or choice to face evidence and conform to it. That evidence is not simply things and their meaningful relation to the person, but most importantly that evidence includes himself and others as needing union with one another in trust to overcome isolation and loneliness. That radical obligation to be open and accept the world and his fellow man leads to the further obligations to be prudent, just, temperate, and courageous in facing the world and forming union with his fellow men. Only subsequent to these moral decisions can man go on to be concerned about the pleasures/pains of the many, to consider the place of animals, embryos, the poor, the refugee, the environment, the place of abortion and euthanasia in moral life. For all these decisions depend upon his radical openness and honesty. These decisions will not be made in a vacuum, but always in some relation to his fellow man. Hence the need for openness and honesty, the need for choosing integrity, the radical choice for every human.

THE CONTRADICTION AND ABSENCE OF MEANING

Singer's ethic has as its foundation a contradiction and a statement that makes his entire effort logically meaningless. The contradiction: "Ethically indefensible behaviour is not always irrational." (314) One defends or justifies a behavior by giving reasons for it. If the behavior is indefensible, no reasons can be given to justify it. If reasons can be given to justify a behavior, it is defensible. Singer's statement is a statement that is grammatically correct, but void of meaning.

The reason for saying Singer's entire effort is meaningless is because he states "Life as a whole has no meaning. . . . It did not happen for any overall purpose." (331) If the whole has no meaning, the parts must be meaningless, too. Since his ethic is a part of human life it is meaningless, too. The additional negative comment that life has no overall purpose is logically, as with all negatives, most difficult to prove. The most that can be said for it is that it is Singer's opinion. The purpose or teleology that can be found in everything from the atom to the brain suggests an overall purpose. The fact and implied meaning of contingent being demands one. In our Chapter 2 we dealt with the God of philosophy, his existence, and our real but limited knowledge of his nature. Briefly, an infinite series of contingent beings cannot explain the fact of contingent being. Therefore there must be a necessary being who is as personal, intelligent, powerful, and purposeful as the intelligent beings that depend upon him for their being and conservation in being. Further, since the necessary being is the fullness of being or perfect being it is impossible that he act imperfectly, without purpose, have an act proceed from him that is not under his direct control and consistent with his intelligent nature. To assert there is no purpose to life is to make a leap from ignorance of possible fact to the assertion of a non-fact. This is all the more illogical in the face of the need to explain the fact of contingent being.

PARTICULAR POINTS OF DISAGREEMENT

THE EQUALITY OF ANIMALS

Singer finds fault with the habit of making sharp distinctions between ourselves and other sentient species (110). But the distinction is there. We reason and talk. They don't. The fact that all of us can suffer means not that we are all essentially the same, but rather that we are all essentially sentient. The fact that a rational animal is an animal, and therefore essentially sentient, does not mean there is no other reality as part of its essence that is the objective reason for habitually distinguishing it sharply from other species. It is precisely this essential characteristic in all the peoples and cultures of our experience that is the reason for speaking of them as human beings—whether they live in the Amazon, the Arctic, the Outback, or Atlanta—they all use arbitrary signs to communicate. They choose to be hostile or friendly, they can learn one another's language and adapt and embrace one another's culture. In a word they transcend the cycle of survival and reproduction and can learn one another's methods of transcending that cycle. Other species have adapted to but none has transcended its environment to move beyond acquiring its essential needs to create the unnecessarily useful and the pleasant—because none of them has the unrestricted desire to know and therefore none is nor can be transcendent. The bird and the monkey may use a twig to dig out a grub or catch a termite, (72) but neither on its own or with the help of manipulative humans develops methods for cultivating and harvesting grubs and termites. Such cultivation and harvesting might be useful and pleasant, but they are not necessary.

Singer clearly wants to diminish the significance of the distinction between man and other sentient beings. The fact that they have different interests and can suffer when deprived of them is not relevant. Interests are interests, no matter whether man's or animals'. Since that is so, the moral principle for ethical man is what Singer calls the principle of equal consideration of interests (21, 55). This is the bridge he uses to say that men and animals are equals and that as it is wrong to exploit man it is equally wrong to exploit animals, except when man needs them for survival (134).

Why the exception? How does the human so differ from the animal that he is justified in inflicting suffering and death on the animal if interests are just interests and nothing more? The only logical reason is that man is superior and the animal is not man's equal. The animal has no absolute right to life but only one relative to man, the superior animal. Since the animal is only relatively independent and equal to man, why should subordination be limited to survival and not to utility and pleasure? Is it really in the interests of the species horse, dog, cat to be domesticated rather than exist in the wild, to be spayed, neutered, and gelded rather than roam free in an ecosystem that in time would balance the various populations? And pushing the logic of survival to the utmost, why would cannibalism be wrong? Or would it? It is wrong because men are independent of one another, not subordinate to one another, whereas animals are not free, not transcendent, and so subordinate to man and can be exploited by him at the very least when necessary for his survival. Not so man who is always man's equal and therefore can never be exploited by him for any purpose.

ABORTION AND INFANTICIDE

The criterion Singer uses for determining the existence of a person are behaviors, namely rationality, autonomy, self-awareness. He finds these in some animals and does not find them in the embryo, fetus, or the week old infant. Since the behaviors are not there, the person is not there, and since the person is not present, there is no question of a right to life. If no other consideration of rights are involved, all of these may be directly killed with moral impunity. Nothing morally bad is done, no guilt should be incurred. Singer says that embryonic life is only a cluster of cells (157). This is another negative that is hard to prove. And the available evidence points in another direction.

First, we are talking about human life, that which develops into the adult person; it does not develop into a tree, a fish, a dog, an insect. Consequently, there must be something distinctive about this life that is not found in other lives, especially other animal lives. Second,what must be said is that life (called human) is intrinsically vegetative, sentient, intellectual, and personal in its nature, substance, essence because it can and does direct its material aspect to constant acts of ever higher forms of being— the needed conditions for vegetative, sentient, intellectual, and personal being. The life, from its very beginning is personal because its purposeful development is to create conditions for activities that surpass the activities of mere animals and produce the unrestricted desire to know, choose, create, trust. This visible reality called man that can do these things is the natural symbol of the one specific life within it.

We must recall that life is a philosophical concept, a meaning derived from observable phenomena in purposeful motion. It is not those phenomena. It is not simply a cluster of cells in motion. Purpose is present in addition to cells in motion. The question that must be asked and given a reasonable answer is: What is that purpose? The answer is that we understand that purpose from watching the action it directs until it reaches its completion. In the case of the human "cluster of cells" that purpose directing them is to develop through nutrition a vegetative, sentient, intellectual, volitional, personal being that not only can understand, but use that understanding to meet other humans in a union of trust. The life and the purposeful activity that it pursues is primarily personal because the vegetative and sentient powers that it produces are subordinate to, exist for, and serve the intellectual and personal. Put another way the life, the spirit, the soul, the psyche, the animating principle expresses itself first by means of body organs and then by using those organs to give an ever more complete expression of what it can do if it is nourished and allowed to mature. Those physical and intellectual expressions are the natural symbol, the natural expression, of its life that is present from the beginning until its death. The life is radically personal, radically free and independent, with rights to life, liberty and the pursuit of happiness. A natural scientist may be excused from deciding whether the cluster of cells is a person; but a philsopher, and ethics is moral philosophy, must go beyond phenomena and affirm meaning of phenomena. The meaning is that the embryo, the fetus, the infant who does not reason, is not self-aware, is nonetheless personal in the most fundamental meaning of its life. Consequently, taking that life without sufficient reason is immoral. The killer becomes by that act an unjust and bad person.

Singer feels that the embryo splitting into identical twins illustrates the absurdity of holding that the embryo is a person. (157) Did we begin with Mary and then get Jane, or did Mary leave and we now have Helen and

Jane? One can smile at all this and say Mary never left, Helen never came and Jane was there from the beginning. The cell did not split; rather they split the cell. How else account for duality of independent actions without duality of actors? That would not imply that the split was accomplished by two rational choices and acts. But it would imply that two distinct principles of personal human life are the sufficient explanation for the two distinct acts of separating or moving away from one another with each going its own independent way of development.

ANIMALS AS PERSONS

Singer's position that animals are personal is refuted by the fact that they do not perform acts that transcend their environment. Nowhere does Singer use the word "instinct" as clearly distinguished from intelligence. In fact the word does not appear in the book. He does not consider the difference from being trained through positive reinforcement and being educated through insight. The example of the chimpanzee deceiving and planning against the dominant chimpanzee (115,116) is not altogether different from the mother bird pretending to be wounded and fluttering away from her nested chicks in order to distract and lead away man, the fox, bobcat, or other presumed predator. A clear distinction between instinctive behavior and intelligent behavior is needed before humans are to be persuaded that some animals are persons in the strict, proper, and not metaphorical sense.

　　We have already seen why animals are not equal to humans and therefore have no right to escape subordination to man not only in the matter of his survival, but also for his utility and pleasure. The moral use of animals is simply to use them for his benefit, his progress in understanding, and benefiting from mastering his environment. Proper use, therefore supposes that no or minimal pain be inflicted upon them during that use. Use that has pain and suffering as an unavoidable consequence is a moral use. It would be an abuse and therefore immoral use to permit avoidable suffering. For that is irrational, purposeless, without meaning. For rational man to act irrationally is to act against his nature and hence is an immoral act. Singer's principle about the environment is applicable to animals, i.e., anything that is unnecessarily harmful is plainly wrong.

LIFE AS SACRED

Strictly speaking the most sacred thing in our experience is not God or God's word, nor God's gift of life. The most sacred thing is our intelligence, for it is the source of our understanding and attributing sacredness to any reality. Only if intelligence is inviolate can anything of value be recognized as good or sacred. For it is by means of his intelligence that man uses and disposes of his world, his life, and his self. Consequently, to act blindly, to act on unexamined and unvalidated authority, is to abdicate reason and to attempt to escape responsibility for acts of omission and commission. Thus to avoid taking life, whether one's own or another's, simply because one believes it is from God, deliberately conserved by God, is a refusal to see what that divine gift really is. It is not a gift as we usually understand that term, e.g., a birthday, wedding, or Christmas present. Rather that gift of life is the gift of freedom, intelligence, and power to do the meaningful and to stop the meaningless, e.g., the meaningless suffering of the terminally ill and the meaningless life of the person we are capable of forcing to live as a vegetable.

We must ask ourselves what is our responsibility when faced with such evidence. What is the cowardly act? What is the courageous act? What act makes us the responsible person which the gift of life demands we be?

Granting the powerful Hebrew-Christian tradition to the contrary, within that tradition is the belief that one must act upon what one understands to be true. In the face of evidence that responsible life is or will be impossible, or where the quality of life is nothing but pain, direct taking of life is reasonable and moral. Not to do so is cowardice and immoral because it is to run away from evidence and refuse to accept what the intellect tells us is true. The only restriction on such an act is evidence that causes us to doubt what is apparently true. If there is reasonable doubt that the individual in question can or will be able to decide for himself, then that person must be given the benefit of the doubt. To do otherwise is to be willing to take life against the wishes of its possessor and so act unjustly.

Thus suicide, assisted suicide, and euthanasia can be morally good, even heroic acts.

How this principle is to be applied in specific instances is a matter of supreme importance. The application cannot be allowed to be the first step down the slippery slope toward condoning murder or state genocide. But that is a separate moral problem and challenge. Until such challenge is sufficiently met, we can be reasonably assured that direct killing of those in absolute pain or those who are permanently physically incompetent of free choice will not be universally accepted as a morally justified act, even though in particular instances it should be.

One may well say this so called challenge is a moral monstrosity. It is also monstrous to refuse to think about and devise some solution to the problem of the suffering of the terminally ill and the problem of life for the totally incompentent. Thoughts to meet such a challenge might be as follows. First, let the competent terminally ill choose to be assisted in their suicide. Second, let the relatives decide on the death of the personally totally incompetent. Then let that decision be supported or denied by the family physician or psychiatrist. Then let the state's health officer confirm or deny those decisions. Finally, if the decisions favor euthanasia, let the relative(s) administer the lethal action in accord with procedures prescribed by the state. Thus moral responsibility would be with the relatives, and social responsibility would be with the state.

SOCIAL PROBLEMS: THE REFUGEE, THE POOR, THE ENVIRONMENT

THE REFUGEE

Singer's position on refugees (247 ff) makes sense, though it can be considered inadequate, especially in light of recent events in Bosnia, Rwanda, and Haiti. Instead of accepting as many refugees as is reasonable, we should consider preventing the cause of their being refugees, namely occupation and overthrow of the persecuting government. To appreciate the reasonableness of such an action one need only recall the U. S. overthrow and occupation of Japan. By means of a constitution political power was transferred from the emperor to the people, 200,000 were declared ineligible for political office, land reform enabled farmers to own their own land, zaibatsu firms were broken up and labor unions established. After these changes were imposed and and supported for three years, the U. S. gradually surrendered its control and by 1952 the occupation officially ended. Both peoples benefited from those forcibly imposed changes. There were no refugees involved, but the former government, had it been allowed to continue, could have led to the same situation that ultimately caused war.

The moral principle involved in intervening in a persecuting and unjust government is the same as that when a person sees a child drowning in a pool. The need is obvious, the resources are present, a human in distress calls to a human in power, the human in power must answer with a "No" or a "Yes" or a "I wonder if I should get involved." He has no other alternatives. The last answer is, of course, a "Not now" answer and is a decision not to be united to another, a decision to be closed, and so immoral. Saving the dying results in gratitude from the saved and the experience of a personal union between both. If there is no answer to the call, the caller dies and the called knows he did not do what he could and should have done. He shut himself off, closed himself off from his neighbor and is not only left alone, but left alone with the fact that he could have made a friend by saving him. He is guilty of an immoral act of omission.

THE POOR

Much the same is true with the case of the absolute affluent and the absolute poor. One of the first questions that must be asked when trying to correct a poverty that is beneath any reasonable definition of human decency (231) is: How did it happen? And a second question should be asked: How did the affluent become so? Beyond question, the widespread affluence is found primarily in the West and has come out of Western civilization. Why did not the same thing happen in Africa, China, Russia, South America, India, the Arab countries? Democracy, freedom from superstition and freedom of and from religion, abundance of natural resources, devotion to learning and especially to philosophy and the natural sciences led to the industrial revolution and to the advances in technology that have brought wealth and affluence to the West. Therefore one of many reasons why so much of the world is in poverty is because it has not done what the West did. A partial solution, and only a partial one, to the problem of absolute poverty is for the poor to begin imitating the West. This does not ignore the effects of limited resources, the injutice and insensitivity of comfortable and affluent nations. It considers only a part of the problem and part of the solution for the absolute poor.

If the poor so hold onto religious beliefs, cultural practices, and ethnic divisiveness that prevent peaceful cooperation in the management of natural resources, then one can expect suffering. When natural disasters occur such as drought, flooding, famine, and disease one can expect massive death. Such pain may cause some among them to say we must live differently, we must have different leaders who will help us see our way out of this continuous cycle of misery.

That being said what is the West, the affluent nations and the affluent individuals, obligated to do? The first obligation is to continue its unrestricted desire to know, to create, to engineer, to create societies that insure justice as men freely pursue these goals. Within those general obligations will be the particular ones, the ones that oblige the individual and him alone. Being free to look at his world and himself in it, he will see what fits him, what he must do to be happy, at peace with himself. Out of those individual obligations will come the decisions to improve and reform his government, to do research, to create works of music and art, to travel, to communicate with other peoples, to work with other peoples, etc. One cannot predict what a free man will feel he must do nor predict what he will actually do, precisely because he is free. The reason why the West must continue to do these things is the same reason why poor should have done them long ago: Namely they are, as all men, free, transcendent, open to the knowledge of anything and everything as well as the relations existing among them. And the reason the individual must see how he fits in and act accordingly is because he is a unique being and so must be true to what he is not only as a human among humans, but as this human among these humans.

That being said what must the affluent nations and affluent individuals do now, and why must they do it?

Singer's position is that the nations should give at least 0.7% of their Gross National Product (222) to help alleviate the misery of the absolute poor. An affluent individual should give 10% of his income for the same purpose. Singer describes the absolute poor in the words of former World Bank President, Robert Macnamara, as ". . .severely deprived human beings struggling to survive in a set of squalid and degraded circumstances almost beyond the power of our sophisticated nations and privileged circumstances to conceive(219). . .[with] per capita incomes under $200 a year" (222). The affluent are such ". . . by any reasonable definition of human needs. [They] choose their food for the pleasures of the palate, not to stop hunger; they buy clothes to look good, not to keep warm; they move from house to house to have a better neighbourhood . . . not to keep out of the rain; and after all this there is still money to spend on stereo systems, video-cameras, and overseas holidays." (221) Granted the truth of this, there is also another truth found in the maxim "The luxuries of today are the necessities of tomorrow." Example: Years ago every engineer had an expensive slide rule. A high school senior may have had one costing fifty cents. Today every high school junior needs a scientific calculator, which costs less than the expensive slide rules of old. The luxuries become necessities dependent upon the technological progress of the society in which one lives.

But something else must always be kept in mind. First animals and vegetation are related as food to the rational animal man. They nourish him. But he is more than an animal. His ideal is not to become one with nature nor to be just another species that is born, forages or hunts and kills and eats his victim, reproduces his own and then dies. It is not his goal and purpose to eat all his food raw, nor to drink only water, and that from lakes, streams, and puddles. He is not only a part of the material world, he transcends it. Therefore he is able to understand food and thereby create beverages and cuisine. He is able to put art into food and thereby sustain himself as a man and not merely as an animal. In doing this he is not merely satisfying his hunger, nor his hunger and palate, but both of those and his need to eat in a social setting with family and friends. Consquently the raising of sentient animals for food is justified on two counts: First they are structured to nourish him, and second as food they can and do contribute to his social life. The proper use of food is governed by the virtue of temperance. The proper use of animals is to be governed by the general principle governing the use of the planet: Use it in such a way as to leave it for our fellow man as well off or better than we inherited it from our forbearers.

Why must individuals and nations pay to alleviate some of the absolute poor? Singer says they must pay because they can do so without sacrificing anything of comparable moral significance (231). To illustrate the sacrifice he uses the example of the professor on the way to give a lecture and sees a child drowning in a pool or pond. His sacrifice is that he dirties and perhaps ruins his clothes, and is late or misses his appointment altogether. That loss does not compare with the loss of the child's life, therefore he must make the sacrifice. Similarly, if we as a nation or as individuals do not make the recommended sacrifices people in absolute poverty will die. Though we can't save all of them, we can save some. If we don't, we let people die, and this is comparable to negligent manslaughter wherein I like the luxury of speed, have no intention of killing someone, but I do. I am indifferent to the consequences of speeding, just as I am indifferent to the consequences of luxury, i.e., the starving do not get my money for their food because I spend it on my luxury. (227)

Singer's conclusion that one's self and one's nation must help the absolute poor, is one that I accept, but I would see the obligation coming from the fact the humans involved are made for union with one another, that the poor are crying out to us, not by their voices, but by the very fact of their existence known to us all through travel and the media of print and television. They call and we must answer because we hear them.

But what must that answer be? First, it seems that one should do something as a citizen working through his government[2], and secondly as an individual acting independently of his government. As a citizen I should learn what my government is doing and consider whether that is the right thing and enough of the right thing. As an individual acting independently, I should look to myself and ask what I can do through the various non-profit agencies designed to help these people, and select the one that makes most sense to me. It is not at all clear that the gift of 0.7% of GNP and 10% of an individual's income is just right, too little, or too much. The point to remember in all this is: What happens to me as a person, not as a thing that will now have as he gives to the poor, but what becomes of me when I act, or procrastinate, or simply refuse to give. What happens to my openness, my integrity in the face of the evident absolute poor? Do I accept the evidence and act upon it? Or do I ignore it? The answer I give to that question is not merely a matter of life and death to some of the absolute poor, but it is a matter of my goodness or lack thereof, a matter of my honesty and integrity as I look at the poor and as I look at myself.

THE ENVIRONMENT

After reading Singer's very thoughtful and forceful "Developing and Environmental Ethic" (284-288) one can hardly believe that he means what he

---

2. As a matter of hindsight one could ask whether a government should have gone into Somalia, subdued by force the various warlords, set up a new government, and supervised it for a few years of occupation, somewhat as was done in Japan by the United States.

says later on "Life *as a whole* has no meaning." He affirms, he makes an act of faith in the meaning of life when he illustrates and condemns all sorts of extravagances harmful to the environment and recommends personal relationships as the radical pleasures of life. He talks the utilitarian language of pleasure when he writes

> the pleasures it [environmental ethic] values do not come from conspicuous consumption. They come, instead, from warm personal and sexual relationships, from being close to children and friends, from conversation, from sports and recreations that are in harmony with our environment instead of being harmful to it; from food that is not based on the exploitation of sentient creatures and does not cost the earth; from creative activity and work of all kinds; and (with due care so as not to ruin precisely what is valued) from appreciating the unspoiled places in the world in which we live. (288)

He speaks empirically; I speak philosophically. He speaks of pleasure from human relationships and using the world in proper order. I speak of the meaning of man as being the communication in trust with his fellow man. Ethically speaking, we are not far apart. Philosophically speaking we are miles apart, mainly because Singer won't descend explicitly to metaphysics. His ethic is empirical: Pleasure not moral goodness, experience not meaning of phenomena, the largest number not universal human nature—these are his criteria to determine whether an act is morally good or not. He does not ask "What is the good man, but what is the ethical man." His answer is "He whose act brings the most pleasure to the most." He does not realize that pleasure and happiness result from a conscious being experiencing its own goodness, its own being in order with itself and its world. Consequently the fundamental ethical or moral question is not what brings happiness or pleasure, but rather what choices are consistent with and completing of his transcendental nature. Those choices are the meaning of his life. What they specifically are to be will be learned by experience and study of himself and his world. The basic obligation, the obligation that can never be rejected without perverting himself, is the obligation to face reality and to be open in trust with his fellow man. This is the only choice that can produce personal, as opposed to intellectual pleasure (e.g., invention, creation, problem solving), animal pleasure (e.g., food, drink, sex) and intellectual-animal pleasure (e.g., beauty of nature and fine arts).

He does not go any deeper than that, namely to the transcendent nature of man that is open to all reality, open to unity, goodness, truth, beauty. He does not see the human nature and substance as essentially capable and needing integrity through assenting to reality, especially the reality of his fellow human being who needs him and whom he needs in a union of trust.

I must admit that Singer's data and concern for the apparent extravagances of modern life, e.g., factory farming, factory animal production, the use of 38% of the world's grain to produce beef, pork, and poultry, the effect of fossil fuels and fluorocarbons on the atmosphere, etc. makes me reconsider my own present and past behavior. What he has done in this respect is to change his readers from being pathetic persons contributing to their own harm into tragic persons who now realize that many of their behaviors are irrational, senseless and should be stopped. Otherwise they will lose their integrity, for now they know better.

What is the practical thing to do? First, decide to change. Then as was said earlier, act as a citizen and then act as an independent person. Acting as a citizen means to take some political action suggested by one's insight. Acting independently means changing one's wasteful behaviors into reasonable ones and, if possible, join and work through some environmental group that seems most reasonable.

What has happened largely because of Singer and those who have preceded him is that people are seeing the inadequacies and harmful consequences associated with their activities to transcend mere surviving and perpetuating the human species. Capitalism and free enterprise have created wealth, leisure, liberation from grinding poverty and disease so that people can not only live, but live well. But those successes have created air and water pollution, carcinogens, holes in the ozone layer, atomic wastes, destruction of rain forests etc.— side effects that were not immediately known and appreciated in the euphoria of the creative moment. We have learned something. We are not as reckless as we once were. Some of us, working as citizens and as individuals are trying to respect both the creativity of men as well as the possible deleterious effects of those creations. We attempt to prevent them by law. This is to do as Lippmann says: Our government demanding justice of us as we conduct our affairs in freedom. Part and parcel of that just behavior is the realization that private property must be limited by individuals and governments in such a way that this planet and universe is to be used not abused, that it is to be passed on to those who come after us in a condition that is as good or better than it came to us. At best we can own it for the three or four score and ten, then we leave it. During that time the honest thing to do is to understand it and choose to adapt to it, i.e., see how it can help us remove poverty and disease, overcome oppression, promote union and peace. The idea that we as individuals or corporations or nations should harm, destroy or exhaust any of its resources for our own ninety years of life is irrational. For that is to ignore that we, as our forefathers were, are a part of human life, a segment of that life which has a past and a future. And that as we have benfited from what they have done and suffered because of their mistakes and crimes, so we must build on their successes and learn from their mistakes and crimes. Our goal is to be more moral , more ethical than they were because we can. We have the unrestricted desire to know , to know how, to do the truth about the world and about ourselves.

A final comment on Singer's work. I found it admirable for its research and learning; but the quality I admired most is his integrity exemplified in his changing his position because of the insight of a fellow scholar, Derek Parfit (365).

ADDENDUM

Shortly after this manuscript was submitted to my publishers, my son gave me a copy of the articulate and learned *Shadows of Forgotten Ancestors*[3] by Carl Sagan and Ann Druyan. I do not question any of the instances of animal behavior documented by the authors. But I do question that the difference between human beings and other animals, e.g., chimpanzees, bonobos, and perhaps apes, is merely one of degree and not of kind.

The authors find that the traditional essential characteristics differentiating man from his simian ancestors are invalid.[4] Invalid because similar characteristics, e.g., intelligence, language, tool making, tool using, a form of religion, can be found in animals. And yet they speak of the human species as being unique (403), our greater intelligence is the hallmark of our species (407). Such language connotes more than a graudal difference of our species from others.

As has been said earlier in this book, man is the unrestricted desire to know. Being is the proper object of the intellect, anything that is is knowable, and science is the knowledge of causes. Man asks how, why, what is the cuase, and he has found answers again and again. Man has done so not merely to survive and propagate himself, but has pusued science and art for the sake of themselves. Knowledge and art are their own reward.

Further, Sagan and Druyan say that the human species "must" and "should" use intelligence (406, 407) to better out condition. They urge us to stop extinguishing "another speices every few minutes"; and they blame us as "faithless heirs, squandering the family inheritance with little thought for the generations to come." (413) But obligation, blame, and the ability to hear, understand, and choose—all these suppose freedom. Yet nowhere in their work do the authors mention freedom, responsibility, obligation.

---

3. Carl Sagan and Ann Druyan, *Shadows of Forgotten Ancestors*, Ballantine Books, New York, 1993.
4. See in particular the last three chapters of their book: "19 What is Human," 20 The Animal Within," and "21 Shadows of Forgotten Ancestors."

And, as with Peter Singer, the idea of instinctive behavior is not mentioned, let alone distinguished from the "intelligent" behavior of animals. Implicity the authors affirm a determinism, brought about by a random evolution, in those animals that do not shed blood within the group, avoid parental and sibling incest, mass murder, and main-force warfare (406). The characteristic that distinguishes man specifically from his "intelligent" ancestors is not simply the fact that he understands number, being, cause, effect, justice, rights, and relations as such, but that intelligence is a property of his free being. This substantial and transcendent freedom not only makes arbitrary signs (language) possible, it also makes free choice and moral virtue and immorality possible. The authors nowhere attribute justice or injustice to our ancestors, nor praise nor blame them for their behaviors, yet they do appeal to our freedom and try to persuade us to give up our bad and destructive behavior. We cannot wait for evolution to rid us of these destructive behaviors (414). Implicity, therefore, they admit an essential difference, a difference of kind rather than degree, between us and our ancestors. That difference is our substantial transcendent freedom.

I agree with the authors that we ought to know more about our animality. They have shown us how very similar we are to our ancestors. But similarity is not identify, simian life is not human life. To say that it is to speak metaphorically. Simian life is simply different from human life, but somewhat the same. That similarity is one of anatomy, anatomical structure. But the principle of life, the soul, the psyche of the animal, that principle which gives it unity of being and action, does not give it the freedom found in understanding being, cause, effect, number, justice, rights, etc. Nor does it give the animal the possiblity of free and responsible choice and allow it to be worthy of praise or blame.

There is an essential difference, a differnece of kind and not of degree. That difference is the transcendent, and therefore free, spirit of mankind. Mankind is free to commit incest, shed blood within his home, neighborhood, city, etc. He is free to organize and practice main-force warfare. Apparently our simian ancestors are not. Had they committed these "crimes," they would have rendered themselves extinct. (406) Man can do these things because he can see immediate good for himself and his and at the same time distract himself from the probable or even necessary evil consequences of such actions. Conversely, he can both recognize and respect the freedom and rights of others, whether they be his children, neighbors or members of different countries, tribes, and races. Not only that, but he can be not only just but also charitable—by choice, not by custom, nor by instinct, but by seeing that it is good for himself and for others to be just and charitable. Freedom is the essential difference between the animals that are human and those animals that are not human.

16

Summary and Conclusion

I attempted to do two things in writing this book: 1) To show that the basis of human morality and ethics is expressed in the American political doctrine of freedom, equality, and inalienable rights, and 2) To show that discussing morality and ethics is essentially a philosophical discussion which implies the use of metaphysics and logic. Throughout the discussion, therefore, I had to use the concepts of substance, accident, causality, relation, one, good, true, evil imperfect, etc. And I constantly had to distinguish between proper and metaphorical or analogous predication.

We saw that the nature of man is a complex unit. That one nature is vegetative, sensory, intellectual, volitional, personal. By virtue of his intellect he is transcendent, i.e., open to the understanding of anything that is. This openness is dynamic, not static. It reaches out of being as such; it is the unrestricted desire or appetite to know. Further, this transcendence not only seeks to grasp and know things or objects, but it also is open to the other transcendent, the other person, and seeks to be united to that person in honesty and trust. It does this by means of communication. That honest communication will produce trust and peace between the persons. We saw that man is meant for union with the other; and that loneliness is bad for him. He cannot be at peace if he is alone with no one to accept him and no one for him to accept in the act of trust. Consequently the fundamental ethical and moral act occurs when man accepts or rejects his fellow human being.

Consequently, we had to discuss the nature of human communication and how that trust was to be accomplished. The method, in brief, is to remain open, to listen, to ask factual questions, to be willing to change positions in light of evidence, and to stand firm in one's own position of certitude, opinion, or doubt until sufficient evidence forces a change. The radical moral act therefore is first the internal decision to be open and social, and then the external act of actually implementing that decision as he meets the world and his fellow man. We looked at two types of communication that went beyond the day to day verbal communication, namely sexual communication and the communication in business. We looked at the nature of both and saw that trust was essential to each, trust in the exchange of goods and trust in the exchange of sexual actions.

We saw that the transcendent substance of man, whose essential parts are matter and spirit, implied inalienable rights of life liberty, and the pursuit of happiness, because the foundation for those rights were in man and could not be removed without destroying his nature. That same rational animal nature, since it is common to all men, imposes the obligation of being common, of being an intelligent part of community. Thus man's freedom is limited and circumscribed by the fact that he is one among and with many. He must not only respect their inalienable rights, but he must respect their right to community, to peace among equals. Thus he must participate in achieving the common good through law. That common good is an extension of the peace and trust that occurs in communication among individuals, friends, spouses, family, neighbors, city, state, nation, and nations among themselves.

We considered animal rights for two reasons. First, the issue is prominent, and secondly, it can only be understood if one sees the difference between right in the proper sense and right in the metaphorical sense . The difference is based on the freedom of man and his need for justice, and the absence of freedom in the animal kingdom and so the impossibility of justice there. Man as an animal also lives in the wild where there is no authority to create and sanction prescriptions and prohibitions among his fellow animals. As an inhabitant of the jungle, he is constrained alone by the law of might makes right. He uses the might of his body and mind to subject the animal to his needs, utility, and pleasure. The only "right" an animal has proceeds from the duty man has to himself to use the animal, as any other creature, rationally.

We looked at homosexuality and said that it was a biological perversion that exists within the personal integrity of the gay person. Our main concern was not with the morality of the homosexual but with the morality or immorality of the person who accepts or rejects the homosexual. It seemed a far worse moral evil to pervert one's openness by refusing to trust the gay person than to pervert one's biological structure.

We considered abortion, primarily as a moral, not legal, issue. Though we found much to admire in the method of Tribe's book, *Abortion: The Clash of Absolutes*, we disagreed with its basic position and the philosophy that leads to it. We showed that the fetus is not part of the mother, that gender differences are not to be legally annulled in the name of equality, but rather further investigated so that their correlative relationship can be understood. Such an understanding would contribute to both the male and female's personal maturity. Finally, we raised the question of whether it is ethical to act in doubt, i.e., whether it is moral to kill the fetus while one is in a state of doubt as to whether the fetus is a person or not.

We critiqued the books of Pirsig, Wilson, and Singer because they are recent studies of the issue of morality. Though we admired much in all three, we found philosophical inadequacies in each. Pirsig rejected the metaphysical notion of substance, but held out for some undefined Dynamic Quality that was given a host of metaphorical names. We saw that quality is just as much a metaphysical term as substance. Wilson's insight that man had an essential desire for attachment, we felt, could be identified with the dynamic transcendence of man which we saw as the explanation of freedom. We found fault with Wilson's doubt about the uniformity of human nature and his entertaining the possibility that its openness was limited in the individuals of some cultures. We felt he could not consistently reject a morality based on cultural relativism without having some criterion by which to judge cultures. that criterion is the transcendence of man or his desire for attachment, and a culture is to be judged as good or bad insofar as it helps or impedes the person in his tendency to be united with any other person, regardless of that person's cultural background.

Singer showed a great concern for sentient creatures, the environment, the poor, the refugee. He was consistent in his reasoning about suicide, assisted suicide, and euthanasia. However we found fault with his philosophy of man. He really does not have one. He can not admit the existence of a common human substance that is essentially intelligent, volitional, personal whose purpose is to be united with other in trust through communication by means of arbitrary signs. Consequently, the universality of his ethic is arbitrary, founded in the agreement of other moral philosophers. We disagreed with him on one other major point, namely, that life on the whole has no meaning. We pointed out that the values of his ill-founded ethic were essentially the same as those we proposed, namely those deriving from the transcendent nature of man.

CONCLUSION

In my opinion, the most immediate and urgent need is for America to harken to Pirsig's insight and advice. Intelligent and rational society must overcome the brute forces of the jungle that are encroaching upon it. The jungle element in the politician, entrepreneur, and professional must be forcibly contained and suppressed. Whether that should occur before, during, or after the violent brute is contained is open to question. One thing is sure, however; society and its drive for peace, seems to be losing its battle against the jungle. Right now crime is worth the insignificant inconvenience of sanction.

In the long view a far more dangerous situation exists in our lack of philosophy and logic. When a distinguished author and scholar can make a

casual remark that people ". . . recognize that the saying 'all men are created equal' is not true," others of less stature can and will say the same
thing and worse. Such a statement is totally destructive of all that America
stands for. As an idea it must be vanquished if American is to continue its
tradition of equality and justice for all. Someone has to see and be able to
distinguish within the one human person substantial humanity, accidental
differences, and personal uniqueness. In other words we have to get over
our fear of natural law philosophy and aggressively develop one. This obligation is inescapable if we admit that freedom and rights exist in human
nature prior to positive law. If we don't develop such a philosophy, then our
way of life will always be threatened by the attractive, learned, eminently
honest, self-confident, rhetorical, articulate person who, unskilled in logic
and metaphysics, is erroneous and casually remarks, "Everyone knows that
all men are not created equal."

Along with this need for a natural law philosophy is the need for logic
and for truly adult discussion. As for logic we need to be able to distinguish
between proper and metaphorical language; be aware of the differences
between sense and metaphysical knowledge. As for discussion, the guide-
lines set down by Carl Rogers along with the principles of transactional
analysis could assure this. Adult must speak to adult with mutual respect
and in a fact finding, problem solving mode. It is time to mature out of the
immature talk show format that is found not only in television and radio,
but even in the classroom.

That format has as its object to present everything from the most bizarre
positions (and persons) to the opinions of the most qualified and conservative experts. But there is never a resolution of the issue. Everyone is equal,
and the assumption is that the opinions are equally valid. Factually that is
impossible, and good research (questioning) will show that one opinion is
actually fact, and its opposite has no validity. That can only happen if the
talk show moderator or teacher is concerned with the issue and the facts,
and has no fear of embarrassing either the bizarre or expert person by
exposing the facts.

On the supposition that both the bizarre and the expert person are open
to evidence, willing to accept it, the discussion moderator can ignore some
or even most of the participants and question those who have relevant facts
to offer. He can and should refuse recognition to those who change the
topic or otherwise offer irrelevant comments. The end result should be
that one or more participants say something like "I'll have to agree with
you an say you are right. We should make the change you suggest."

This rarely happens in panel or classroom discussions; not even in the
more temperate panel discussions seen on public television forums. Why
not? I submit that the embarrassment of admitting my position is wrong is

too punishing both for participant and moderator to be overcome by the reward of learning something new from him/her who differs from me. The moderator lets me off the hook by asking a similar question to another participant. The topic is changed just a bit; the embarrassment is avoided. All the panelists are treated democratically, all get due recognition even though they have less or nothing to offer. Reality and effective action to deal with reality is postponed. The tyranny of reality is overcome by democracy of person and thought; but the tyrant reality will hurt and perhaps kill us later on.

We do not have many role models in the art of adult discussion of issues. Tribe in his book on abortion is clearly one of the best. So, too, are Pringle, Wilson, and Singer, in their very objective presentation of data on animal rights, the environment, and the issue of the moral sense. None of these gentlemen is likely to receive the wide attention their excellent manners deserve. Fortunately, there is an author whose manner is much like theirs and frequently will give up a position to take another in the light of new evidence. Fortunately, millions witness this behavior again and again over the years. Her name is Ann Landers.

Anyone who has read her over any length of time knows two things about her. She does research. She seeks out and gets the opinion of experts in order to offer accurate answers. And most relevant to our topic here, she can eat crow gracefully.[1] Often she has admitted that her advice was wrong; and she gives the reasons, facts sent in by her many readers. This characteristic, in my view, does more for the maturity of Americans than any advice she has ever given. It is the habitual manifestation of integrity, the deliberate choice to be open to the facts. She chooses to become by choice what she is by nature, transcendent, open to reality.

That will always be the struggle and choice for all of us: Either the white lie and the dodge in the face of reality, or the ultimate moral and ethical achievement and reward, personal integrity.

---

1. Hawking and Einstein can do this, too. Hawking writes: "...one of my students...found that in a slightly more complicated model, the collapse of the universe was very different from the expansion. I realized that I had made a mistake...What should you do when you find you have made a mistake like that? Some people never admit they are wrong and continue to find new, and often mutually inconsistent, arguments to support their case—as Eddington did in opposing black hole theory. ... It seems to me much better and less confusing if you admit in print that you were wrong. A good example of this was Einstein, who called the cosmological constant, which he introduced when he was trying to make a static model of the universe, the biggest mistake of his life." Hawking, *A Brief History of Time*, 150, 151.

GLOSSARY

Accident — that which exists in another and cannot exist in itself, e.g., color, weight, movement, etc.

Art — correct way of making something. Implies science, i.e. knowledge of materials and knowledge/skill in using them to accomplish the end intended. Useful art: e.g., carpentry. Fine art: e.g., poetry

Beautiful — that which when perceived pleases the beholder.

Being — that which exists, a transcendental concept and therefore predicated analogously.

Contingent Being — that which exists as dependent upon another for both its existence and essence.

Necessary Being — the uncaused being, the required being for the fact of contingent being, the God inferred by philosophy from the fact of contingent being, the fullness of being, pure act, incapable of internal change because change implies growth in or loss of being. Both are impossible for the fullness of being.

Possible Being — the non-existent that is capable of being brought into existence. The absence of contradiction in its essential elements.

Being, possible or actual — that which can or does exist.

Cause — a principle or source from which a change or difference proceeds, the raison d'etre or justification or explanation of why and how a thing is or differs.

Types of Causality — kinds or classes of being to which the term "cause" can be properly applied.

Efficient cause — the agent that acts purposefully according to chosen design to bring something into being or change an already existing being.

Exemplary cause — the model, plan, or design that guides the efficient cause as it seeks to bring something into being or change something for its own purposes.

Final cause — the purpose or good that moves the efficient cause to act and bring something to be or be changed. There is no purposeless action. Intelligent or instinctive action is always purposeful. A specific nature always seeks its own good. Purpose, end, or good are other words for final cause and determine and explain the action of the efficient cause.

185

Formal cause — the internal source from which the difference or specification of the being proceeds, e.g., the spirit or soul of the human is that from which proceeds his animality and rationality. It informs matter to make possible rationality and animality.

Instrumental cause — a tool used by the agent to effect a change. The effect manifests both the form or species of the tool and that of the agent on the effect, e.g., script shows both the intelligence of the human and the character of the pen and ink.

Material cause — the internal source, which when informed by an animating principle, causes extension, weight, mass of the physical material being.

Moral cause — strictly speaking this is not a cause for it does not bring into being nor change an existing being. It attempts to move a free being to act freely. It presents to a fellow human a good to be sought or an evil to be avoided in the hope that the human will avoid the evil and choose the good.

Extrinsic causes — sources or principles from which things come to be specifically this or that or come to be changed. The two extrinsic cause are are purpose or final cause and efficient cause. Purpose drives the agent to put wood together in the form of a chair. The agent is also extrinsic to the chair; he puts the wood together in the form of the chair.

Intrinsic causes — the source of the change or difference is internal to the thing changed or differentiated, e.g., the specific nature of man causes him to be human, the specific nature of the apple tree causes it to be that kind of tree. Those natures are intrinsic to the particular or individual being. Formal and material causes are intrinsic to the being, e.g., the wooden chair is made of different material from that of the steel chair. Steel or wood is intrinsic to them. Snake and mouse are different species of animal life. The specific vitality of the snake is intrinsic to the snake and causes it to be different from the mouse.

Caveat emptor: — Latin expression: Let the buyer beware.

Conscience — the experience of self as good, evil, indifferent, guilty, honorable as the result of making a choice. It is double knowledge, knowledge of self and knowldege of what one has done.

Corruptio optimi pessima — Latin expression: The corruption of the best is the worst corruption of all.

Effect — a change on something or a difference among things. Each demands an explanation, an answer to the questions of how and why. Without such answers there can be no science nor any art.

Equality — two or more things having the same nature, qualities, size etc. are said to be equal regarding nature or quality or size etc.

Essence — that which determines the specific nature of a being and causes it to be this rather than that, having this name rather than some other.

Ethics/Morality — used interchangeably. The science of what man must freely choose to do to acquire the goodness for which he is designed, i.e. peace as a person and as a social being. The science of obligation.

Evil/Bad — the privation of being or good that should be present in something.

Existence — the act whereby the essence is real rather than purely possible. Essence and existence are components of contingent being. The necessary being's essence is identical with its existence. The necessary being is not composed for that would imply an extrinsic composer.

Fortitude — the habit of standing firm against the difficulties surrounding man's efforts to lead a good life. It is subordinate to prudence and therefore excludes recklessness. It overcomes apathy.

Freedom — the being independent of and transcending limitation.

Good — being considered as perfecting or completing.

Common good — that benefit of law or just government whereby man can conduct his affairs in freedom. The peace and security that permits the full exercise of freedom.

Habit — an abiding moral disposition or inclination to act in a certain way. Sometimes called "second nature" because it imitates the radical or "first" nature of man which disposes him to behave as a rational animal. The habit is acquired through practice and can be for good or evil.

Imperfect — being on the way to completion and more being, e.g., child growing into adolescence and adulthood.

Institutions — the organized and/or customary ways in which society operates., e.g., the government and its programs.

Justice — the habit of giving or rendering to each his due, the habit of respecting the rights of others, whether those others be individuals or societies.

Law, natural — the structure of man that must be respected if he is to maintain and acquire the goods for which he is designed. That structure is both unique and common, individual and social.

Law, positive — an ordination of reason created, sanctioned, and promulgated by those in authority to achieve the common good.

Logic — the forms of human thought about the real world; the principles of argu-mentation and proof whereby one comes to certitude or knowledge rather than mere opinion, probability, or doubt.

Metaphor — an implied comparison between two different things, an analogy, e.g., he is an ox, meaning he is large and strong as an ox is large and strong.

Metaphysics — the science or knowledge of being in its various causal functions within phenomena. Since being is in all reality, knowledge of being is the most universal and exact of all knowledge. The principle of contradiction, substance, essence, nature, cause, purpose, relationship, accident, quality, quantity are examples of the manners in which being is shared or participated in. Metaphysics gives the ultimate meaning, understanding, knowledge of reality.

Murder — intentional or deliberate killing innocent human life.

Nature — substance as specified for this rather than that action or characteristic. It is the specific nature that determines the type of action or characteristic that will necessarily flow from it. Intelligent action comes from the nature of man. Instinctive action comes from the nature of animals, specific fruit from different species of trees, etc. Thus the philosophic dicta: action follows being, nature is for act, nature will out, etc.

Human nature — rational animal. The essential and inseparable elements of man's nature are his rationality and his animality.

Norms of morality/ethics — guides, prescriptions and prohibitions directing man to his individual and social good.

One — that which is undivided in itself and is divided from all others.

Order — parts uniting or united to accomplish a unfied effect, end, goal, purpose, whole.

Part — correlative to the whole, its total meaning is in reference to something more than and in some sense outside of itself, an end, purpose, an effect.

Pathetic — the pain or suffering that comes to a person through no fault of his own. Any accidental suffering or pain, e.g., the victim of natural disasters, victims of murder, molestation, physical abuse,etc.

Peace — dynamic tranquility of order.

Person — the individualized human nature, the individualized rational animal, this particular human substance.

Power, moral — the ability to act or determine oneself freely. This supposes freedom from instinct, physical restraint, or coercion.

Power, physical — the ability to move or restrain other bodies.

Predication — attributing to a subject a name or a condition.

Analogous predication — The same predicate attributed to each subject fits them in similar, not in identical, manners. God is alive, man is alive, the fox is alive or God is a being, man is a being, the fox is a being, etc. — the predicates alive and being fit all those different subjects in simply different manners, but in some sense the same.

Proper or univocal predication — the predicate attributed or ascribed to the subject is identical as far as can be with the subject, i.e., John is a man,

John is strong, John is cancerous, etc. — those predicates fit him perfectly.

Prudence — the habit of carefully considering the relevant evidence that will
guide one in the free choice one is about to make

Punishment — specific pain produced by restricting the freedom of another against his will, thus punishment is essentially brutal for it violates
the human being's freedom. It is an essential part of law, for by it the
citizen knows that the prescribed sanction for violating the law will be
realized. The sanction is, therefore, a real threat designed to deter the
citizen from lawbreaking.

Corporal punishment — pain prescribed by law inflicted on the body.

Real — that which exists or can exist.

Religion — that part of ethics describing man's obligation to God.

Right — a moral power based in the freedom and independence of the
individual. It is caused by the individual's relationship to a good that
his nature or his society demands he must have.

Right, animal — a metaphor. They are not moral beings and therefore have
no moral powers. They are of a subordinate order of being to that of
man. He has an obligation to use them in accord with that subordination, but that obligation is to himself, as one respecting the order in
which he exists.

Right, legal — the moral power caused by society, e.g., to operate within traf-
fic laws.

Right, natural — the moral power caused by one's nature, e.g. to live, to
own, to speak.

Sanction — the threat of punishment prescribed in the law.

Science — knowledge of causes, e.g., knowledge phenomena—natural science,
knowledge of number—math, knowledge of being—metaphysics.

Substance — that which exists in and for itself and not in another, e.g., man,
fox, ant, etc.

Temperance — the habit of subordinating pleasure to one's overall good.
Any satisfied appetite, whether of the body or of the mind, by definition, means the achievement of its proper good and that is necessarily
pleasing. Food, drink, work, all can be pursued intemperately.

Torture — undefined pain inflicted against the free will of the human, but
designed to give the torturer vengance or to coerce a confession or the
giving of information. As undefined it is essentially arbitrary and ceases only with the satisfaction of the avenger or the act of confession or
informing.

Tragic — that pain or suffering that is a result of a deliberate action that
exceeds moderation, e.g., ambition is good, but when it is immoderate
it can lead to deceit, injustice, greed, betrayal, murder, etc. These in

turn lead to loss of reputation, friends, even life if the law executes the murderer. Immoderate ambition or other practices create pity and fear in those who watch the good man become immoderate. They fear he will destroy himself, they feel sorry for him as he deliberately moves toward his own destruction.

Transactional analysis — Transactions are communications. The analysis of these is the determination of the particular ego-state (parent or adult or child) from which the parties express themselves to one another. Those mutual communications or transactions can be described thus: P-P, P-A, P-C, A-A, A-C, i.e., parent to parent, parent to adult or adult to parent, parent to child or child to parent, etc.

Transcendence — literally "a going across," therefore not confined by limits, therefore free of limitation. Man is said to transcend matter because his acts of intelligence are not confined to specific types of expression, i.e., he freely develops a language proper to him and his associates of family, tribe, nation. Man is transcendent, relatively free of specific limtation by matter, e.g., it is not the nature of man to be confined to one language, but it is of his nature to freely use some signs to communicate with others.

Transcendental Concepts — these are not limited to one or other kind or class of being, but go beyond all classification and fit all being. The transcendental concepts are: being, one, good, true, and, according to many, beautiful. Since these concepts fit all different things, they are therefore predicated analogously. The being of the man is not the being of the ant, nor is his unity, nor his goodness, nor his objective truth, nor his beauty. Yet both he and the ant have being, unity, goodness, truth, and beauty. Therefore I say the man is good and the ant is good, etc.

True — conformity of a being to its proper design or concept. Called objectively true.

Truth — conformity of the mind by means of a judgment or proposition to reality. Called subjective truth because the subject, man, is conformed mentally to the real world. Sometimes called logical truth, truth of the mind, and contrasted with ontological turth, truth of the reality conformed to its proper design.

Virtue — a moral habit of doing what is good for the human subject in which the habit exists.

Cardinal Virtues — cardinal from the Latin word "cardo" meaning hinge. Prudence, justice, temperance, fortitude are the cardinal virtues. All other virtues hinge on these, i.e., are subordinate to and are to be controlled by these, e.g., charity that is not prudent can be wasteful, unjust, etc.

BIBLIOGRAPHY

Arthur Ashe (and Arnold Rampersad), *Days of Grace, A Memoir,* Ballantine Books, New York, 1993.

Bartlett's Familiar Quotations, 15th Edition, Little, Brown & Co., Boston, 1980.

Eric Berne, *Transactional Analysis in Psychotherapy, A Systematic Individual and Social Psychiatry,* Grove Press, New York, 1961.

Allan Bloom, *The Closing of the American Mind,* Simon & Schuster, First Touchstone Edition, New York, 1988.

John Boslough, *Stephen Hawking's Universe,* Avon Books, New York, 1989.

Francis Herbert Bradley, *Essays on Truth and Reality,* London, 1914.

Joseph Campbell, *The Power of Myth,* with Bill Moyers, Betty Sue Flowers, William Morrow and Company, Inc. New York 1984.

Albert Z. Carr, "Is Business Bluffing Ethical?" *Essentials of Business Ethics, A Collection of Articles by Top Social Thinkers,* edited by Peter Madsen, and Jay M. Shafritz, New York, 1990.

Don Clark, Ph. D., *Loving Someone Gay,* Celestial Arts, Berkeley, 1977, rev. 1987.

Paul Davies, *The Cosmic Blueprint,* Touchstone Book, Simon and Schuster, 1989.

"Face to Face with Connie Chung." Earvin Johnson Interview, CBS, 12/11/91, transcription by Burrell's Information Services, Livingston, NJ.

Robert Seitz Frey and Nancy Thompson Frey, *The Silent and the Damned, The Murder of Mary Phagan and the Lynching of Leo Frank,* Madison Books, New York, 1988.

Milton Friedman, "The Social Responsibility of Business is to Increase Its Profits," *Essentials of Business Ethics, A Collection of Articles by Top Social Thinkers,* edited by Peter Madsen, and Jay M. Shafritz, New York, 1990.

Charles A. Gardner, "Is an Embryo A Person?" *Nation,* 11/13/89.

Steven Jay Gould, *Moral Controversies, Race, Class, and Gender in Applied Ethics,* Wadsworth Publishing Co., Belmont, CA., 1993.

Joram Graf Haber, Being and Doing, *Readings in Moral Philosophy,* Macmillan, N. Y., 1993.

Stephen H. Hawking, *A Brief History of Time, From the Big Bang to Black Holes,* Bantam Books, New York, 1988.

Gerard Manley Hopkins, "The Wreck of the Deutschland," Stanza 5, *Gerard Manley Hopkins, Poems and Prose,* Selected with an Introduction and notes by W. H. Gardner, Penguin Books, 1985.

INC magazine, "Corporate Do-gooder: Control Data's Bill Norris," *Essentials of Business Ethics, A Collection of Articles by Top Social Thinkers,* edited by Peter Madsen, and Jay M. Shafritz, New York, 1990.

Deborah Laake, *Secret Ceremonies, A Mormon Woman's Intimate Diary of Marriage and Beyond,* William Morrow and Company Inc., New York, 1993.

Walter Lippmann, *The Good Society,* George Allen and Unwin, Ltd., London, 1937.

JoAnn Loulan, *Lesbian Sex,* Spinsters Ink, Minneapolis, l984.

Myron Magnet, "The Decline and Fall of Business Ethics," *Essentials of Business Ethics, A Collection of Articles by Top Social Thinkers,* edited by Peter Madsen, and Jay M. Shafritz, New York, 1990.

Karl Menninger, M.D., *The Crime of Punishment,* Viking Press, New York, 1968.

Robert K.Merton, *Social Theory and Social Structure,* 1968 Enlarged Edition, The Free Press, New York, 1968,

Lawrence Miller, *The American Spirit, Visions of a New Corporate Culture,* William Morrow and Company, Inc., New York, 1984.

Richard S. Miller, "Ecology," *The World Book Encyclopedia,* VI, World Book, Inc., 1982.

Robert M. Pirsig, *Lila, An Inquiry into Morals,* Bantam Books, New York, 1991.

Laurence Pringle, *The Animal Rights Controversy,* Harcourt Brace Janovich, New York, 1989.

Productivity and the Self-Fulfilling Prophecy: The Pygmalion Effect, a video tape from CRM Productions, McGraw-Hill, Inc.

Karl Rahner, "The Experience of Self and the Experience of God," *Theological Investigations,* XIII, Tr. David Bourke, Crossroad, Seabury, New York, 1975, 122-132. "Reflections on the Unity of the Love of Neighbour and the Love of God," *T.I.,* VI, Tr. Karl-H. and Boniface Kruger, Crossroad, New York, 1982, 231-249. "The Anonymous Christian," *T.I.,* VI, 390-398.

Carl Rogers and F. J. Roethlisberger, "Barriers and Gateways to Communication," *Harvard Business Review,* July-August, 1952.

Robert Rosenthal and Lenore Jacobson, *Pygmalion in the Classroom, Teacher Expectations and Pupils' Intellectual Development,* Holt Rinehart, and Winston, New York, 1968.

Carl Sagan and Ann Druyan, *Shadows of Forgotten Ancestors,* Ballantine Books, New York, 1993.

Science, "Evidence for Homosexuality Gene," 7/16/93, Vol. 261.

H. G. Stoker, *Das Gewissen, Erscheinungsformen und Theorien,* Friedrich Cohen, Bonn, 1925.

Laurence H. Tribe, *Abortion, The Clash of Absolutes,* W. H. Norton & Co., New York, 1990,

Richard A. Wasserstrom , *Today's Moral Problems,* Macmillan , N.Y., 1985.

James Q. Wilson, *The Moral Sense,* The Free Press, Macmillan, New York, 1993.

INDEX